EXTREMISM IN NORTH EAST INDIA

About the Editor

Bimal J. Deb was formerly Professor and Head, Department of Political Science, North Eastern Hill University, Shillong. He is currently National Fellow, Indian Council of Social Science Research, New Delhi. He is also President of North East India Council for Social Science Research, Shillong.

EXTREMISM IN NORTH EAST INDIA

Edited by

Bimal J. Deb

CONCEPT PUBLISHING COMPANY PVT. LTD.
NEW DELHI-110059

ISBN-13 : 978-93-5125-140-8

First Published 2015

Published and Printed by

Concept
Since 1974

Concept Publishing Company Pvt. Ltd.
A/15-16, Commercial Block, Mohan Garden
New Delhi-110059 (India)
T: 25351460, 25351794, *F*: 091-11-25357109
E: publishing@conceptpub.com, W: www.conceptpub.com
Editorial Office: H-13, Bali Nagar, New Delhi-110 015, India.

Cataloging in Publication Data—*Courtesy:* D.K. Agencies (P) Ltd. <docinfo@dkagencies.com>

Extremism in North East India / edited by Bimal J. Deb.
pages cm
Includes bibliographical references and index.
ISBN 9789351251408

1. Radicalism—India, Northeastern—Congresses. 2. Insurgency—India, Northeastern- -Congresses. 3. Terrorism—Social aspects—India, Northeastern—Congresses. 4. Terrorism—Economic aspects—India, Northeastern—Congresses. 5. India,

DDC 320.5309541 23

Preface

Political dynamics in post-independent North East India comprising seven states was particularly characterized by numerous identity assertions articulated by educated elite and emerging middle class in a manner somewhat unconventional in nature but largely drawing vitality and strength from mass mobilization in defence of political aspirations held to be *sine qua non* for preservation of ethnic and cultural distinctiveness. Significantly, the means adopted for articulation, of political aspirations have been both constitutional and extra-constitutional in nature which confronted the might of the state even though it needs to be realized that introduction of liberal democracy in the region largely provided the soil for such assertions, distinctively different from administrative and political arrangements prevalent in excluded and partially excluded era encompassing the greater part of the region which was the homeland of numerous ethnic groups, big and small.

All this coupled with growing alienation of the ethnic groups and communities from mainstream India provided the springboard for a spurt of regional sentiments manifesting ultimately in insurgency and secessionist movements and outbursts. What was inevitable was a clash of interests involving articulation of political aspirations and employment of counter-insurgency measures. It is in this background that the great debate on security and development of the region came to the forefront. In such a situation, the growth of extremist and militant outfits sounded a discordant note in an environment surcharged with promotion of straight jacket mechanism devised in the form of Sixth Schedule to the Constitution compounded by attempted imposition of political solution without the consent of the people.

The discourse in the region centring self-determination and sovereignty ignited by identity thrust, economic and administrative neglect and rampant human rights abuse needs to be understood in proper perspective and particularly in the context of growing discontent and alienation of people belonging to various communities. Negotiation process in the region no doubt accorded political legitimacy to the insurgent organizations and several accords have already brought about perceptible change in the political scenario. Nevertheless, economic issues and instruments have remained relatively neglected elements in the peace process in North East India. No one can deny the fact that any post-conflict situation ought to look beyond the supposed short-term gains from any political settlement. Admittedly, along with political solution, economic recovery plan is a driving force for sustaining peace so that a narrow elite does not reap most of the benefits of peace dynamics. This book has attempted to understand cross-currents and undercurrents of contemporary discourse on extremism and militancy in various parts of the region so that a sustainable peace emerges on the plank of governance and development.

B.J. Deb

Acknowledgements

It gives me great pleasure to state that publication of this volume is another milestone in the research activity of the Council based on proceedings of a National Seminar. We are indeed thankful to the then Governor of Meghalaya for providing valuable inputs while inaugurating the Seminar. We deeply acknowledge the research contribution of our members while writing papers. We are also thankful to Shri Nitin Mittal, Managing Director of Concept Publishing Co. Pvt. Ltd. for publishing this volume.

Shillong

Prof. Zahid Husain Qureshi
Secretary,
North East India Council
for Social Science Research

Contents

List of Contributors

Biswajit Mahapatra (Dr.), Associate Professor of Political Science, NEHU, Shillong.

Chandana Bhattacharjee (Dr.), Head, Department of Anthropology, Women's College, Shillong.

D.D. Mali (Dr.), Former Director of Entrepreneurship Development, Assam.

Debojyoti Das (Dr.), Scholar, Meghalaya.

Dipankar Chakrabarti (Dr.), Head, Department of English, Government Degree College, Khumulwng, Jirania, Tripura (W).

Dipesh Ch. Bhagabati (Dr.), Head, Department of Education, Titiu College, Assam.

Harekrishna Deka (Mr.), Former Director General of Police, Assam.

Jagadish Ch. Sarma (Dr.), Sr. Lecturer, Barnagar College, Sorbhog.

Kshireswar Borah (Dr.), Head, Department of Philosophy, Arya Vidyapeeth College, Guwahati.

Kundan Hazarika (Mr.), Research Scholar, Assam.

L. Seityabati Devi (Dr.), Lecturer of Political Science, Kamakhya Pemton College, Hiyangthang, Imphal.

Malabika Das Gupta (Dr.), Professor of Economics (Retd.), Tripura University.

Manoranjan Goswami (Mr.), Retired Colonel, Indian Army and Scholar.

Oinam Sareeta Devi (Ms.), Lecturer, Home Science Department, Kakching Khunou College, Manipur.

P.C. Dutta (Dr.), Faculty, S.S. College, Hailakandi, Assam.

P. K. Ryngnga (Dr.), Associate Professor of Geography, NEHU, Assam.

Prakash Sarma (Dr.), Scholar, Assam.

R.C. Borpatra Gohain (Dr.), Professor of Law, Guwahati University, Assam.

Rajiv Kumar Roy (Mr.), Research Scholar, NEHU, Shillong.

Ranjit S. Mooshahary (Mr.), Former Governor of Meghalaya.

S. Thangboi Zou (Dr.), Scholar, Meghalaya.

Sanjeeb Kakoty (Dr.), Faculty, I.I.M., Shillong.

Somingam Mawon (Mr.), Research Scholar, NEHU, Shillong.

Sumana Paul (Ms.), Faculty, Department of Education, Women's College, Shillong.

Surajit Sen (Mr.), Lecturer, Department of English, Women's College, Shillong.

T. Ninghorla Zimik (Dr.), Faculty, G.P. Women's College, Manipur.

Th. Binanai Devi (Dr.), Sr. Lecturer of Political Science, G.P. Women's College, Imphal.

Xavier P. Mao (Dr.), Professor of Philosophy, NEHU, Shillong.

1

North East India

Maladies and Remedies

Ranjit S. Mooshahary

North-Eeast is the most volatile territory in our country. Home of many autochthonous tribes who had lived on clan loyalties and in glorious isolation from each other in time and clime, the region is not a melting pot of a pan-tribal society but a veritable remake of the Tower of Babel with the tribes speaking in different tongues, expressing different thoughts and following different faiths and practices. Often they are at war with each other for supremacy or for preserving their identities from the assimilative advances of outsiders making the region hotbed of political irreconcilabilities.

The problem of the North East people in a broader frame is, therefore, twofold: (i) among themselves and (ii) with the rest of India. All the conflicts and clashes, contradictions and confrontations—be it the demand for sovereignty or separate statehood, special status for linguistic or cultural distinctiveness or for sixth schedule status issue forth from these two main roots. The fear of identity extinction runs deep in the veins of the north-easterners and it makes them emotive whenever they apprehend any threat to their identity. They are effusive in their joys and aggressive in their fears and like the turbulent Brahmaputra in summer months slicing its way through the friable soil wreaking havoc on the people they can create waves of lawlessness in the region and its attendant human misery.

Of the seven northeastern states, Assam has the highest diversity and density of population. Historically, she is the mother state as from her womb other states have derived their entities in the crucible of history. The problems of Assam are extraordinarily complex—insurgency, terrorism, kidnapping, extortion, killings, demographic aggression, ethnic heterogeneity, student politics, border disputes with the neighbouring states, flood, poverty, unemployment and underdevelopment have mired the state in an imbroglio with no parallel anywhere.

The crux of the matter is that what happens in Assam has cascading impacts in the other six states of the region. The corridor to the North East runs through the Bodoland area in Kokrajhar district of Assam and also partly through Dhubri district of the state. The district is subjected to 50-55 days bandhs of various types a year effectively blocking the vital lifeline to the region. The West Bengal-Assam interstate border checkposts at Srirampur and Chagalia are the bottlenecks restricting the flow of economic activities. An enquiry by a senior state government functionary, whose report was made public through an RTI petition, revealed glaring mismanagement and unchecked corruption in these check-posts for which the people of the North East as a whole are made to bear higher cost of commodities.

Nagaland is the mother of insurgency. For over six decades the state has passed through various stages of insurgency situation, though the state has not witnessed any large scale violence after the ceasefire agreement with the NSCN, which is in force for 12 years now. Nevertheless, the underground runs its own affairs of governance in a challenge to the constitutionally elected government. The demand of sovereignty by the NSCN has practically become a thing of the past and settlement within the constitutional framework appears likely provided the main demand for Nagalim is addressed with a positive concern.

Manipur is virtually in a state of continuing insurgency with over thirty armed outfits running parallel administration and creating continuous violence and blood-shed. The valley inhabitants — the Meiteis — and the tribes in the surrounding hills are so completely divided that there seems no hope of their ever coming together again. There is no immediate prospect of insurgency and violence ceasing in Manipur.

Tripura is a state surrounded on three sides by Bangladesh and prone to the trans-border criminal exploits. It is one of the better governed states in the country and no doubt the best in the

North East. It is an example of how good governance can resolve human conflicts despite geographical disadvantage.

Meghalaya and Mizoram are peaceful states. Both these states had their share of militancy and violence but today these two states are as the islands of peace signifying the fact that there is a way to violence and there is also a way to peace. The fact that ethnically both the states are more homogeneous than others has helped in the return of peace.

Arunachal Pradesh is too sparsely populated and too spread over and underdeveloped to harbour armed movement right now. But it has the potential for conflict in future when education and development would arouse people's expectation. Its tribal heterogeneity may lead to social disharmony along the ethnic lines.

Common Maladies of North East

The region has been ravaged by terrorism and militancy by both underground and over-ground actors. There are also disguised terrorists who subvert the system to advance their agenda and are actually more harmful to the society and the people.

All the states of North East, Tripura expected, suffer from the syndrome of governance deficit. Absence of effective, responsive and transparent governance make people desperate and it leads to anger and violence.

Total absence of any mechanism to curb corruption has only made it no risk high return industry thereby accentuating the deprivation quotient, which fuels militancy and violence.

Immunized corruption is the twin brother of extortion; both misappropriate resources with impunity.

All the states in the region have to depend heavily on central assistance on financial matters. Their own revenue collection is not enough even to pay their employees' salary. If corruption is controlled their revenue collection will improve.

Sclerotic civil administration not only hampers development pace but also makes people cynical as they lose faith in the system. This is one reason why in the North East we see so many organizations trying to destroy the system to derive personal aggrandizement.

Militancy and terrorism have become money spinners in the region; there are vested interests who do not want them to end.

Only an efficient political leadership as in Tripura can check this menace.

People are by nature apprehensive of the intention of outsiders and it fuels the crisis of confidence, which often erupts in violence.

Common Remedies

- Efficient and effective political leadership can stem the rot. The region requires visionary and dynamic political leadership. Political parties—the national parties in particular—need to ponder on this and encourage people to join them.
- States need to create institutional mechanisms to fight corruption. This can be easily done if there is will, but since many are involved in this lucrative practice of corruption it is difficult to curb it. Civil society must create people's war against corruption through protests and demonstrations, exposure and non-cooperation.
- Political resolution of issues is the key to control violence. Too long operation by the armed forces becomes counterproductive and there is immediate need to strengthen the civil police to enable them to take control of the situation.
- Pace of development must be accelerated and employment generation through micro, small and medium projects to be rapidly created. DONER and NEC can play much larger role in addressing the development issues.

Suggestions and Combating Terrorism

- Terrorism cannot be put down merely by enacting new laws howsoever stringent such laws may be. We introduced death penalty in the IPC by inserting Section 364(A) in 1993 for the crime of kidnapping for ransom with the objective of curbing the menace of kidnapping. It was believed that capital punishment, which is provided only in murder case under Section 302 IPC, would deter people from committing the crime of kidnapping for ransom. But today we find kidnapping has become an industry in many parts of the country even where there is no insurgency or militancy. It is so because we have failed to send even a single kidnapper to the gallows.

- Law is value neutral. It is its implementation that makes it effective. Therefore, more important than law is the quality of the enforcement personnel. We have to train and motivate the enforcement officers and facilitate their efficient functioning by providing them with the tools and techniques for implementing the law.
- We over deploy our uniformed personnel. India is the only country where even the VVIP security is done with visible presence of men in uniform, which is rather a disadvantage. Demonstrative deployment of men in uniform is necessary to control crowd, regulate traffic, procession etc. but such deployment to prevent terrorism, it is counter-productive. Instead we should emphasize on plain cloth police deployment to oversee the activities of the terrorists. The cities and towns/villages can be divided into policing zones and assigned to specific groups of plain cloth policemen making them accountable for securing the area from the visitation of crimes and militancy.
- Intelligence can never be perfect. It is analytical interpretation of it that leads to actionable inputs and that is where we fail. There is need for enhancing the quality of intelligence gathering and its analysis that will help intelligence units to correlate different types of inputs.

The Merging of the North East with the Mainstream

It is an encouraging sign that today the North East is much closer to the mainstream. People have come to realize that India offers opportunities for development without having to abandon one's faith and practices, custom and culture and that democracy in India is better than anywhere among our neighbours. This is a paradigm shift in the mindset of the people of North East and with the passage of time the bond of integration of its people with the rest of India is going to be even stronger. This will resolve many issues that tend to distance this region from India now.

Note: Speech delivered by Shri Ranjit S. Mooshahary, Governor of Meghalaya at the seminar organized by the North East India Council for Social Science Research on "Extremists in North East India"on March 6, 2009 at Shillong.

2

Extremism and Conflict Resolution

(In the Context of Militancy in Assam)

Harekrishna Deka

It is necessary to be clear about the term 'extremism' before I undertake further discussion on my subject. This term is found used in historical context particularly when the historians were dealing with India's struggle for national independence in the early part of the twentieth century. With the change of time and with tremendous changes in the socio-political scenario occurring in this country since independence, the term appears to have acquired a different connotation and it is even in the process of being replaced by another 'terrorism', which, of course, was also used in the past but with a meaning distinctly different from the other term. The Oxford English Reference Dictionary, which I often consult, has not defined 'extremism' and indicates that it is a noun derivative of the adjective 'extremist', who is 'a person who holds extreme or fanatical political or religious views and esp. resorts to and advocates extreme action.' In today's context, when violence has become an everyday affair, it is often presumed that violence is a necessary ingredient of extreme actions. But during the early part of India's national struggle, those who were called the extremists were those who did not speak of violent actions though they wanted to radicalize the methodology of the struggle to achieve *Swaraj*. Bal Gangadhar Tilak and Bipin Chandra Pal were the examples of such extremists, unlike the moderates like Gokhale. Instead of direct action advocated by the extremists, which were, of course, non-violent, the moderates believed in petition and representation and at the most wanted recognition of the Indian's political rights through constitutional method.[1] Interestingly, a Gandhian, Martin Luther King, who launched a non-violent struggle for the civil rights of the black people in America did not hesitate to use the word extremist, when he said 'the question is not whether we will be extremists, but what kind of extremists we will be...The nation and the world are in dire need of creative extremists.' Though his words have a tinge of sarcasm, since it referred to what others said of his methodology, his coinage of the term 'creative extremism' is novel and points to his non-violent strategy.

I notice that, the present trend in our country is to define 'extremism' in the context of violent actions adopted by radicalized groups seeking political change. When I was in the intelligence Branch of Assam Police, I found the term mainly used to describe the kind of activities the Naxalite groups were indulging in and we referred to this mode of political violence as 'left-wing extremism'. I think this description is still in use. On the other hand, it became customary to name the mode of actions of the radicalized groups of the North East who particularly adopted the National Socialist Council of Nagaland (NSCN) pattern of hostility as 'insurgency'. The most recent term 'terrorism' has been defined in many ways, though, each differ subtly from the other. This term usually refers to the extremely violent actions of the non-state political groups who aim at creating panic in civilian population to weaken an established rule in a state of traumatizing a recalcitrant community with a view to compelling them to concede demands on issues of politico-religious, politico-ethnic or politico-economic nature. With the frequency of bomb blasts occurring in Assam, the term 'terrorism' now finds mention while describing the activities of the militant groups active in the state.

Roger Scruton considers 'extremism' to be a vague term[2], which means — (1) a political idea with the intention not only to confront but also to *eliminate* opposition, (2) intolerance towards all views other than one's own, and (3) adoption of means to political ends which disregard accepted standard of conduct, in particular which show disregard for the life, liberty and human rights of others.

While I do not question Scruton's categorization, my focus will be on a kind of extremism which fits the third category given by him. In my discussion, I will not make any reference to the form of actions adopted by non-violent political actors advocating direct action to achieve political goals. My discussion will remain confined to a form of extreme action where violence is adopted as a necessary radical means in disregard of life, liberty and human rights of others. Though it is done at the cost of human lives, the radicalized group may seek legitimacy from a segment of a people amongst whom it works and whom it may consider its constituency. Under this rubric, the militancy of United Liberation Front of Assam (ULFA), which is often termed insurgency, is a kind of extremism. There is a tendency to dismiss ULFA as a group of misadventurists intolerant of human values but while their actions are dangerously subversive of accepted standards of conduct, their own conduct sprang from the social soil—a soil of which the foundation got weakened due to non-realization of socio-economic expectations. Therefore, dealing with ULFA is not just dealing with a group of people intolerant of others but is addressing the underlying societal failures which surfaced through the minds of these people as lack and manifested as political demands.

The ULFA in adopting a form of extremism with its attended violence set Assam's liberation from India as its mission. This outfit was not the first to demand severance of ties from India. Even when the idea of a pan-Indian nationalism was sweeping through the minds of the people of British India, the question of Assam's inclusion was raised by Jnannath Bora, an Assamese intellectual in 1936 and 1938. Even before that Kamalakanta Bhattacharyya (1855-1936), editor of Assamese magazine, *'Asom Hitoishi'* advocated for an independent and self-reliant Assam.[3] Though the Indian nationalistic upsurge had a stronger impact on the Assamese middle class, there were still many who subscribed to the views expressed by the Late Bora. In the post-Independence era, disillusionment with the national leadership was growing and it stemmed mainly from the slow rate of economic development with its concomitant unemployment problem, which was politically expressed as neglect of a peripheral region by a unitary centre alleged to be concerned mainly with the well-being of a heartland. An undercurrent of linguistic nationalism has continued to be there amongst major linguistic groups of this country from the days of the national struggle and it took shape even when Indian nationalism was being formulated. This found expression when the states were reorganized on linguistic basis.[4] Language was the main formula around which the major linguistic groups under the dominance of the middle class elite foregrounded their identity. The Assamese also cherished a similar linguistic identity and conceptually it was nationalistic. The smaller people-groups, particularly who did not have a long tradition of literary culture formulated their identity around the idea of ethnicity. And this also took nationalistic turn in many instances. A particular instance is the Naga people whose ethnic identity as one people was formed during the British rule when different Naga tribes shared common administration and common religion. They even adopted a common language Nagamese derived from Assamese as a communicating link. It may be said that Naga pride was so much based on this identity that it even rebelled against the idea of sharing sovereignty with the Indian Union when it came into being. Effort at integration through different political strategies adopted by the Centre has, of course, succeeded in mellowing this strong sense of separate identity in recent time but the Centre need to move cautiously so that the pride of Naga identity does not get hurt. I leave this context here as my discussion mainly centres on security scenario in Assam.

The Assamese having found themselves at a lower trajectory of development than the rest of the country after the first decade of Independence developed an anti-outsider syndrome. At first accepting the alleged blame that the community was slow in enterprise to grab opportunities, it soon discovered other causes for the negative growth of the region and found that most middle class opportunities had been grabbed by the outsiders except in the State Government services. Trade and commerce went to the hands of the Marwaries, tea capital slipped to Kolkata, the Bengalis dominated the service sector except in the State Government services, Biharis dominated the labour segment and the immigrants from the erstwhile East Bengal, later Bangladesh, gradually spread over to all vacant lands and became an important political factor in vote-bank politics. Actually, all this happened in an economic situation when India's adoption of Mahalanobis model[5] for development, that banked on heavy industry, did not create any opportunity for capital formation in a region where poor communication and its frontier character became disadvantage for economic take off on this model. Regional imbalance became pronounced and the heartland-vision of the Centre also failed to address this lack in time to remove the sense of neglect. Economic underdevelopment coupled with demographic changes created a feeling amongst the Assamese that their identity was threatened at home and they were being marginalized. Among the youth, two different readings were taken. The All Assam Students Union, whose leadership had their schooling in the linguistic nationalism and in whose vein this ran as sub-nationalism without supplanting the Pan-Indian nationalism, read that the ills lay in continuous migration from outside the state – initially assumed to be from the East and the North of the country, when the term *'Bahiragata'* was coined, but later modifying the reading as demographic invasion from erstwhile East Bengal (Bangladesh), as it became clear from the census reports[6] . But a radical group took a different reading. They read it as exploitation of the region's resources by a colonial Centre, only the dramatis personae having changed, i.e. the Indian colonialists substituting the British. The radical group adopted a nationalistic concept and aimed for national liberation. Thus manifested ULFA. Unlike All Assam Students' Union (AASU) adopting a strategy of democratic movement to preserve the Assamese identity within the nation called India, it embarked on a violent liberation movement having adopted the NSCN model of insurgency. Like all other North East groups having schooled in the lessons of insurgency by the Naga rebels, ULFA too adopted the NSCN model in this respect.

Though ULFA accepted the NSCN as a role model, and the core concept of their demand emanated from a sense of nationalism, both nationalisms (of NSCN and ULFA) differed in substance. As said already, a common British administration allowed the Naga tribes living in isolation to come together and the concept of Naga as one nation developed. While the British administered them loosely allowing customary laws to prevail, they facilitated a common system of Western education and the missionaries gave them a common church. From my reading, these appear to be the three pillars on which Naga nationalism took birth and it was claimed as sovereign. I admit that my reading may be wrong. But I feel that a sense of nationhood gave them a sense of territorial separation and an urge to preserve this. If in course of time a major part of this Naga nation has reconciled itself to remain in the Indian Union their own sense of nation has not evaporated from their psyche. A nation in its pride does not want to remain at subsistence level and wants economic development in order to earn a place of pride in human society. So the economic factor plays its role even if the sense of nationalism sprang from other factors. To preserve its national identity, the Naga wants its territorial integrity and wants to develop economically. By giving a state within the Union and providing the hope of developing the state economically India has partially fulfilled these conditions and the participation of the Nagas in the democratic process of the country has become a reality. But yet this has not satisfied the rebels. They are yet to give up the demand for sovereignty will get mellowed over time and the concept itself will get re-formulated to bring it nearer to the concept of autonomy but the more difficult question may be territorial integrity of the Naga nation.

The ULFA's formulation of Assamese nation has also a territorial concept but it is confusing. It refers to Assam as it existed before the Yandaboo Treaty but at the same time it also refers to the *Kalika Purana* where the kingdom of Kamarupa is said to have spread over to areas beyond North Bengal. But the main formulation of its nationalism is linked to the concept of colonialism. Economic exploitation is the theme, which is in fact grounded in real situation, that underlies the identity formulation of both the AASU and the ULFA, but read differently by each as already indicated. Hence, the economic factor is a primary factor in ULFA's formulation of nationhood, though sought to be realized through sovereignty. The AASU has seen it as the neglect of a sub-nation by a Nation because of which is the exploitation by others. In ULFA's eyes it is exploitation of one Nation by another Nation, which is colonization.

In case of AASU's movement, the State sought to deal with it initially as a law and order problem. But when the movement took an upswing then the Government read it as a political problem to be solved politically. By the time negotiations started it became a mass movement, which the leaders of the agitation ironically exploited to come to power instead of asking for a solution through a developmental strategy based on specific agenda to remove regional inequality. The Assam Accord reached through negotiations was a compromise between the leaders of the agitation and the Government but it failed to satisfy the people. The leaders of the agitation who came to power could not deliver the goods promised to the people. ULFA had appeared in the scene as the agitation was going on in full-swing but could not make headway as long as the people continued to support the agitation. It gained space only when the people became disillusioned with the agitation leaders turned rulers who failed to address the developmental issues with the sense of purpose they should have had. Against this background, ULFA tried to gain a foothold in the popular mind undertaking some rudimentary social agenda through an overground front in rural areas, showcasing these as people-oriented developmental programmes. By this strategy, it not only developed a constituency in highly backward rural areas but even did get some foothold in the middle class mind already disillusioned with the leaders of the agitation who became failed rulers. I am raising this point here to emphasize that behind the political issues lurked the social need for economic development as a key factor. ULFA continues to have influence in very backward areas where the people have not seen the administration at work though it has lost much ground amongst the influential urban middle class because of reckless violence it unleashed showing its terror-teeth to a people who abhor violence. Even then, the popular demand is that the Government negotiate with them instead of seeking a military solution. Extremism is a complex phenomenon and many factors play and interplay in bringing about this complexity. Often the state tries to tackle its manifestations, but the root causes which spring from the psycho-social soil deprived of economic nourishment remain unattended. Social imbalances do not get corrected and as a result extremism tries to take a deeper root. But the actors who are drawn to extremism for a kind of justice and aim for redressal of societal imbalances through a violent doctrine, too, in course of their actions lose touch with reality, over-interprete their capability and start confusing between what is form and what is substance. The form of violence then becomes the end and not the means to reach the goal aimed at. This degeneration results in terrorism.

Far too long the State Government has adopted a counter-insurgency strategy in the military mode stressing on form rather than on content of the rebellion. In this mode, the success is calculated in numbers that is how many guerillas are eliminated or neutralized. The root causes that emanate from socio-economic discontent are not properly addressed. A cycle of violence is created in which the rebel's action is met with counter-action, human rights violations take place either by mistake or by design, innocents suffer in between, this causes disaffection in the midst of ordinary sufferers, from amongst the sufferers new volunteers join the rebel camp, more counter actions take place and discontent further extends. Thus instead of the cycle of violence being broken it expands or moves to a new era. This counter-insurgency strategy has been followed for several decades in the North East but has achieved only temporary successes mainly in causing split in the outfit. Such splits cannot be called real successes because insurgency with various intensity has continued in Assam and in other parts of the North East. The only success in the North East was in Mizoram but here the solution was found politically and after promises were made to provide developmental aid. The rebels after accepting the constitutional ways became the ruling party in the state (then Union Territory).

It is quite necessary that the root causes of all forms of protected socio-political conflicts are identified and attempts made to remove those causes so that the frustration arising out of these causes do not find expression in explosive violence. As Late Edward Azar, a Lebanese social scientist who conducted a large number of case-studies in protracted social violence in the 1990s said once,

> "Reducing overt conflict requires reduction in levels of underdevelopment. Groups which seek to satisfy their identity and security needs through conflict are in effect seeking change in the structure in their society. Conflict resolution can truly occur and last if satisfactory amelioration of underdevelopment occurs as well."

He also said that the critical factor in protracted social conflict was that it represented the prolonged and often violent struggle by communal groups for such basic needs as security, recognition and acceptance, fair access to political institutions and economic participation.[7] In place of 'communal group' we may use the term 'ethnic group' so far as the North East of India is concerned.

Counter-insurgency strategy undertaken in the military mode is a strategy of containment and does not lead to the resolution of the main problem. I have emphasized elsewhere the role of civil society in reducing social tension and for seeking an alternative to violence by democratic means. Remaining apart from the State and untouched by a doctrine of violence, civil society can have a clearer vision from a neutral standpoint. Antonio Gramci thought that civil society is a contested area and often the ruling class tries to appropriate it. Louis Althusser said that the 'Ideological State Apparatuses' are the means by which the ideology of the ruling classes is injected into the subject and they are thus manipulated to imagine the same to be real. On the other hand, Robert Putnam argued that a kind of social capital is formed in civil society and democratic values are sustained by means of such social capital. Religious institutions like Satras, Namghars, Churches, Social Clubs, educational institutions, Worker's Unions, Associations, Women's organizations etc. all bring groups of people together and social values develop through their fraternal relationship. Putnam believed that networking of civil society is an important way through which social capital could be produced. What I see is this—the State through its governmental mechanism develops an official discourse which circumscribes its perspective. Being boxed into the narrow confines of this discourse, it cannot emerge to locate an alternative discourse. On the other hand, the non-state actors who choose the extremist path to challenge the State's monopoly on law and the use of force are also boxed into a counter-discourse from which they refuse or fail to grow out. Civil society through their dialogic discourses can acquire a different kind of social capital and can remain clear of this contested zone. Therefore, they can provide a neutral voice *vis-à-vis* the voices of the two contested sides and can generate an alternative discourse for untangling the complexity. Of course, this could happen only if the State is inclined to fulfil the following conditions: (1) it has to make some room for civil society institutions to freely activate society's goodwill in form of social capital, and (2) the governmental obligations for economic development and for balancing divergent socio-political elements need to be met so that the development fruits reach all sections of the people in an equitable manner. Even civil society may get frozen if the masses remain highly dissatisfied.

I believe that extremism in the long run fails as a strategy to achieve a mission and it often degenerates into terrorism. When this happens it loses direction and becomes a self-defeating doctrine. But at the same time, the state cannot dismiss it simply as a senseless ideology and itself use only extreme measures to crush the extremists abandoning all other modes of action or strategy. Often groups seeking recognition or justice resort to extremism in desperation when there is absence of a dialogic path. The state's response to extremism has to be a combination of hard options and soft power. I recognize that the state needs to exercise hard option when a culture of violence is deliberately spread by certain elements but the state should avail this choice for the purpose of restoring rule of law only when it tends to break down under the weight of culture of violence. An important component of the state's strategy has to be reduction of social discontent by means of developmental plan and political dialogue. Terrorism may be self-defeating, but what causes terrorism becomes enduring and contaminates the social soil if the soil is not nourished properly.

NOTES

1. See *India's Struggle for Independence* by Bipan Chandra (Penguin).
2. See *Dictionary of Political Thought* by Roger Scruton (Palgrave Macmillan).
3. See *Periphery Strikes Back,* Chapter-IV by Udayon Mishra (Indian Institute of Advanced Studies, Simla).
4. Ramchandra Guha has amply discussed this in his book *India After Gandhi* (Picador India).
5. Manmohan Agarwal and Sudip Ranjan Basu have discussed the effect of the Mahalanobis Development Strategy in their article 'Development Strategy and Regional Inequality in India' included in *'India's North East, Development Issues in a Historical Perspective'* edited by Alokesh Barua (Manohar).
6. In 1978, Guwahati city witnessed a wall-writing and postering campaign against the so-called Indian outsiders. But by 1979, the campaign turned against the illegal migrants from Bangladesh and then the Assam Movement against foreign nationals took birth. This happened due to convergence of several factors: (1) Myron Weiner's book *'Sons of the Soil'* published in 1978 highlighted the immigration problem affecting Assam's demography, (2) M.L. Sakhder, the then Chief Election Commissioner spoke about suspected non-citizens' names finding large-scale entry in the electoral rolls, referring particularly to Assam, while addressing a conference of state election commissioners in 1978, (3) In 1979, the revision of electoral rolls of the Mangaldai constituency in Assam was taken up for a bye-election

following the death of the sitting M.P. Hiralal Patowary. During this exercise numerous complaints were raised against inclusion of the names of a large number of suspects who were illegal migrants, and (4) Two new political parties were formed on sub-nationalist agenda in 1978 and 1979. They were Purbanchaliya Loka Parishad and Asom Jatiyatabadi Dal respectively. The PLP particularly raised the question of 'native identity' from the beginning.

7. For a discussion on this see Chapter IV of the book *'Contemporary Conflict Resolution'*, second edition written by Oliver Ramsbotham, Tom Woodhouse and High Mial (Poloty). Azar was a Lebanese intellectual who moved to the U.S.A. He died in 1991. The world has become more violent since his death, but many of the points he made are still valid.

3

Extremism and Security in North East

Manoranjan Goswami

History and geography do live together and in case of North East of India, we must not try to deal with the problem of insurgency of extremism that engulfs the region today, without considering the geographical location of the region and the history of the region together. The North East, barring Assam and Tripura, is mostly a region with hilly areas and at the same time is an area of almost separate history from the rest of country, whether we talk about independent kingdomship or culture of the ethnic groups that the region have, which are indistinctly different from the rest of the country. Even Assam and Tripura has a history of long independence and autonomy rule with least interference from outside. The modernity of history touched the region rather late and though British rule did bring unity and modernization in administration, the feeling of commonality with rest of India did take time to sink in and still there are groups who feel 'dominated by outsiders'. There is a psychological barrier, particularly, among distant ethnic groups and it requires deep understanding of politics and history of the people before the state machinery puts all its might and force as a measure of control on those who rebel. Geographically too, North East is tagged in a corner really with five foreign countries, not friendly necessarily, surrounding the region, but also it is connected with the mainland of India with a very 'thin neck' of just 20 km wide, which too give a 'feeling of a separation' from the rest. The surrounding countries, China, Myanmar, Bhutan, Nepal and

Bangladesh, are adding to this feeling of alienation by their hostile attitude to India and sometimes 'overfriendliness' to those groups who are going against the interest of unity and integrity of the country. North East, is therefore, a complex problem and cannot be or should not be just treated as a 'law and order' problem only. The problem of insurgency, extremism or terrorism, whichever way we brand it, is to be tackled with not just strong hand, but with strong mind and understanding too.

At the time of independence, Assam, as it was then a combination of six states, all independent states within India now, had a per capita income of 4 per cent above the national average. Today, combined or severally, North East states are among the poorest lots in India. The Central Government's apathy towards this region for a long time after independence or rather till the insurgency made its mark, is one reason for the feeling of alienation of the people of North East. Secondly, there seems to have a conflict between politics and security as we see the problem of mass scale infiltration of unauthorized people from the neighbouring country Bangladesh. This issue of illegal migration from Bangladesh, mostly to Assam is not only changing the demography of the State of Assam, but also it is becoming a great security threat for the country as a whole. Immigration and extremism are two different matters, but still they are connected, more so, for the unabated and unchecked influx from Bangladesh to the North East States, having an access for the militant groups to cross over.

The Islamic militant groups like Harkat-ul-Jihad-e-Islami (HUJI) or LeT are not only seeking their root in Bangladesh, but even Inter-Services Intelligence (ISI) of Pakistan seems to have established a strong base in that country. It should be appreciated and understood that it is not Kashmir, but North East today, which can be major centre of activities where Islamic fanaticism may take its root. The recent militant activities spreading across Assam including reported hoisting of Pakistani Flag somewhere, is a clear indicator that Infiltration in mass scale from across the border is not just an issue of illegal citizenship, but more serious aspect is that it is linked with subversive design to destroy the integrity of India. Added to it, whether it is United Liberation Front of Assam (ULFA) or Bodo militant group, they are getting patronization from Bangladesh and that country has become the sanctuary of many terrorist groups from North India. We are still talking about extradition of militant like Anup Chetia, for example India hopes that new democratic Government in Bangladesh will change history so far as relation with India is concerned. The recent BDR mutiny, however, suggests that there may be an element who does oppose this change, but hopefully, the support base of North East militants in that country will be eroded sooner than later and cross border terrorism across the border will be down. As it stands now, Pakistan is trying to carry out its operation from North East rather more with the help from our neighbour through induction of arms, ammunition and fund. Even in 2008, the number of civilian deaths due to terrorist activity in North East is 1057 against 539 in J & K. The Centre and state must act together in its effort to wipe out terrorism and a common programme has to be evaluated and placed in position. Sophisticated threat must be met with sophisticated state machinery and honest diplomacy.

When we talk of sophisticated machinery to deal with extremism, we must first of all upgrade our Police Force and modernize it both from human resource point of view and weaponry it holds. The Police Force, dealing with terrorism or extremism must have a separate specialized training programme and cannot be clubbed up with the normal police training. The Police cannot, at the same time, act in isolation and in conflict with local people around. They need support, both physical and moral from local population as much as they need uninterfered support from the Government. We also must remember that left wing extremism and insurgency in North East is more home-grown and that is where the understanding of psychology and causes for feeling of alienation should be appreciated. Police, though, must act firmly, but must not be perceived as symbol of 'State terrorism'. Insurgency in the North East has been fuelled by increasing proliferation of small arms in the region and support received from external militant outfits. It is a complex issue where there is restlessness and frustration among local youths and at the same time subversive assistance from alien countries.

Military operation should be taken as the last resort, but more than that, the Centre should have willingness and a desire to recognize and appreciate the regional and ethnic aspiration of the people of the area concerned and meet them to the extent possible, without sacrificing the sovereignty and integrity of the nation, though. Winning heart through a genuineness of feeling of understanding and on ground action for economic development of the region must go hand in hand. Special development in North East through investment and also through local based institute like Hill Council in Meghalaya to meet the aspiration of the people is equally important.

There are three kinds of challenges to internal Security – Insurgency, Naxalism and Terror groups. The security and sovereignty cannot be compromised and Security machineries of the State must be modernized, motivated and trained with latest weapons, no doubt, but the Government must also understand the cause and origin of the discontentment. That does not in anyway mean that state can slacken the effort to control any damaging activities resorted by the extremist group. Considering the threat to the human, economic and national security that the extremism poses, it has become very important to re-examine the strategy presently adopted in the North East and it has become all the more important to bring about alternative counter-insurgency plan. As we have tried to impress upon, that while the psychology and cause of discontentment has to be appreciated, the Police cannot take back seat or be shifted back. Sense of fear for the Police is important for the state and the people, but Police also must understand that they are part of the society and must be considered friend of the law abiding people. Rough treatment to the total population of suspected area and indiscriminate third degree method may cause fear, but cannot wipe out root of insurgency. 'Be tough, but understand your fellowmen' – should be the guiding factor. Military deployment leaving the Police in the back seat may have disastrous consequence. Firstly, Military is really not trained to deal with civilian law breakers and secondly, Military should not be exposed to the local civil population too much and too frequent, because that does affect its operational role when called upon by the country. One other aspect which has become a hindrance to effective counter-insurgency operation is rampant corruption among Government officials. The people must understand that extremists will take advantage of this menace of the society.

The Police or the state machinery to control extremism has grown in size and education, but at the same time the extremist groups, whether we call them insurgents or other militants, are also getting modernized and equipped with new arms, technique and equipments. The hand from the foreign countries, more prominently, Pakistan in our case, is adding to the challenges that we are facing. Not only our Police should have separate dedicated wing to face extremist groups with all modern gadgets, equipments and weaponry, but our Army too should have a specialized wing to deal with the terrorist groups when ultimately called up. At the same time the Police, particularly, must be trained to understand the psyche of the terrorists. Even Indian Air Force is planning to deploy Unarmed Aerial Vehicle (UAV) to combat insurgency in North East as a new step towards meeting the terrorist groups hidden in thick jungles. The Army is, in fact, upgrading its anti-insurgents training everyday. It is felt that Police of the North East States should have a separate training establishment in direct liaison with Army where anti-terror and anti-extremism training can be imparted with absolute professionalism. A common forum for intelligence sharing among the North East States' Police Forces is also called for. We cannot afford the 'luxury' of each state Police to have their water-tight intelligence organization within itself. Sharing intelligence is the call of the day.

The Army has amply shown their efficiency and dedication while dealing with the Mumbai carnage of 26/11 through National Security Guard operation, but I would say, NSG deployment will get diluted if called upon at slightest provocation. In fact, my personal opinion is that there should be NSG hubs in nooks and corner of the country, as demanded now from much quarters. We must not dilute the gravity of Army operation or of NSG as a normal course of internal security.

Let there also be serious study on 'conflict management', among the young boys and girls across North East and left to themselves, they will find solution too. The politicians, who sometimes do refuel the situation, should not involve themselves or should not unnecessarily interface and better leave the situation to be tackled by the Police and available State resources with trust and confidence. Constant research as to why a section likes to take arms against their own people or their own state must be an ongoing exercise along with strong determined Police action. We cannot leave one for the other. I will conclude again emphasizing that this beautiful land of North East cannot be allowed to be destroyed by fear and sense of insecurity created from within and outside and we shall solve it together. The North East will smile as ever.

4

Extremism and Sustainable Development of North East India

Dipankar Chakrabarti

North East India is a land of lush green virginity with a rich biodiversity and a unique blend of people, culture and traditions. Though rich with strong natural and human resources, it has remained economically backward and politically turbulent, even after sixty seven years of Independence.

When we look back over the last five decades of government policies towards the North East region, perhaps mainly due to the politico-insurgent vandalism, we find almost all policies have failed miserably.

The central policy of Government of India towards North East region had undergone five paradigms:

(a) In 1950s: Cultural Paradigm.
(b) In 1960s: Security Paradigm.
(c) In 1970s: Politics Paradigm.
(d) In 1980s: Development Paradigm.
(e) In 1990s: Package Paradigm.

But nothing changed significantly in North East region. Here arises an obvious question to ask why, after 40 or 50 years of playing around with different paradigms the region is still in a crisis ?

The North East raises the issues of Indian State's ability to deal with militancy, secessionism and violence. North East is a challenge to our foreign policy. It is the challenge to the nature of governance.

It is a question mark on our developmental strategy. More than anything else, it should induce us to review the nation building processes followed after we gained independence.

The region has been facing insurgencies or separatist movements from over 50 groups. Although each conflict has its own roots and history, the issues they raise include language and ethnicity, tribal rivalry, migration, control over local resources, access to water, and a widespread feeling of exploitation and alienation from the Indian state. From the National perspective, these movements represent not just domestic discontent, but the danger of destabilization by Chinese or Pakistani intelligence activities. People from India's smaller North-eastern neighbours, Nepal and Bangladesh, have swelled the destabilizing migrations at the root of some of these insurgencies, and dissident groups have used these countries, as well as Bhutan and Myanmar, for sanctuary.

North East has always been viewed as the 'sensitive' area and a significant part of the GDP is going down the drain without much being achieved in terms of meaningful development, restoring peace, and bringing back the North East region into the mainstream ensuring sustained socio-economic development.

However, as compared to 'sensitive', the North East region is far more 'strategic' to the nation, in its huge potential of untapped resources, tourism, trading link of the nation with the ASEAN countries, etc.

Exploiting the potentials of the North East Region, as such, needs an effective re-orientation of the policies at the National level to result in a faster, balanced and sustainable socio-economic development of the North East Region.

The present policy framework for the North East Region is based on its political economy and a cultural approach, adjusted with a regional planning model. It is implemented mainly through the Planning Commission and the North East Council. Despite huge financial investments, this has failed to produce desired results.

The term 'extremism' is often used with reference to those who use or advocate 'violence' against the 'will of society at large'; but it is also used by some to describe those who advocate or use 'violence' to enforce the will of the social body, such as Government or majority of the constituency, those described as 'extremist' would in general not accept that what they practice or advocate constitute 'violence' and would instead speak in terms of 'acts of resistance' or 'militant action' or 'the use of force'. The word 'violence' cannot be regarded as 'value neutral'. Ideology and 'methodology' often become inextricably linked under the single term 'extremism'.

The notion that there is a philosophy which can be described as 'extremist' is considered by some to be suspect. Within Sociology several academics who track (and are critical of) 'extreme right-wing' groups have objected to the term 'extremist' which was popularized by 'centrist' sociologists of the 1960s and 1970s. As Jerome Himmelstein states the cause: 'At best this characterization tells us nothing substantive about the people it labels; at worst it paints a false picture' (Himmelstein, p. 7). The act of labelling a person, group or action as 'extremist' is something claimed to be a technique to further a political goal – especially by Governments seeking to defend the *status quo*, or 'political centrists'. In any event, the term 'extremist'—like the word 'violence'—cannot be regarded as 'value neutral'.

This chapter aims at establishing Extremism as one of the main reasons for the failure of the Central Government's existing policy framework and develop a workable model/solution to bolster a faster pace of balanced development. We believe that extremism jeopardize peace and peace fosters progress or development. Hence, in our postulation extremism alone is sufficient to impede developmental efforts.

The Genesis of the Problems

Historically, the North East had extensive links with the neighbouring region of Tibet, Bhutan, Burma and Indo-China. It formed the southern trail of the silk road. However, as India became an important colony for Great Britain, barriers were erected between Bhutan and Assam, while traditional links with other countries acquired a strategic hue. Soon Burma and Tibet became the Empire's buffer against the French in Indo-China and Russia in the north, disrupting economic ties (Baruah, 2004). The disruption of old trade routes had been seen as 'colonialism's most enduring negative legacy.'

Despite this legacy, prior to 1947, the region comprising the North East had substantial economic and social intercourse with the neighbouring countries. East Bengal (later called East Pakistan and ultimately Bangladesh) was well integrated with the North East. There is evidence that trade and migration into territories today comprising Tibet, Myanmar, Yunnan province of China, Nepal, Bhutan and Sikkim were important to the economy of the region (Baruah, 2004).

However, partition of India and independence to Bangladesh ended whatever remained of this intercourse. The partition transformed the region at the crossroad of emerging Asia, into a landlocked outpost of a large continental economy. It soon lost its natural advantage as its integration with the economy in the south and the west was disrupted by trade and industrial policies pursued by independent India. Though there is little research on the link between the effect of isolation and trade disruption to the extent of poverty in the North East, there is little doubt that the impact on the region was highly regressive (Verghese, 2001).

Bengal Eastern Frontier Regulation (BEFR), 1873: The British Apartheid Mindset at Work

The root cause of the problem is the condition set in place by British rule in the North East since 1826 and the formation of East Pakistan in 1947. New Delhi's inability to integrate the region stems from its failure to recognize that the British Raj had converted North East India into a human zoo, where each tribe was allowed to roam free within its "own territory", but was not allowed to cross the boundaries set forth by their British masters and establish contact with the rest of India.

The British came into the area in the 1820s, following the Burmese conquest of Manipur and parts of Assam. The area had become unstable in the later part of the eighteenth century following the over-extension of the Ahom kingdom, a Burmese-based kingdom that reached into Assam. The Anglo-Burmese war of 1824-26 ended with the British emerging victorious. For the British East India Company, gaining control in the North East of India aided in gaining access to southern China's natural wealth. In 1838, the East India Company assumed charge of the government of Assam, in order to enhance trade and commerce, and sacked the Ahom king, who had been its "protected prince" since 1826.

The decision to isolate the tribals came about in 1873 through the promulgation of the Bengal Eastern Frontier Regulation (BEFR). However, the policy of declaring the North East Frontier Agency (NEFA) a secluded area had been advocated long before. Section 2 of the regulation empowered the company "to prescribe and from time to time alter by notification, a line to be called the Inner Line and to prohibit any subject living outside the area from living or moving therein." The apartheid programme eliminated the North East Frontier Agency from the political map of India and segregated the tribal population from Assam, as the British had done in southern Africa.

Apartheid also helped the British to function freely in this closed environment. Soon enough, the British Crown introduced proselytization of Christianity among the tribal population. Between 1891 and 1901, the number of native Christians increased 128 per cent.

With the partition of Bengal, North East India became practically isolated, connected to the mainland through a narrow corridor. These British policies provide a clue to why North East India has remained a bubbling cauldron and vulnerable to secessionist movements.

The Nation Building Process after the Independence: Poor Governance and Policy Mismatch

Poor governance has been a major problem in the region. This goes back to the first two decades after India's independence when the national leaders were busy addressing the broader economic concerns, giving shape to the country's foreign policy and grappling with the nitty-gritty's of administering the nation. The North-eastern region did not figure high on New Delhi's agenda during this period except, perhaps, the realization that this was a strategic area that needed concentration of military strength. This led to an impression that the Indian leadership actually regarded the region as a buffer against possible foreign aggression and hardly anything else.

What followed is well known to us: the region got caught in the vicious cycle of lack of development breeding insurgency and unrest, and militancy and violence retarding economic growth. By the mid-sixties, when militancy had come to strike roots in the region and gave rise to dangerous-looking insurgency movements with separatist designs, the Union Government started pumping money to the states in the region, hoping that a semblance of economic growth or development could halt this trend. Today, despite the lack of industrialization, the Net State Domestic Product in the region is growing at the rate of 11.2 per cent per annum at $4.2 billion, indicating a high purchasing power of the people in the area compared to those in the rest of the country. But, insurgency continues, and has in fact multiplied and assumed dangerous proportions, with trans-border linkages, making them flush with funds and hardware.

A Measure of Performance of the Central Policies: The Dismal Picture

Other than oil and tea, one would be hard pressed to name any industry capable of generating employment along with forward and backward economic linkages. The fate of public sector units in the mad rush to disinvest is well known. On the other hand, the major industries—tea and oil have remained extractive in essence. Most of the populace is still engaged in the primary sector and dependent on forests, rivers and land. A dismal 5.56 per cent of total North East populace is engaged in industry. The impoverishment of the rural economy goes on unabated. The lack of employment avenues, diminishing return from agricultural production and division of landholdings, has resulted in the potential for more violence. Added to this is the fact that control over scarce resources has become a rallying point for communities and ethnic groups. To complicate matters even further, the government has a blind policy of encouraging individual land use patterns in areas that were either considered to be 'Sixth Schedule' areas, or 'Reserved areas'. Land, which has always been a source of livelihood, is losing its productivity in the commercialised market oriented economy.

On the other hand, the rural sector has little capital and even less investment for the development of industries, or in the health and education sectors. Inevitably, underdevelopment has become the cause of generating violence amongst communities in the region. To talk of 'peace' without taking into consideration, the complex political economy of underdevelopment and social history is nothing but a travesty of great proportions.

In fifty years, the region saw nothing in terms of meaningful economic and industrial development. Social cohesion is at its ebb. Growing terrorism and the consequent militarization of the region are eroding the very social structure. Massive unemployment and under-development are culminating into a sense of deprivation and posing a serious threat to the national integrity.

Agriculture Sector

(i) Foodgrain production in North East India has registered a 37.41 per cent growth during the period 1971-87. Cultivated area has increased from 26.7 lakh hectares in 1970-71 to 35.01 lakh hectares in 1986-87. About 3.72 per cent of the country's population resides in the North East but its share in total food grain production is only 2.6 per cent.

(ii) The total requirement of cereals in 1989 was 5734 thousand tons whereas the production figure for the year shows a shortage of more than 30 per cent.

(iii) Despite an increase in per capita availability of food grain, malnutrition at a high degree continues to exist because of unequal distribution system.

(iv) The percentage of cultivated land to total land is far below the same for the country as a whole during the period 1970-71 to 1990-91. Although the carrying capacity of the land in the region has experienced increase, the actual pressure due to population explosion has more than neutralized the improvement. All-India situation is better in this regard with a carrying capacity of 0.9 persons per hectare in 1985-86.

Yield rate of the region has increased by 54 per cent during the period 1970-94 as against 71 per cent increase in country's yield rate. While observing the traditional agricultural practices and low yield rates, the increase in food grain production over the period may be attributed to enlargement of cultivated land by encroaching forested tracts.

(v) Increasing population pressure on agricultural resources in North East India has been progressively lowering the per capita availability. While comparing agricultural resource availability between North East region and India as a whole by means of set of indicators, viz. per capita cultivated area, per capita food grain production and per capita availability of livestock and poultry, it is found that the region's figures are much below than that of the nation.

(vi) With regard to other agricultural commodities like milk, egg and fish, the percentage of production in North East India to the total production of the country (1.61%, 3.2% and 2.7% for milk, egg and fish respectively), is less than 3.72 per cent, the percentage of North East population to the All-India population. This is also an indication of the excess pressure on these commodities, which is offloaded by import from other parts of the country.

(vii) Hardly 22 per cent of the net sown area in the region is irrigated as against 30 per cent at the All-India level. Virtually, there has been no progress in the creation of irrigation facilities in the region over the last few decades. The existing irrigation system in the region is neither fully dependent nor equally spread over different states. Canal irrigation system does not at all exist in the states of Arunachal Pradesh, Manipur, Mizoram, Meghalaya and Nagaland. Irrigation in the form of tanks, tube wells and other wells is also insignificant in the region. About 50 per cent of the existing irrigated land are supplied with water with very minor irrigation system devised mostly at the farm level and are non-dependable.

Power Sector

(i) The degree of electrification of villages in the region is almost at par with All-India (NER 82.8; All-India 84.4) but per capita consumption of electricity is much less (100 KWH/year against 240 KWH/year in India). Meghalaya is known to be a power-surplus state but only at the cost of the lowest degree of rural electrification and poor per capita consumption of power.

(ii) Power situation is also not satisfactory in the North East. The region has an installed capacity of 1138.8 MW of which Assam and Meghalaya taken together have more than 65 per cent. The central sector has about 23 per cent and the rest 12 per cent by the remaining five states. As far as electrification of villages is concerned it is not lagging behind. Almost 83 per cent of the total villages in the region are electrified when the same is 84 per cent at the All-India level. The per capita consumption of power is very low. It is as low as 83.9 KWH in Tripura. The highest per capita power consumption in the region is in the state of Meghalaya which is hardly 159.4 KWH as against the All-India average consumption of 330.6 KWH.

ICT Sector

(i) Development of postal and telecommunication facilities although seem to be quite adequate, services rendered are considered to be not satisfactory from the consumers' point of view.

(ii) As many as 428 telephone exchanges with 1.26 lakh of switching capacities are installed in the region. It has been able to give as many as 1.02 lakh connections. Over the years, there has been tremendous progress in the telecom facilities. Number of telephone exchanges has increased from 272 in 1983-84 to 428 in 1993-94 and number of connections increased from 30,686 to 1,02,505 during the same period.

(iii) There are 6524 post offices located in different parts of the region. It is estimated that on an average each post office serves 5288 persons in the North East as against 5607 persons at the All-India leveL However, if we examine from the point of view of area served by a post office, it can be said that the region is relatively more backward. Each post office serves a much bigger area of 48.2 sq. kms. on an average in the region as against an area of 21.6 sq. kms. in the country. There has also been greater disparity in the concentration of post offices in different states of the North East.

Large and Medium Scale Industries

As on 1994, the region had only 166 large and medium industries. Many of them have been closed down, or have been declared sick, including all 12 in Nagaland closed down in 2004.

Tourism Sector

The entire region is full of scenic beauty, which has the potential to attract tourists of any taste. The north and the eastern most part of the region have been declared as one of the top 25 biodiversity hotspot in the world (Myers, 2001).

However, unfortunately, the region has been attracting only a negligible number of leisure tourists. Only about 0.15 per cent of the foreign tourists coming to India are visiting the North East Region (Sarma, 2002). The inflow of domestic tourists is also poor and is not enough to sustain the tourism industry on its own.

Infrastructure Sectors

Transport Sector

(i) The ratio of surfaced road to total road length in NER is 0.27 against 0.51 in All-India and road length per 100 sq. km. of area is 46 km. against 64 in the nation. Except in Assam and Tripura, there is hardly any access to the railways.

(ii) The N.E. Region which constitutes 7.8 per cent of the total geographical area of the country has a meagre of 1,16,551 km. of road length. It is estimated that for every 100 sq. km. area, the region has only road length of 45.7 km. as against 62.8 km. in the country. Besides, road condition is far from satisfactory. Hardly 27.1 per cent of the total road length is surfaced in the region in sharp contrast to 50.5 per cent at the All-India level. The state-wise figures reveal that Tripura is in the most advantageous position followed by Assam in regard to road development.

(iii) Development of railways is quite insignificant in the region. There exist only 2466.8 km. of length of railway line in Assam and 45 km. in Tripura. All other states are yet to be connected by railway lines. About 266 km. of length of broad gauge line has been created in the entire region. In other words, only 10.6 per cent of the total railway line in the region is broad gauge and that too it is only in the state of Assam. There has been very minor progress in the development of railway network in the region in the last twenty years. The total gauge has increased hardly from 2378.6 km. in 1983 to 2524.8 km. in 1992.

Recommendations/Findings

(a) The region has been facing insurgencies or separatist movements from over 50 groups. Although each conflict has its own roots and history, the issues they raise include language and ethnicity, tribal rivalry, migration, control over local resources, access to water, and a widespread feeling of exploitation and alienation from the Indian state. From the national perspective, these movements represent not just domestic discontent, but the danger of destabilization by Chinese or Pakistani intelligence activities. People from India's smaller north-eastern neighbours, Nepal and Bangladesh, have swelled the destabilizing migrations at the root of some of these insurgencies, and dissident groups have used these countries, as well as Bhutan and Myanmar, for sanctuary.

(b) This study emphasizes, socio-economic pluralism and inequality in the participation of the development process generating co-operative conflict lie at the root of the insurgency in the North East. Therefore, the distinction between economic development of the geographical areas constituting the region and that of its backward sections must be borne in mind by all those who seek solution to the problem.

(c) The conflict between equity and efficiency is very sharp in the region. If equity especially inter-group equity (group meaning a distinct socio-cultural-ethnic identity) cannot be ensured, development effort will be thwarted by social revolt. Therefore, development projects must be such as is able to receive social approval at the grassroot level, given the diversities of population. This means that it must ensure the participation of the masses of all groups in the development process with reasonable equity in the distribution of costs and benefits.

(d) Concerning to the role of infrastructure in development of the region, the question of balance in infrastructure is very importantly highlighted in most of the studies. Various types of infrastructure must be commensurate with each other so as to produce optimal results.

(e) Lack of inter-departmental cohesion, coordination and synergy are the major issues, and with terrorism and growing insurgency attributed to the prime cause of such non-performance.

(f) Unless the infrastructure is substantially improved, there would be only a limited prospect of horticulture and forest based products if they are to be supplied to the rest of the nation raw and unprocessed (which, even if profitable, would not have been prudent). The same is true with floriculture and mushroom businesses. Good transportation and organized marketing system is called for.

(g) A wide range of literature very strongly justifies tourism as one of the prime potential of this region which can be significantly exploited for the betterment of the region. The entire tourism industry and its infrastructure is an area of unlimited business potential, contributing to employment generation and increased revenue earnings. This is an area where immediate benefits can be reaped. However, it is argued that adequate support and initiatives had not been taken to develop the region as the tourist hub.

(h) There are reasons why there is no much prospect for setting up of large-scale industries in the region at large (some parts of the region may, however be exceptions). One of the reasons is the location of the region at the borders of the nation. The political economy of a frontier region is almost always quite complex and rather opaque. Investment is risky and it becomes more risky due to the location disadvantages and socio-economic adversities.

(i) It is said that the region is capital shy. Due to location disadvantages, the cost of production in the industries operating in the region is quite high and therefore, these industries cannot withstand competition. Cost of production is higher in the region due again to the geographical, institutional and technological reasons.

(j) Business and industries can flourish only if there is a

peaceful and safe environment for them to operate and prosper. Unfortunately, the social atmosphere in the region has not been amiable for investment to come in and the conditions are progressively deteriorating. Capital is not shying away from the region, it is afraid of being in station. Investors are apprehensive and capital is fleeing away from the region.

(k) Another point stressed is that development in the North East must be ecologically sustainable and must not be eco-degrading. Even schemes for infrastructural development like construction of roads and railways and power projects must be so drafted as to involve minimal adverse effects on the ecology. Besides, special attention must be made while going for mining and cement industries. It must be remembered that in the North East, the masses are overwhelmingly dependent on forests, rivers and other natural resources for their daily requirements. Even plans for environment protection must be chalked out with the consent of the people and keeping their interest in view (Ganguly, 1996).

(l) Although statehood under the Indian federation cannot be granted to each sub-national group or each socio-cultural-ethnic entity their distinct identities must be respected. The best way to ensure decision-making power to different groups is to decentralize the political and economic administration. Federal principle should be followed not only in the Centre-State relation but also in the relation between the State Governments and local-level political-administrative units.

(m) The studies seek to empirically investigate how the politics of "recognition" and "representation" of the exclusive rights of a community is being enacted and reflected in the renewed assertion for "recognition" of "traditional political institutions", which are perceived to the institutionalized bearers of "traditionality". In this context, the studies mostly investigate the bases of "political" authority, the nature of the institutional structures, the implications of consensual "political" processes, limits to individual liberty and gender equality and the dichotomous or constitutive relationship between "modern" and "traditional" institutions in rural areas of the states.

(n) Lastly, all study argue that it must be driven home to the people of the North East that they can never attain real political power and development if they depend on the outside funding in all important schemes as at present. Even while accusing the Centre for neglecting the region one cannot deny the fact that most of the State Governments in the region are financially non-viable and they depend largely on the largesse of the Central Government for both plan and non-plan expenditure as evident from their annual budgets.

(o) The way to achieve greater financial and political autonomy and to avoid non-priority expenditures or wastage is local resource generation for local development works. Of course, the resource-transfer from the Centre can never be totally dispensed with. But, if Central resource-transfer is matched by significant amount of resource generation at local levels, it will not only reduce inequality and wastage in the region but will also give the people the real taste of political power.

5

Insurgency, Development and Communities at the Fringes of Nation State—Communities of North East India

Debojyoti Das

Insurgency in North East India is a chronic social phenomenon. Often these organised forms of resistances to state power are seen as products of development deficit by the Indian state. However, I argue in this chapter that people's resistance to state power in North East is historically embedded in colonial and post-colonial practices of articulation and the influence of homogenizing frontier territories that are plural and diverse. The statecraft of colonial intervention and the whole idea of mainstreaming frontier space have created resentment among native communities. Similarly, ethnic identities, the construction of the 'others' is gaining new meaning as autonomy movements have succeeded in instigating federal state in the region. Insurgency in this context has to be understood as a contest over nationalism and a struggle to sustain the plurality of social forms and community life. The ethno-political and ethno-nationalistic demands contest as well as rearticulate the web of political culture that has been formalised by colonial forms of governance, based on power, privilege and patronage in the highlands and foothills of insurgency, militancy, terrorism, underground activity as organised forms of people's response to state power operate in different forms and practice in North East. State responses to such challenge have been brutal as well as benevolent and paternalistic. Cease-fire, negotiations, dialogue have evolved with repressive legislations like Armed Forces Special Power Act (AFSPA), 1958 Disturbed Area Act 1991 and many others among forms of state coercion. The North East as a territorial space is looked upon by the Indian state as a strategic entity of North-eastern borderland, where powers like China merge their frontiers along with Bangladesh and Myanmar to construct complex geo-political and strategic challenges to the territorial integrity of India. This national security perspective has dominated discourses of security and nationalism in mainland India among scholars and policy makers working on the North East. This perspective has undermined the regional autonomy and specific cultural identity of tribes, communities and clans living in the region for centuries and who were isolated and independent before the treaty of Yandabu and the conquest of Burma by the British Empire.

Colonial Historiography is full of resistance movements and indigenous struggles by individual tribes against colonial control before they became subservient and lost autonomy. In the native imagination the British were always superior race. However, British rule was looked upon with hostility and indifference. The post-colonial Indian state continues with the colonial strategies of governance. However in recent decades state intervention have mutated to incorporate people's participation, civil society as dialogue partners and community-led interventions that present more humane state interventions where communities' social capital are invoked, cherished and previliged. By making communities responsible through participation, community development projects, and Self Help Groups, the civil society as brokers and translators in improving landscape that are imaged in the national mindset as uncivilized, barbaric, crude and underdeveloped. However, there is a catch to these representations and aspirations for improvements in native life. By involving civil society state power is not detached but reinscribed through indirect control and monitoring of facts. Similarly, communities have responded differently to development projects of the state. Some people get included while others get excluded in these development programmes. These schemes of improvement have created their own constituencies of beneficiaries. The common answer in public understanding of state intervention has been the failure of state and its machinery to deliver justice, equity and the embedded practice of political non-committed representatives who mismanage development grants and aids.

A cursory look at the economic and social dependence of the region on mainland India proves this fact. Most of the region is aid dependent on central fiscal spending like the economies of Sub-Saharan Africa with the exception of Assam that has limited dependence on central resources. It is said that the per capita central assistance is one of the highest for the North Eastern state. These observations are also countered by local intellectuals from the region, who argue for a core periphery relation and the dependence of the region on mainland India. These processes have to be understood from the specific political histories and strategies of homogenisation of trade, economy and social life with the entry of colonial administration and the spread of Christianity in the region. Before the arrival of the British regional powers, vassal chiefs, village republics, autonomous Kinships, Chiefs, Village Headman's ruled their respective territories and often co-operated as well as collided for disputes over territories, resources and authority over their clans and kinsman. Blood feuds, head hunting, raids and skirmishes were common. To any civilised state making project these political formation were disorderly and presented a state of 'Chaos' which Welsh rightly highlights in his official parchment as 'Chaos' political formation. However, in the other parts of this vast contagious space there were kingdoms that were strong and warring. The Ahoms, Tiparra Kingdom, Rajbhingshis, Manipuri Kingdon flourished in the plains until the advent of the Burmese forces. The Ahoms maintained territorial fraternity with the raiding Nagas. They never interfered into each other's territory. The territorial conquest was never the rule. Colonial intervention in the Hills marked the first systematic incursion into the wilderness. Early colonial records of 1840s refer to all the tribes of Assam as wild, savage, hostile. Even the initial response of the colonial administration was non-interference. However, policies changes as raids grew all-over the Bengal East India frontier. The Miris, Mishmis, Garos, Nagas, Bhutias and the Abors frequently challenged colonial authority and skirmished British controlled villages. The grant of Posa by the Ahom Kingdom as a reciprocal exchange to maintain territorial integrity was constrained by the intervention of the colonial government. Moreover, colonial state controlled trade in the hills and this frustrated the hill tribes in the initial years. Topographical surveys followed and it systematically led to the extension of the British Empire in the hills. These contagious spaces became the frontier tracts where colonial policy was based on personal influence and indirect control.

The political system of the highlands compelled the colonial government to adopt such strategies of governance. Here it becomes important to discuss how power and patronage operates in the highlands. The colonial government did not challenge existing social hierarchies among the indigenous communities. In fact, traditional institutional authorities were mutated and fostered by state sanction. The post of Dobashi and Village Headman facilitated administrative control and helped colonial administration to negotiate with local customary traditions. Similarly, in the post-colonial period we have the planned state with Village Councils, District Councils, Development Blocks as sites of planning and development. The colonial interventions are manifested in far greater levels of sophistication by the post-colonial Indian state.

One of the most popular and strongest instrument of social change has been the party system and the growth of democracy. The democratic deficit as Sanjeeb Baruah points out presents unique challenge to the Indian state. It also creates agendas for political action and inaction. The political culture of the nation is transplanted in the North East through pedagogy of democratisation and govemmental tactics that sets new agendas of state intervention through populist discourses of participation and participatory development.

It is often argued that resistance movements in North East were ingrained in a nationalistic discourse that called for self-determination like the Naga National Movement. In later phase, the Assam movement and today there are multiple forms of resistance and the invention of the past. The cultural invention of a unique historical past. There are also debates on questions of Sons of the Soil, the insider outsider debate, we and the 'others' and a challenge to the Pan-Assamese identity. In recent decades these issues have been complicated by trans-national pan-Islamic movements that are fuelled by intelligence agencies of India's neighbours. The issue of arms trade and its smuggling has today attained a international character, where communities living in the Blanketed space co-operate to challenge state claims over frontier territories. These events register in the national imagination as anti-national and destabilizing activities. But, if we were to ask how much of the Native life is disturbed by policies of state control and boundary making, the answers are difficult to imagine. The birth of politically administered frontiers restricts the free mobility of people and communities. By demarcating boundaries and constructing borders, the Indian state has fledged communities that were once at the heart of trade and exchange. The classic examples are of the Ao, Semas, Khasis, Garos, Tiparra kingdom and the Mishmis, Abors of Arunachal Pradesh. The partition of India as Van Shandle argues created spaces of isolation and completely restricted population mobility across North East frontier. These historical processes have to be imagined before we discuss organised peoples' resistance in the context of North East India.

Insurgency has played an important role in shaping life and times of communities living in the North East. However, insurgencies in their diverse forms have to be understood as processes that were shaped by the political culture and aspirations of territorial control. People's resistance in North East India as a geographical space cannot be looked independently nor in isolation. These have to be understood through a dialogical intervention of people's engagement with other states in South and South East Asia. The classic example stands of Burma. How much of Burma is known today in North East and *vice versa*. The Nagas are spread over Burma. In the common Naga mind they are economically backward and marginal to the whole idea of Burmese Nation state. Thus communities' social, political and cultural identity is constrained by national identities and mainstream politics. The idea of backwardness is projected by mainstream political think tank to identify ideas of backwardness. However, how do citizens realize that they are backward? Backwardness is used as a measure for improvement. When communities are marginal resistance is bound to happen. Resistance can only be negotiated through bringing development. Democratic representation is used as measures of equity in the society, however, these participatory practices create their own power and patronage equation that privileged some and marginalize others. For example in Meghalaya, Khasis are more privileged than Garos. Similarly, the Ao, Angamis, Semas, Lothas and Rengmas see the backward districts of Mon and Tuensang as privileged enjoying 33 per cent reservation in public employment. The statecraft of reservation has gone beyond mainland India in social discrimination based on caste exploitation mitigated through positive discrimination. However, these policies of the state are embedded in a larger politics of improvement where they are made to believe that equity will be achieved one day in future. However, we are not in a position to rethink how these heterogeneous spaces that were once blanketed and untouched by foreign rule became systematically entrenched in state system with unified administration. The homogenisation of jurisprudence, creation of law abiding citizens, uniform polity and centralised marketised exchange create a homogeneous space where citizens behave in a set codes of conduct approved by a higher authority, the state, democracy, nation-state, republic. Communities, clans and individuals who deviate from the established norms are declared bandit, fugitives, traitors, militias, and anti-nationals engaged in sedation and subversion of national interest. Thus, insurgency has to be understood as a more complex political mobilization where various factors play their role for popular mobilization against the state.

The history of integration and popular democratic processes and questions of marginality have to be underpinned in this regard. Marginality as a social process has to be understood in order to understand sub-nationalistic agendas. Marginality is a complex term as there are multiple webs of marginality produced by the 'democratic deficit' and 'political culture' of the nation state.

Insurgency is closely linked with questions of ethnic identity in North East. However, demands for identities have evolved over time. Identities have become stronger and stringent in the North-eastern region. The plural cultural identities that were once under a pan-Assamese identity are today challenged and fragmented. Old identities have started challenging the contemporary ones. As many young minds today feel the North East is not a melting pot of cultures rather communities present a salad bowl where identities are distinct and independent. The cosmetic federal structure that North East presents has led to limited autonomy. However, regional aspirations are growing. This has led to the proliferation of autonomy movements. The state has systematically ossified autonomy movements according to their merit. The creation of BTC (Bodoland Territorial Council) precedes many other struggles in the tea gardens of Upper Assam and Karbi Anglong. Today, Marans, Mataks, Chutias, Deories and Rajbhansis clans to have a distinct historical past. The recreation of identities based on oral tradition and pride for uniqueness has created now identity and indignity movements in Manipur valley, among the Maitis who have revived their age-old tradition and culture. The statecraft of divisiveness creates new identity crisis and political deficit. Insurgency in this context has to be understood through a set practice of state construction and interventions based on nationalist aspirations that underplay the cultural context and social complexity of local life. Insurgency can at one level be understood as people's contest to authority and state intervention. While it also evolves as particular identities become dominant over others. To use the term plurality is tricky as it can trigger struggles for equity. The plurality can be seen in the number of cultural and civil society groups that have emerged with identities as distinct and separate. The contest for autonomy has mutated struggles and claims for difference have been fostered. In this context, insurgency-militancy as defined by state and the political apparatus has to understood in its complexity.

6
Extremism in North East India and Growth of Entrepreneurship

D.D. Mali

Introduction

Entrepreneurs are people who own, operate, manage and take the risk of business venture. They are engaged in entrepreneurship, the process of running a business venture of one's own. They are always alert to see opportunities in their environment. They are capable of gathering resources of men, money and materials to exploit the opportunities to their advantages by assuming risks of business. In the process not only they benefit, the society also is benefited at large.

Some people take up entrepreneurship by choice, some by forces of circumstances, and still some other, by training. Some of those who take up entrepreneurship by choice or by forces of circumstances also take the training route to become entrepreneur. But the motivations of each group of people are different. Individuals taking up entrepreneurship by choice do so for personal satisfaction, to become their own boss, for economic gain, social status or because of achievement motivation, etc. Individuals taking up entrepreneurship because of forces of circumstances do so because they could not get job or take up job; but leave it because of dissatisfaction or frustration or do not get job of their liking or in a place of their choice. They also set up enterprises. In addition, some take up entrepreneurship because of economic compulsion;

some inherit business and have to take up family business for its survival, growth and preservation. Besides, there are people who take up entrepreneurial career after undergoing training. They are created entrepreneurs.

In whatever way a person becomes entrepreneur, he/she is an entrepreneur. The society needs more such persons for their role in economic and social change and development. The entrepreneurs are highly sought after persons. The more the number of entrepreneurs, the higher is the level of economic and industrial development. They are the persons who take risk of business and lead the economy to the path of growth.

Environment and Entrepreneurship

Majority of individuals are, however, influenced by environment in the family, society, resource system and support system. In addition, economic, political, and legal environment and law and order environment further influence the decision making process of individuals. Only a minority of people can control the influence of environment and can carry on their entrepreneurial activities irrespective of positive or negative external environment. Positive environment encourage individuals for entrepreneurship. Negative environment becomes a hurdle for growth of entrepreneurship.

Individual taking up entrepreneurship, needs to have knowledge and skill about the enterprise. But most important is his/her motivation. Only motivation can make the knowledge and skill operative for taking up entrepreneurship. Individual is generally influenced by his/her family in his/her decision making process, at least in our country. He/she will take up such kind of activities which his/her parent wants him/her to take. There are only a few individuals who can go against the wishes of the parents, though there are also exceptions. Family expectation is further influenced by social environment. Both the individual and family are further influenced for entrepreneurship by the availability of resource system technology and technical manpower, existing industries and enterprises, transport and communication facilities, power, raw materials, market, etc. All the three systems are further influenced by the support system, that is, the support organisations, including banks and financial organisations, their policy and programmes and the organisational climate in the growth of entrepreneurship in any society. Entrepreneurship has been the outcome of the total interaction between these four systems (Pareek & Nadkarni, 1978).

Political environment relate to policy support for encouraging or discouraging growth of enterprise. In India policy of protection was followed till the country initiated economic reforms. This has been replaced by the policy of promotion. Supportive policy encourages enterprises to grow.

Economic environment may either increase employment or lead to lay-off or even job loss. While economic prosperity will lead to greater employment opportunities, and also opportunities for self-employment and entrepreneurship, depression will lead to displacement of individual. This will lay the foundation for entrepreneurship. More individuals take up entrepreneurship in such a situation due to forces of circumstances.

Cultural environment may also lead to displacement arising out of reservation of jobs based on caste, creed, race, religion etc. Such displacement will force those who are displaced to take up entrepreneurial activities.

Law and order can help or hinder the growth of entrepreneurship. In North East India, this is a problem. This problem is further aggravated because of problem of extremism. Extremism is not law and order problem as such, but is much more serious problem which affects every aspect of individual's life including his desire for entrepreneurship.

Situation in North East India

In the North East India parents generally want their children to take up employment and not self-employment or entrepreneurship. This is because society gives higher status to a person who is employed, and not to one who is self-employed or take up entrepreneurship. But the situation has been changing for the better.

The number of industries has been growing. This has also some demonstration effect in encouraging individuals for entrepreneurship. But the region is still to depend on outside skilled and technical persons for some kinds of industries. Even for labour in construction industry, the region is to depend on immigrant labour. It is estimated that the region requires 22 lakh persons for construction industry; but it can supply 3 lakh labours only.

Transport and communication have improved to a great extent. But road condition is still very bad, particularly in Assam. Even in Guwahati, the gateway to the North East India, the roads are bad by any standard. Development of roads helps in emergence of entrepreneurship.

Power situation is bad, except perhaps in Meghalaya. Power is one of the most important infrastructures. Uninterrupted and quality power is needed for any kind of entrepreneurial activity.

The support system comprises a number of peripheral, regulatory, development organisations and banks and financial institutions. Peripheral organisations such as organisations or departments providing land revenue record or permission for construction of work-shed or workshop have a minor role in the growth of entrepreneurship; but they are most often cause of concern for would-be entrepreneurs. The delay in getting the documents or permissions will delay the process of launching project and hence, cost overrun. Most often the would-be entrepreneurs also require permanent resident certificate. Getting these documents is not an easy task.

Regulatory organisations, such as the authorities issuing trade licence, no objection certificate for pollution, or permission etc. can create problem. These documents are required at the initial stage. At a later stage, the requirement will be different. For instance, payment of tax, submission of reports and meeting the requirement of different authorities can create problem.

Organisational climate in development organisation is also much to be desired. Delay is a major concern almost in all organisations. Some delays are understandable. But most of the delays in doing a work are avoidable.

Banks and financial institutions have been helping in the development of trade, commerce and industry. However, procedural formalities, delay and insistence on collateral security even for a small loan most often discourages would-be entrepreneurs.

What the entrepreneurs do to get this kind of permission or document or avoid the delays that are avoidable? They take a short-cut to overcome the difficulties faced in their entrepreneurial pursuit. Most of them pay 'speed money' to manage this situation. In other words, they get the permissions/clearances or no objection certificate at a cost. Whether in getting electrical connection, land document, no objection certificate for pollution, nothing comes free. Everything has a price tag. Of course, that money does not go to the coffer of the government. This is known to the power-that-be; but everybody considers this to be small favour to be shown to the concern people. Any departure from this practice will delay the process of project launching, if a person is to start his project, and lead to delay in launching their project and hence, cost overrun. Practically nobody wants to displease these people because of the fear of facing trouble at a later date. Hence, the practice continues openly. Those who do not want to pay 'speed money' will suffer and may even abandon their desire to become entrepreneur or businessman.

Almost all the entrepreneurs are affected by this kind of environment; but most of them also 'manage environment' to carry on their business.

Environment of Extremism

Environment of extremism is much more a bigger problem than the problem of law and order. The problem of extremism has not occurred in a year or two. Besides, the causes of extremism are also diverse and complex.

Social and economic deprivation, problem of unemployment, high level of corruption, political support to extremist groups for political gain, unwillingness to solve this problem for one reason or other, apathy and allowing problem to grow till it becomes unmanageable are some of the causes that have created the problem of extremism. This problem has thrived over the years. This has in fact now become an industry. When easy money can be obtained with extortion notice, intimidation, and similar tactics, extremism thrives not necessarily for any ideology (Prakash, 2008).

I had an opportunity to meet surrendered extremists in Assam, Tripura and Manipur and interact with them. Most of them narrated how they became a part of the extremist groups. They became part of extremist because of compelling circumstances. Some became part of extremist groups when they were working as messengers for such groups. Some were lured by such groups because they were educated, but remained unemployed. Some (in Tripura) even left their job to join the extremist groups because they considered that by joining such groups they would be able to change the prevailing situation in their state.

Extremists resort to different kind of tactics to extort money. In states of North East India, every entrepreneur may not be paying money to extremists. But those who pay they pay for their security and also for running their enterprise. They live in this environment. In course of time it becomes a normal situation for them. They forget and people also forget about the extremists till they resurface again. Extremists thrive. Businesses also continue. The losers are the consumers who are to pay higher price almost for everything. In other words, entrepreneurs 'manage environment'. They pay for services they get from various organisations or institutions or departments and live with this environment.

As per Newspaper report (Khabar, 2009) outside entrepreneurs (investors) are reluctant to come to North East, particularly to Assam because of environment of extremism. About a dozen of investors who had proposals to set up enterprises in Assam left the state immediately after the bomb blast on 30 October, 2008. Among those who left Assam had proposals to set up transformer manufacturing unit, detergent making, agro-products, washing machines, menthol products, etc. They asked for security from Assam Government; but the Government could not give such assurance. Hence, they left. Indigenous entrepreneurs also can go out of the region and set up enterprises in other states. But except a very few entrepreneurs who left Assam, all others are continuing in the region itself, in February 2009, while announcing the Assam Government's Industrial Policy 2008, the Minister of Industries and Commerce, Assani stated that the state has proposals worth Rs. 2100 crore in the pipeline indicating that those who want to start enterprise in Assam, they can do so and the environment of extremism should not be a major inhibiting factor for them.

Positive environment definitely encourages more entrepreneurs to emerge. This is more so in the present socio-economic environment. Job opportunities declining, individuals are forced to take up entrepreneurship. Individuals taking up entrepreneurship by forces of circumstances will continue to grow because of changing social and economic environment, that is, liberalisation, privatisation and globalisation. More people will to take up entrepreneurship because of forces of circumstances. More people will also become entrepreneurs on their own. But their number will still remain small. There will be more individuals to take the training route to become entrepreneurs.

In the region, more than 70,000 registered small scale industries (SSI) were set up till 2002-03 (NEC, 2006). In 1997-98, the region had 53,729 SSI units. It means that 31.4 per cent units were set up at a time when extremism also continues. The number has been growing. In Assam, there were 48,567 units in 2004. In 2005, the number has gone up to 50,694 (Assam, 2008). Besides, good number of individuals are taking up entrepreneurship in different field of activities. But more entrepreneurs are emerging in the service sector. Many have been taking up agro-based activities.

Conclusion

Environment may slow down; but it cannot stop the growth of entrepreneurship in any society. Most of the entrepreneurs are affected by environment. But how much they are affected because of general environment and environment of extremism is difficult to be quantified. As far as my knowledge goes no researcher has made any attempt to make an empirical study of this situation and assess the impact on the growth of entrepreneurship. Such a study will reveal the real state of affairs about the ease of doing business in North East India.

We need more entrepreneurs. More important, we need an enterprising society where everybody will be entrepreneurial in their approach and behaviour. Environment has become a barrier in slowing down the growth of entrepreneurship. Removal of this barrier should be the major concern for all. However, governments have to play a major role in making an entrepreneur-friendly environment in North East India for rapid growth of entrepreneurship.

REFERENCES

Asomiya Khabar, February 2009.

Assam, Department of Economics & Statistics: *Handbook of Statistics 2008*.

Col. Ved Prakash: *Terrorism in India's North East 2008* (Volume 1).

North Eastern Council: *Basic Statistics of NER 2006*.

Uday Pareek and Monohar Nadkami in T.V. Rao (ed) *Development of Entrepreneurship — A Conceptual Model in Developing Entrepreneurship*, 1978, Delhi.

7

State Response to Violence in North East India

(With Special Reference to the Surrender Issue in Assam)

Dipesh Ch. Bhagabati

Surrendering of some of the members of extremist group has created some novel problems in the social milieu of Assam. Though there are several reasons behind the surrender of the members belonging to the extremist groups, temptation of the Government machinery in the form of material gain and comfort has sent an unwanted signal to join such groups in order to have a life with full of physical comfort and security. It has been attempted in this chapter to highlight the negative outcomes of the Government's approach in dealing with the surrendered members of the extremist groups like United Liberation Front of Assam (ULFA).

In the early part of the last decade, a contingent of the ULFA (henceforth will be stated as Ulfa) cadres came out of their hide-outs to lay down their arms before the state authority. One must keep in mind that the Ulfa began its arm struggle for long three decades back to achieve sovereignty for Assam. However, the episode of surrender of its cadres was a move to marginalize the strength of the underground extremist organisation creating a split within itself and this gradually emerged as a common practice with almost all the extremist groups in the state. The same practice is in vogue till date. The cadres of Ulfa who deserted the organisation and surrendered before the authority to join the so-called mainstream is popularly known as 'Sulfa' (i.e. surrendered Ulfa). This band of the cadres apparently laid down their arms and vowed themselves to the laws laid down by the Constitution of India. The authority also on behalf of the Government greeted them with bouquet, *gamocha,* shaking hands with a smile (as, usually aired in the media for public information) while creating a perception that henceforth everything would run normal for everybody. Meanwhile, the practice became common to the other extremist groups of the state as well. It has been attempted here to highlight the consequence of this practice in social life in the state and to come to a conclusion whether such a policy should be allowed to go ahead or not. However, it is important to be aware of the reasons behind the surrender by some of the cadres of a fully active extremist group.

The reasons behind the phenomena in question are multiple in numbers, such as:

(i) Self-realization
(ii) Persuasion
(iii) Personal cause
(iv) Compulsory leave from the organization
(v) Internal conflict
(vi) Temptation from the state authority etc.

The first three of the above causes are quite obvious with any cadre of an organization. Out of the remaining three causes, serial No. iv. may not be a matter of serious concern unless it becomes an outcome of a misunderstanding with the leadership. Unfortunately, if it happens so, what most likely comes out is a feeling of hostility, which tends to be revengeful towards each other.

Significantly, the last one is the part of the Government's strategy of tackling the extremists in Assam. The reason behind the Government's preference for taking up such a strategy is inherent in the organization itself (Bora, 1997). It is stated that unlike the movement launched by the other ethnic groups in the North East, Ulfa's struggle for liberation of Assam is a "movement from the mainstream". The Government of India prefers to resist such assault on the so-called mainstream by bringing back the rebels into the mainstream "with promises of riches to the returnees on the one hand and crushing the movement out of existence by brute force on the other" (Bora, 1997). This is a two pronged strategy in which the packages and promises offered to make the returnees rich and prosperous has worked as most appealing temptation to leave the organisation midway by surrendering to the authority. Note that the government resorted to such a game plan with Ulfa alone; the same approach was applied to other extremist organizations of the state too, resulting multiplying their number in thousands till date. To the contrary, those who have adhered to their organizational responsibilities have continued to struggle for the cause.

It is not the whole story what is aired in the media, as stated previously, so far as surrender ceremony is concerned. The early birds in this marathon were motivated with lots of temptations with multiple facilities like –

(i) Offering a job,
(ii) Granting of loan of higher amount,
(iii) Dropping of charges against the person concerned,
(iv) Allowed to possess arms on the plea of self-defence etc.

There may be no discontent with the provision offered to them for their safety of life. But the other provisions which have immediate impact on the economic front leading to a life with full of luxury and disproportionate prosperity transmit some far reaching message to the other segment of the youth, which may provoke them to join hands with such organisation with ulterior motive to reach the aforesaid status within the shortest possible segment of time. None can deny the fact that the prevailing socio-economic situation in the state is responsible for developing such tendencies in the young minds. For example,

(1) The state is now overburdened with more than twenty lakh of unemployed as per record of the live register of the DGE&T (GOA, 2007). For years together, the State Government could not recruit personnel to man the various Departments. Unlike some other states of India, Assam fails to offer any optimistic ground particularly in the farm and industry sector. Government's failure to check the ever-growing problem of unemployment among the educated itself is a failure in handling with the problem of growing extremist tendency in the state. It has ultimately raised political discontent, among all sections of people in general, and the mediocre youths of the low middle-class in

particular, some of whom looking for a respite from the prevailing economic uncertainty, do prefer to join hands with either of the extremist groups (Sinha, 1997). Dependence on salaried job has emerged as most sought after way for subsistence, particularly for the youth with middle class background, and in its absence unfortunately, a sizable proportion of them have joined various extremist groups. Representation of youth in higher number belonging to this segment in the extremist groups substantiates the fact.

(2) Once they surrender, the law enforcing authorities become their friend and not enemy at all. All the registered charges against them remain idle without progress in investigation. They are otherwise enabled to enjoy a comfortable life, which transmits a signal that life may be enjoyed even after joining the extremist group if one proceeds through the formalities of surrender.

(3) The post-liberalization era in the societies has witnessed a transition in value judgment. People are no more concerned about how much serious crime one has committed if one makes much material contribution for the comfort of the society or group. There is no dearth of examples to substantiate such a proposition in the contemporary society in Assam. Thus, to earn a comfortable social status is also not a difficult task (if it is felt necessary for the person concerned) even after joining an extremist group.

It is undeniable fact that some of the members of the extremist groups do surrender following realization of the futility of the way they resorted to for the sake of the sought after liberation. Quite a good number of already surrendered members have joined the mainstream and continued to contribute to the society as its responsible members.

The other side of the reality also cannot be overlooked. Contrary to the mainstreamed contingent, the other group is not lagging behind in enjoying some extra privileges in civil life. It is alleged that many a time the security forces use them in counter-insurgency operation in exchange of which they enjoy some undue advantages even without daring to take law and order in their own hands. The reluctance of the law enforcing authority to bring such law breakers to the book reflects some unhealthy attitude of the state machinery towards them. Thus, the game plan of the authority to marginalize the extremists has resulted in an undesirable atmosphere for the common people and state machinery as well.

The Government's approach to 'crush the movement out of existence by brute force' is also not welcome at all. The civil society never supports the act of violence from any end at all. Since the outcome of such approach is not so encouraging, a paradigm shift in the State's approach is of utmost necessity. It has been spelt out time and again from various corners that the issue must not be tackled as just an issue of law and order. With all sincerity, whole hearted approach must be chalked out to bring this movement to an end for which the Government must play the lead role. No doubt, the people of Assam become more and more aware about the discrimination meted upon them with perceptible regional imbalances so far as development is concerned. But then, the common people are, by and large peace lovers who look for removal of all imbalances not in exchange of flesh and blood. That is why, off late, people from every corner are demanding meaningful dialogue to find out a respectable solution of the issue. The Government should consider for mobilizing the public opinion to marginalize the extremist groups in a well organized way in which removal of regional imbalances must enjoy top priority.

It is clear that the approach played by a democratic government, like that of ours to control the extremists' problem in no way be termed as sound as it was supposed to be. Since the strategy to infuse the tendency to surrender in exchange of some gainful bait has created some new problems, the Government should come forward with more realistic approaches than diplomatic ones.

The Government must not give a blind eye to gross lapses in the security and intelligence fronts as it is going on at present. The incidences of serial blasts on October 30 (2008) and January 1 (2009) in the city of Guwahati are more than sufficient to convince the inactivity of the Government machinery to curb the violence by anti-social forces. Government must prove its accountability in providing security to people's life and property for which it must go ahead with all sincerity.

The episode of surrender of some of the members of the extremist groups in exchange of material gain and physical comfort never deserves appreciation at all. Continuation of such exercise reveals weakness in policy and practices at both the ends, i.e. Government and the respective extremist group. We the people of Assam are worst sufferer of regional imbalances for which our political leaders coming to the power at different times are no less responsible than the leaders at Delhi. Let us sweat more and more and no bleeding at all in leading the struggle for our development. Any movement or struggle, if launched for the people, must satisfy the interest of the people. The people of Assam is looking for freedom from poverty, unemployment, flood and erosion, ill-health, poor communication, lack of industrialization, and multiple of constraints hampering development. We want to have a peaceful and decent living. The lesson received so far is not able to convince us that the gun-battle will make it possible to achieve all these in the near future. The ongoing situation must be brought to an end as early as possible for which unconditional talk between the fighting groups and the Government authority is a must. There is nothing to be delighted for the Government in multiplying the numbers of surrendered. Those who desire to surrender bidding an adieu to extremism may be offered a chance to rehabilitate by hard working only. Further, who of them want to pursue education may be offered free studentship whatsoever the course may be. In no case, the facilities accorded to them be read as an incentive to join extremist group first and then come back for surrender.

REFERENCES

Bhattacharjee, J.B. (2007), *Roots of Insurgency in North East India,* Akansha Publishing House, New Delhi.

Bora, Dhrubajyoti (1997), *Insurgency in the Mainstream: A Study of Assam* (in Pakem, B.).

Ganguly, J.B. (1997), *Insurgency in North East India: An Assessment* (in Pakem, B.).

Government of Assam (2008), *Statistical Hand Book of Assam 2007.* Government Press, Guwahati.

Hajarika, Sanjay (1997), *Insurgency in North East India* (in Pakem B.).

_______(2008), *Writing on the Wall Reflections on the North East.* Penguin Books, New Delhi.

Pakem, B. (Ed) (1997), *Insurgency in North East India.* Omsons Publications. New Delhi.

Sinha, A.P. (1997), *Insurgency in the North East India* (in Pakem, B.).

8

ULFA's Extremism

A Nemesis for Assam

Chandana Bhattacharjee and *Rajiv Kumar Roy*

The terrorist attack in Mumbai, India, on 26th November 2008, has alarmed the citizens of the country. The attack received condemnation from the American and European countries as well. A combined pressure was exerted on the governments on whose political boundary these elements are nurtured. We, too, registered our voice against such heinous crimes, frequently committed,—term it *extremist, terrorists, insurgent groups* or any other. When we look back at the last terror strike (30th October, 2008) all-over Assam, and compare it with 26/11 Mumbai attack, do we actually see any difference between the two? Of the hundreds of terror attacks all-over the country, we are comparing only the above-mentioned two cases, as for example. The difference lies basically in planning, the style of attack, the degree of damage and so on. Whatsoever may be the degree of damage there are extreme steps adopted by certain groups of people,—destruction and terrorizing happens to be the ultimate goal—of these extremist groups. The question, however, remains that why is it so that the Mumbai attack alarmed the people from all walks of life, within and outside the country while the same did not happen during Assam serial blast?

Some answers lie within which may or may not be true and it depends on the reader how he/she takes it:

1. The Assam State Government acted promptly to cover up the extent of damage, including the loss of life;

2. Adopting immediately, therefore, all the measures to hide to the rest of the world the impact by severing sources of contacts. Media coverage was also very limited; and
3. The public protest from within the state was surprisingly negligible against such terrorist attack,—leaving little or no scope for the rest of the countrymen to join hand and fight for its cause.

"Extremism", as defined by Merriam Webster Dictionary, "is a quality or state of being extreme, especially advocacy of extreme political measures." It can also be described as a "political theory savouring immoderate, uncompromising policies. It can also be defined as threat or use of violence, often against civilian population and social ends to intimidate opponents or to publicize grievances often coupled with specific demands."

The nation-states in the present world are facing the problem of extremism in the process of governance. Extremism has become a global menace. South Asia is facing multi-faceted challenges, both as a region and in inter-state relations. The worsening of the security situation and the rise in extremism in many of South Asian States has created an immensely complicated situation in an already turmoil-ridden environment.

The Britishers sowed the seeds of separatism and secessionism in the region. When the freedom dawned, the North East region of the country comprised the state of Assam and two princely states of Manipur and Tripura. The phrase North East got wide currency only after the re-organization of the region. The North East region is home to over 200 tribal groups and sub-groups, many of whose historical rivalries continue today. Historically, tribal populations were divided between states. The extensive fragmentation of ethnic communities and their identity aspirations led to resentment and resistance among the tribes. The political environment was further effected by the influx of people from other regions as well as neighbouring countries like Bangladesh and Myanmar. There are mainly three kinds of insurgent outfits in the region based on their demands and issue. They are—

(1) Secessionist outfits;
(2) Outfits demanding separate state within India; and
(3) Outfits demanding Autonomous District Councils.

But despite their difference, one thing which is common among these insurgent outfits of the region is that they base their demands and issues on separate ethnic identity assertion.

Geographical isolation, colonial legacies, deprivation of indigenous population, post-Independence policies are some of the factors in explaining the birth and growth of extremism in this part of the country. However, these reasons do not hold valid today in any State of this region and especially Assam. In many States of the North East India, the situation, beyond doubt, is out of control now. The terror attack in Assam on 30th October, 2008 bears the testimony of the subject, long been discussed and little have been done to tackle it. Today, fear psychosis runs high among the people, more than the awareness about the necessary actions to be taken, which essentially demands mass involvement. Stress should be laid on action and not words alone any longer. Tough words, combined with stem actions against the extremist outfits of the States including United Liberation Front of Assam (ULFA).

The ULFA resistance movement, started in 1979, was founded on ideology of Assamese nationalism and its slogan was to establish a Swadhin Asom (Independent Assam) comprising the ethnic Assamese speaking people. In the beginning, it did manage to garner support from the Assamese people. Over time, however, its ideological degeneration, terror tactics, extortion, external linkages and acceptance of illegal Bangladeshi migrants in Assam have seriously eroded its popular support. Significantly, the historical narrative on which the ULFA based its resistance movement has also been challenged by mainstream Assamese intellectuals like Udayon Misra, who argue that ULFA's methodology of historical interpretation reflects a selective bias. While other scholars have been critical of the outfit's tactics of targeting innocent civilians, ULFA has never attempted to take the people of Assam into confidence regarding its organizational structure, tactics and strategy. It has also disregarded the views of other ethnic groups of Assam like the Bodos, Dimasas, Deuris, Karbis, Tiwas, and others. ULFA is hardly representative of the Assamese people.

ULFA once borne and nourished by the people of Assam, sharing common interest, aims and objectives, today appears to be an organization ruining the people's life and the assets of the State. This outfit with the aid of the neighbouring countries, involve in activities all-over Assam. Established network with the neighbouring countries and eventual attacks on the civilians, calls for the reassessment of this organization, ULFA along with other extremist outfits are acting as a major impediment even to the economic development of the State. All these and many more factors taken together, have given rise to a series of other problems, making the State scenario a much complex one. Our main objective here is to attempt to highlight the shift in the working of the ULFA in the recent past, involvement of Inter-Services Intelligence (ISI) of Pakistan and Directorate General of Forces Intelligence (DGFI) of Bangladesh as support system to ULFA, its influence and its shift from violence to talks.

The ULFA is a militant group from Assam, among many other such groups in North-East India. The Government of India classifies it as a terrorist group, while the U.S. State Department (2006) lists ULFA under "Other Groups of Concern".[1] ULFA claims to have been founded at the historic Ahom structure Rang Ghar on April 7th, 1979. It is reported that in 1986, it came into contact with NSCN and the MA operating in Myanmar. Later it established its camp in Bangladesh in late 1980s and initiated a series of major violent activities thereafter. The Government of India has classified ULFA as a terrorist organization and banned it under the Unlawful Activities (Prevention) Act, 1967 on 28th November, 1990. The Government of India accuses ULFA of maintaining links with the ISI of Pakistan and the DGFI of Bangladesh and waging a proxy-war on their behalf against India. The preceding years witnessed the continuing agitation and its momentum resulted in the enforcement of the Assam Disturbed Area Act and the Armed Forces (Special Powers) Act on 6th April, 1980. ULFA initiated major violent activities in 1990s. Consequently, the Government launched Operation Bajrang by the Army in 1990, to improve the law and order situation in Assam. The success of Operation Bajrang can be gauged from the success of a subsequent follow-up operation, Operation Rhino in the month of September 1991. Operation Bajrang and Operation Rhino were also marked by increased accusation against the army of atrocities and excesses. But most of these were examples of the ULFA's propaganda machinery at work.

As the Operations progressed, the number of ULFA surrenders started increasing and finally, overtook the number of those killed or captured. This was suitably encouraged by a generous policy of rehabilitation instituted by the Chief Minister for the surrendered ULFA, i.e. SULFA. The preceding years also saw the improvement in the law and order situation, with an ever-increasing co-operation between the Government, local population, security forces and SULFA. The total number of ULFA cadres to have laid down arms has gone up to 8,718 between 1991 and 2005. With an ever-increasing number of ULFA cadres surrendering to the government, the SULFA became active and further weakened the militants. The security forces, learning from the past mistakes, organized a 'Unified Command Structure' from January 1997 to enable better co-ordination of various civil. military, para-military and police force departments. This improved the efficiency and understanding between the security forces and other actors in the operations, further increasing pressure on the ULFA. But ULFA continued to attempt ambushes and sporadic attacks on Government officials and security forces and innocent civilians too.

"ULFA was able to become a large outfit primarily due to the tacit support provided by the first AGP regime under Prafulla Kumar Mahanta. The outfit was running a parallel government in Assam during that period."[2] It is not alone the State Government, but also the bureaucrats and big business personnels who helped this group in their own ways. Illegal arms sale to the ULFA cadres have also been reported.[3] Moreover, some media people have been sympathetic towards the cause of this organization. Some of them even have stepped further to help the outfit by receiving, typing, photocopying messages for them. They also extended their services to distribute ULFA's statements among other journalists, etc.[4] Networking among the outfit groups within the region increased (including arms training), fund, shelter, visas and passports for the leaders which enabled them an easy movement in different countries. Our bordering countries like China, Pakistan, Bangladesh, Myanmar provided shelter to the members and leaders of such organizations.[5] Due to such kind of supports, money laundering by ULFA leaders (ignoring the lower rung cadres) and their leading of luxurious life, were well known facts. ULFA has stepped far beyond these and surprised the people when a leading U.S. think-tank stated that the ULFA had funded over six million dollars to political parties in Bangladesh during the 2007 election of that country.[6] ISI has facilitated cooperation between ULFA and other militant outfits of North East India, Jammu and Kashmir, LTTE in Sri Lanka and Al Qaeda linked Jehadi groups operating in the region.[7] Indian militants run 172 training camps in various parts of Bangladesh. Indian security forces revealed that ULFA did not have many Muslim cadres in its fold in the past, but the increasing flow of Bangladeshi refugees across the border has given the group more and more capable members willing to sacrifice their lives for the group's cause with nudging from the ISI. Top ULFA leaders including Paresh Baruah and Arbinda Rajkhowa were believed to be operating from Bangladesh. Thus, Bangladesh has certainly become the nerve-centre of international terrorism.[8]

The ULFA has a history of resorting to acts of terror ahead of important events to pressurize both the Central and State Governments to make some concessions. ULFA's sporadic activities, largely consisted of blasts on oil pipelines in deserted areas and the killings of unprotected and unarmed migrant workers, provided substantial indications of the group's largely diminished ability to carry out high-quality attacks. This indicated significant reversals in an outfit that has only been in business for nearly three decades, but is also known to have been backed up by the Inter-Services Intelligence (ISI) of Pakistan and the Bangladeshi Directorate General of Forces Intelligence (DGFI), for a considerable period. This has lent credence to the assertions by the security forces (SFs) that, while ULFA has weakened over years, the current operations would incapacitate it even further. It is claimed that ULFA has been forced to rely on a band of young recruits in adequate preparation and insufficiently trained to use sophisticated weapons and explosives. Similarly, ULFA is known to be using newly formed groups like the All Adivasi National Liberation Army (AANLA)—which is believed to have been armed by the ULFA—to carry out extortion in the tea estates in the tea districts. The group is now hiring unemployed youth and even school and college students to lob grenades, distribute extortion notes and collect ransom from the businessmen and government officials. It will, however, be premature to predict the end of ULFA. The group clearly has its back against the wall, but is adopting new survival tactics which are yet to be neutralized by an effective strategy of response from the state.

Over the years, the Government of India has been expressing its desire to hold direct talks with the ULFA. However, its past experience has not been encouraging due to the ULFA's intransigence. The ULFA's offer to hold talks with the Centre during major security operations has been aimed at getting the security forces off its back. This happened during Operation Bajrang in 1990 and Operation Rhino in 1991. In 1992, in response to ULFA's offer to hold talks, the Centre released five of its senior leaders. But soon after the first round of talks, the leaders slipped into Bangladesh and never returned to the negotiating table. Similarly, in the aftermath of Operation All Clear in 2003, when its bases in Bhutan were destroyed and most of its cadres killed or arrested, the ULFA once again expressed a desire for talks in 2005. The ULFA's demands for talks was based on three pre-conditions. These are:

1. Talks to be held in a mutually acceptable location outside India;
2. Talks to be held under the supervision of the United Nations; and
3. The main issue to be discussed would be the 'sovereignty' of Assam.

ULFA informed the Prime Minister's Office, New Delhi, on 7th September, 2005 that the organization would constitute a citizens group for preliminary discussion with the Government. This group christened as Peoples' Consultative Group (PCG) consisted eleven eminent persons from various walks of life, viz., lawyers, journalists, Human rights activists and sports personality (also a childhood friend of Paresh Barua, ULFA Commander-in Chief) formed in September 2005. Gnanpith award winning author and novelist—Indira (Mamoni Raisom) Goswarni, was selected its chief mediator. While three rounds of talks were held with the PCG, they broke down, as the Centre wanted the ULFA's assurance that it would shun violence and participate in direct talks. The ULFA, on the other hand, insisted on the release of its five top leaders lodged in jails. Both the Centre and the ULFA has failed to compromise their respective stands. In August 2006, the Central Government unilaterally announced a ceasefire with the outfit and the ULFA also responded by promising to end hostilities. However, after a period of six weeks, the government called off the ceasefire and resumed military operations on the ground that the ULFA had not kept its promise of not indulging in violent activities in the state. On September 27, 2006, the PCG withdrew from negotiations protesting against the Central Government's decision to resume military operations against the outfit. Thus, the peace talks came to an abrupt end even before they really took off.

The Central Government ruled out acceding to the pre-conditions for talks laid down by ULFA. The members of the PCG (2005) picked by the ULFA leaders and not through the mandate of the people, raised eyebrows of a section of the people. Thus, neither the ULFA nor the PCG are, in reality the choice of the people. This clearly is a conflicting situation. The *'Sovereignty of Assam'* as the ultimate goal of ULFA does not have anything to do with the common citizens of Assam. Therefore, the wise observers believe that the illegal migration from Bangladesh, which has caused a socio-economic imbalance within the state, should be the priority agenda during talks with the Centre so that some consensus can be reached to deal with such a serious issue.

However, ULFA pushed afar the people of the state by following a violent path. It created panic among the non-Assamese people by killing 74 innocent Biharis in 2007-2008. It also irated a section of the Assamese people by the diktat issued to "all Hindi-speaking people to leave the state", deviating from its earlier slogan of 'unity' of all communities within Assam for its cause. Bangladeshi immigrants have been regularly used as a vote bank by the Congress in the State since the time of Smt. Indira Gandhi, "Influx of Muslim illegal immigrants from Bangladesh, today is virtually controlled by a pan-Islamic organization. A fact that is creating room for the Islamisation of the territory and threatening the same indigenous Assamese identity which the ULFA promised its supporters."[9] According to a study, a total of 1,298,754 illegal Bangladeshi migrants have entered into Assam between 1951 and 1991.[10] Thus, ULFA has retreated from its own agenda of 'detection', 'deletion' and 'deportation' of illegal Bangladeshi immigrants from Assam.

The concept of peace talk was yet to bear any fruit. More than thirty years long insurgent activities of ULFA have left the people of the state exhausted and devastated. The ULFA, too, on its part has taken to more and more diversionary strategies. The initial ULFA promise against the Islamisation of its territory has, over the years, proved to be just its opposite. The people of the state, who initially provided support to this organization, have withdrawn its support very silently. No explicit protest was shown in support of ULFA by the common people of the state.

The rise of extremism has provided the government with the opportunity to enact laws granting it extraordinary powers. Over the years, the Indian government has passed a series of anti-terrorism bills. These include the Assam Disturbed Area Act and the Armed Forces (Special Powers) Act. But can the mere enforcement of these draconian laws put an end to all law and order problems in the state ? What is required is a radical change in the present state's approach towards the decades old ULFA's extremism. The effective implementation of the Illegal Migrants (Determination by Tribunals) Act, 1983 can help in solving the present problem. But again if this has to be done, then some of the political parties—like Congress—will have to compromise with their (Bangladeshi) vote bank, and this is something which is unlikely to happen in the present scenario. Neither the Congress nor the AGP led government has been successful in solving the influx problem of the state. It is quite interesting to note that the Centre is blamed for every wrong things in the state whether it be underdevelopment or unemployment. But the same finger which blames the Centre forgets/fails to point about the failure of the state leadership and also the failure of the local people to pressurize their political leaders to bring about development in the state.

The previous NDA Government was strong in rhetoric relating to terrorism, but weak in action. The present UPA Government is weak in rhetoric as well as in action. It seems to believe in confidence-building measures with neighbours—especially Bangladesh. However, it is quite true that ULFA's social base will survive till such time when the Indian government succeeds in persuading the common people of the State that, under its aegis, they would be guaranteed economic justice and also all-round development.

What is urgently required is that the people and the civil society of the state must also respond, try to bring back to the right track ULFA cadres and other such organization members, show them some right direction and compel them to continue the peace talks with the Centre, for it is the common ordinary citizens' lives which are at stake always and not the lives of the political leaders.

NOTES

1. *The Shillong Times*, 2nd May, 2007.
2. *DIALOGUE*, Vol. 8, No. 2, B.B. Kumar, p. 166.
3. *Ibid.*, p. 171.
4. *Ibid.*, pp. 172-173.
5. *DIALOGUE*, Vol. 8, No. 2, B.B. Kumar, pp. 174-175.
6. *The Shillong Times*, 26th February, 2007.
7. *Ibid.*, 24 April, 2007.
8. Ravi Pratap Singh, *South Asia Politics*, "Insurgency and Illegal Immigration in North East: The Great Game of Pakistan and Bangladesh", January 2008.
9. *The Shillong Times*, 5th February, 2007.
10. "NGO report on illegal migrants in Assam", *Hindustan Times*, (New Delhi), May 15, 2002. Internet Source —www.satp.org.

9

Preventing Extremism

Role of Education

Sumana Paul

Extremism is the taking of concessions for which there is no basis or truth. It is a tendency or disposition to go to extremes. We have always had extremism which leads to violence and death. Extremism may be defined as "When you do not allow for a different point of view; when you hold your own views as being quite exclusive, when you don't allow for the possibility of difference" (Archbishop Desmond Tutu on a debate in Doha, Qatar). L. Davies of University of Birmingham added, "And when you want to impose these views on others using violence if necessary."

Some definitions say that extremism is the use of violence in order that a population forces their governments to the table of negotiation or to some changes in their policies—that is extremism is not just about views, but has a political end. The word Extremism may also be used to describe a flammable mixture of ideology, methodology and religion without differentiation. The term extremism which generally has a religious flavour attached to it is a serious threat to our secularism.

Now let us see who are Extremists? In simple words, extremists are those who advocate violence against society at large. Extremists may be termed as suicide extremists, or Islamic fundamentalists etc. But whatever may be the terminology they have a common goal and that is to compel modern democracies to withdraw military forces from the territory that the extremists consider to their homeland. Extremism does not originate haphazardly. It must indeed have causes and motivation. Knowledge of the causes is essential to enable us to define remedy, which medically speaking must always be preceded by diagnosis. But diagnosis is impossible when causes are not known.

We must realize at the outset that no cause is wholly responsible for the spread of extremism. It is a complex phenomenon with numerous interrelated causes. Some of which are direct, others indirect; some found in the distant past, others in the present. Consequently, we should not focus on one cause and totally ignore the others. The causes of extremism could be religious, political, social, economic, psychological, intellectual or a combination of all of these. Religion is rarely a root cause, although it is often used as tool by various extremist groups in recruiting and in other efforts in service of the broader strategic objective. Individuals join extremist groups for a number of reasons, including the desire to achieve specific political goals, as well as a variety of financial, spiritual and emotional incentives and rewards (they earn much more/family members also receive financial and material rewards such as better housing etc.).

However, the root causes of extremism in North East India may be enumerated in the following way:

1. The problems of poverty and corruption and exploitation of the vulnerable sections of the society.
2. Sometimes young people become extremists because they have a feeling of having discriminated against and treated as second class citizens.
3. The appalling gap between the rich and poor, the privileged and unprivileged.
4. Ignorance of the common masses with reference to the actual geographical and cultural contribution of the people of North East India.
5. Inadequate employment opportunities, lack of access to resources, underdeveloped agriculture, geographical isolation, industrial backwardness etc.
6. Provocation by outsiders and influence of External Forces.
7. The concept of 'sons of soil' is likely to have some sort of a regional arrogance, which might have culminated in the form of extremism in the region.

8. People of North East India had been frustrated due to negligence by consecutive State and Central Governments. Ultimately in utter desperation these frustrated persons take up guns. Another prime cause may be the failure of the government to address the overwhelming challenges of development arising from rapid social, demographic and economic changes over the last century.

There is an urgency to improve the conditions of rural life as majority people live in villages. Majority of the people who live in rural areas are poor and susceptible to some level to the appeal of the extremist groups. Now the question is—How do we prevent individuals from joining extremist or violent movements? Or How do we enable people to make challenges to extremist movements? There may be political and military solutions to extremism, but these are not permanent solutions. Law and order is not enough to deal with extremism. We need to address the underlying issues that can drive young people to reject the message of extremism and help to bring about a safer society. Now, I want to look at some of the educational strategies to prevent or to fight against extremism.

In my opinion it is education which has the power to help people to reject cruelty and violence and promote our core values of tolerance, trust, mutual respect, liberty, fairness and respect of the rule of law. Trust, mutual respect and goodwill have a very strong role to play in holding the people belonging to diverse faiths together. If we do not prevent extremism it will destabilize its social fabric thereby weakening its democratic base and consequently putting into risk its own survival. Our basic values, which are part and parcel of Indian society can only be retained through an integrated approach to value education. We should learn how to say no to extremism. And only education can help to change the mindset of our younger generation by promoting peace education. Peace education as well as value education equips our younger generation to reject the arguments of those who preach hate.

Prosperity of the nation is important not only for the prosperity of the world but it is important to avoid conflicts and war. In this respect education enables us to formulate ideas and systems to bring prosperity and reduce disparity.

So far as North East India is concerned, there is an urgency to improve the conditions of rural life and this could be achieved by better knowledge connectivity. It is a known fact that level of extremism decreases when a country becomes wealthier, more powerful and more socially concerned, and this is possible through imparting quality education.

Role of Schools and Colleges in Preventing Extremism

Education globally has a vital role to play in the challenge to extremism. Schools and colleges can play a key role in empowering people to reject the message of extremism. It is possible to build a stronger, safer society through inculcation of core values in the students at school level. Real education should enable one to utilize the knowledge one has acquired to meet the challenges of life and to make all human beings happy as far as possible. In order to achieve this real education, children should learn certain values at the very initial state of their learning process, because the children of today are the adults of tomorrow and it is expected that whatever they are taught at the formative years of their life is responsible for molding them for their future life. The methods and approaches for teaching values could be—

- *Curricular approach*—lecture method, story telling method, group activities, books and supplementary reading materials etc.
- *Co-curricular approach*—sports and games, drama, debates on social problem. Awareness programmes against the various extremist groups, prayer (during everyday assembly in order to help the students think positively) social service programmes like NCC, NSS, services to the poor, services to hospitals etc. have immense importance in imbibing values among students.

Colleges too play a greater role in promoting community cohesion and preventing extremism. Colleges have a responsibility to foster our shared values and protect their students and staff from those who wish to promote violence. College teachers can play a great role by providing support to vulnerable students and offering appropriate advice, guidance to all students. Through various activities (like debate, panel discussion, lectures on sensitive issues by eminent personalities) organized in the college, the students should be made aware of their roles in preventing extremism. There is no denying the fact that the power of rumour and distorted information is significant in spreading violence. And here comes the role of teachers. Teachers can enable young and adult learners to engage in critical analysis of newspapers and T.V reporting. This is an essential survival skill at individual and national level.

Schools and colleges also play a key role in helping young people to recognize and reject those violent movies that could draw them into extremism. Groups which challenge the message of extremism should be supported. It may also be mentioned that Teachers Training Programme may be a very important area where teachers should be oriented in developing skills towards teaching controversial issues.

Again at school and college level the predominate need is to have a peaceful climate, a peace culture by developing attitude and behaviour of appreciation, cooperation, belongingness, trust, mutual respects and spirit of learning. In such a culture the students will naturally absorb the spirit of peace and adopt a living system of peace, values, norms and practice it into the daily life. Hence, it would be necessary to change the teacher-centred classroom approach to student-centred learning. When there is active and participative learning in the classroom using interesting teaching and learning methods in a friendly and lively atmosphere marked by creative expressions of potentials and self-discipline, peace will emerge naturally. Teachers have to identify effective strategies and practices that could transform the educational institutions into a place of harmony.

Conclusion

The struggle against extremism will be difficult to win unless we make sincere efforts to make our education value based. Our schools and colleges should preserve, develop and create a culture of peace which would ultimately build the peace for the new millennium. Education has the power to prepare our younger generation to address the problems of extremism in the region in a peaceful manner. In my opinion, it is the education which offers positive solution to the problem of extremism. Value based education and peace education will not only give a shape to our personality or character but also promote understanding, tolerance and friendship among all nations, racial and religious groups.

10

Communal Extremism can Promote Terrorism

Sanjeeb Kakoty

Though Assam is no stranger to violence, yet the eighteen simultaneous blasts in October 2008 that killed and maimed hundreds of people in different parts of the state was quite unprecedented. The scale, spread and amazingly synchronized nature of the blasts speak of meticulous planning and good logistics. The question of who masterminded the blasts raises the disconcerting possibility of the involvement of *Jihadi* elements. When the blasts are seen in tandem with the growing communal fault-lines in the body politic of Assam, the picture carries fearful connotations. The problem is exacerbated by the fact that the question of communal extremism is normally kept out of the realm of public debate. This is so because anyone talking of a growing communal divide in Assam is branded as an advocate of communalism! In this atmosphere, it is hardly surprising that no politician or political commentator, have had the courage to delve into the ground reality of happenings in Assam just prior to the blasts. One has to ask whether the large scale disturbance, especially in the districts of Darrang and Udalguri, were essentially communal in nature and whether the blasts were somehow related to it.

It may sound amazing, but the fact remains, that the spark that lit the flame of recent violence in Assam was a silly dispute over the ownership of a chicken! What ambient conditions fed the flame and transformed it into a raging fire that consumed hundreds of lives and thousands of hearths and homes? It is in the numerous refugee camps that one can discern the most tell tale signs of the nature of the violence. On the one side are the Muslim refugee camps and on the other side are camps that house Bodos, Assamese, Santhals, Garos, and other non-Muslims. Each side has harrowing tales to recount and the fear of returning to their own homes has ensured that the camps continue to exist.

As the world outside began to take cognizance of the humanitarian plight of displaced people, the reality of the communal overtones of the clashes also became increasingly apparent. Interestingly, it was at this juncture that the happenings of a single day decisively shifted public attention. Media attention and public consciousness changed focus from the agony of people forced to live in refugee camps in one's own country, to the naked terror of a series of devastating bomb blasts in public places. From the growing communal divide in Assam, to the realm of raw terror and fear, the transition seems to have been achieved instantaneously. The huge loss of life and property has not only triggered extreme emotions but has also created a stifling atmosphere of fear. In such an emotionally surcharged situation, the biggest casualty has been truth and reason.

Probably the best example of reason having taken a back seat was the classic statement made by a prominent Assam Minister. In response to a question, in the immediate aftermath of the blasts, the Government spokesman, Health Minister Himanata Biswa Sharma, angrily refuted the suggestion that there was any kind of intelligence failure that led to the blasts! Soon after this famous statement, began the circus of the blame game! From the initial government response of *Jihadi* elements being responsible, to the appearance of a SMS from a little known Islamic outfit claiming responsibility for the blasts, the accusations have come a full circle to encompass the National Democratic Front of Bodoland (NDFB) and the United Liberation Front of Assam (ULFA). Interestingly, the investigations have been done with the media in full attendance, and the public made privy, to the minutest clue, imagined or unearthed by investigators!

The manner of conducting the investigations seems to have veered away from the basic purpose of ascertaining the truth behind the conspiracy and identifying the forces and people responsible for it. Instead there seems to be a singular effort, with the help of a pliant media, to paint some of the accused as guilty without any trial. It stands to reason that once the postulate "the guilty have been nabbed", is reasonably established in people's minds, the case will fade away from public consciousness. But until another bomb rips away the peace and normalcy that supposedly prevails in Assam, the questions that need to be asked are:

1. What was the motive behind the blasts ?
2. Who hatched the conspiracy ?
3. Who planned and financed it ?
4. Who executed the plan ?

If reason and logic has any place in our minds, it would be difficult to brush aside the suggestions that the blasts are somehow linked to the violence in Darrang and Udalguri. The scale, precision, magnitude and places of occurrence of the blasts points towards the involvement of Islamic fundamentalists at some stage, be it conspiracy, financing or planning. Were the blasts meant to send a signal to one and all, that violence against the community could have serious repercussions elsewhere? Does the news of Harkatul-Jihad-e-Islami (HUJI) militants being killed in an encounter in lower Assam: the inputs from the Army and the Director General of the Border Security Force (BSF), regarding the activities of Islamic Militants in the region; the violence in Darrang and Udalguri; the reported rising of Pakistani flags in certain troubled areas followed by meticulously planned, well coordinated and effectively executed bomb attacks all add up to something tangible? This certainly seems an opportune time to consider the fact that there are new entrants to the ranks of extremist outfits operating in the state, and their *raison d'etre* is basically communal.

It should be of immense interest to security planners that the blasts might hold lessons about the merging shadow lines of the extremist outfits. Mutual help and sharing of logistics among extremist groups in the region is not something new. But the entry of Islamic Militant elements to this fraternity would add a new dimension with major consequences. If recent government revelations are to be believed, the execution of the plan for the serial blasts, may have been delegated to local contacts. If the majority of the suspects, as the investigators are telling us, belong to the NDFB, where does it put the onus ?

Probably one would do well to look into the ground realities of Assam to have some understanding of the conspiracy angle. The first reality is the simple fact that the political fault-lines of Assam are drawn on basic communal lines. The second, terrorism as a method of achieving political goals and exerting pressure, has come to stay. From this standpoint, it may be said that the recent bomb blasts were a means of exerting pressure. By whom and for what, are question the investigators would need to answer.

For a start, it has to be accepted that the danger of the communal divide in Assam was always present. Can anybody deny the fact that grouping scheme during the time of independence which almost placed Assam with Muslim majority East Pakistan. and the subsequent successful fight to reverse it, was essentially politics fought on communal lines? It is remarkable that the All Assam Students' Union led anti-foreigner movement did not degenerate into a communal hate campaign, though the people at the receiving end of the agitation were largely Muslims. This is not to suggest that communal violence did not take place during the period of the agitation. As a matter of fact, Assam did witness some of the worst communal violence in the 1980s. But the basic character of the agitation never endorsed a communal position.

Interestingly, it was in the post accord Assam, that the communal fault-lines became clearly visible. The emergence of the political grouping called the United Minorities Front (UMF), that positioned itself as the champion of the minority community was the best example of the communal polarization that Assam was undergoing. In order to halt the erosion of the immigrant Muslim vote bank, something the Congress in Assam had assiduously cultivated, the party sought to hijack the agenda of the UMF by positioning itself as being more pro-minority than the UMF itself! In time, the Congress was able to wean away a large chunk of the UMF leaders and supporters, and not surprisingly, the UMF gradually faded away. The disappearance of the UMF from the political firmament did not mark the end of communal politics it merely marked the adoption of their partisan agenda by mainstream political parties. While the Congress sought to monopolize the votes of the immigrant Muslims, the Bhartiya Janata Party (BJP) dreamed of consolidating their Hindu constituency by seeking to make a distinction between Muslim and Hindu infiltrators. Interestingly, the child of the Assam agitation, the Asom Gana Parishad (AGP), sought to maintain an enigmatic silence, thereby exposing its lack of deep ideological moorings. Bereft of ideological anchorage, its subsequent disintegration into numerous personality dominated factions is quite understandable.

In this murky political tug of war of communal polarization, what party occupied which space remained unclear. While the Bharatiya Janata Party (BJP) occupied one end of the spectrum, the Congress sought to straddle the entire spectrum and also play the communal card whenever necessary. The only regional party of some standing, the Assam Gana Parishad (AGP) neither took a strident anti-immigrant stand nor worked on developing a strong regional agenda. To make matters worse, it also displayed an utter lack of concern to understand or address the concerns and aspirations of indigenous communities. Under the circumstances, it was inevitable that there would emerge both ultra regional and overtly communal groupings. This fact was evidenced by the emergence of numerous autonomy movements, the most notable being that of the Bodos, and also an assertion of Muslim interests, as espoused by the All-India United Democratic Front (AUDF). At this stage, the creation of the Bodoland Autonomous Council did create some democratic space that attracted a large section of the Bodo extremists, most notably the Bodo Liberation Tigers (BLT) to vie for it. The Bodo political grouping calling itself the Bodo People's Party (BPP) or the Bodoland Peoples Front (BPF) not only captured power in the autonomous council but also won most of the seats in Bodo dominated constituencies of the state assembly. For the first time in Assam's history, the successful electioneering on communal lines by the Bodos, saw the emergence of their party as a decisive force in Government making. This had two major consequences. On the one hand, it brought the Bodos to the thick of governance in Dispur and Kokrajhar, and on the flip side, denied parties with a minority support base, any bargaining power in the process of government formation. In a major break from the past, the survival of the new government in the state was not dependant on the minorities. Understandably, this put parties, such as the AUDF, firmly on the back foot. With its support rendered inconsequential for the continuance of the government, the party found itself helpless to effectively champion the minority cause. Probably, had it not been for the acumen and charisma of its founder and millionaire businessman Badruddin Ajmal, the party would have gone the UMF way. Though it continues to survive it is apparent that it is losing ground. Like all other parties in the opposition, it espouses moral superiority but betrays utter impotence in providing substantive criticism to government policies. This has caused these political groupings to concede emotional space to new voices speaking a more extreme language. The extremists have often lambasted the inability of political parties in safeguarding minority interests. These radical voices have liberally sown the seeds of militancy. In this backdrop, the recent attempts to rally the moderate Muslim voice, under the leadership of Ajmal, and the issuance of *fatwa* against violence, in the aftermath of the serial bomb blasts, are significant developments. This move, opens the window of opportunity, to isolate the extremists from the moderates. Used in tandem with the public outrage against senseless violence, it may prove useful in isolating all extremist elements, irrespective of communal affiliations. To that end, the investigating agencies have to get to the bottom of the blast conspiracy.

At this crucial juncture, Assam requires political leadership of the highest order. Sadly, good leadership is a rare commodity in the state. Scoring Brownie points over political opponents is merely a quality that can never be confused with leadership. One party had a leader who was prudent enough to issue a *fatwa* against violence. Assam is waiting with bated breath to see if there exists more such leaders who will seize the opportunity to help shape a tomorrow of peace and hope!

11
Religion and Politics
Church Leaders in the Naga Political Movement

Somingam Mawon

Introduction

With the end of Cold War and the collapse of communist regimes in Eastern Europe and the former Soviet Union, many hoped the page had turned to a more peaceful chapter in the World History. However, one also witnessed the outbreak or continuation of sectarian violence and secessionist or other political movements in the Balkan, Africa, the Middle East, South Asia and other corners of the globe; the emergence of a more lethal and global brand of terrorism; and a growing cultural divide dashed many of those hopes. In other words, it has created skepticism about the prospects for peace, security, dialogue and discussion among parties in conflict (Wallensteen, 2004: Preface). In it, the influence of religion was observable.

Religion operates as a form of power and mobilization almost everywhere in any form of political movement. In Eastern Europe, religion—mostly Christianity and Islam—played an important role in the diffusion of the communist monopoly. In Africa, the Middle East, South America, Central Asia, the Indian subcontinent and South East Asia, religion harnessed many nationalist causes (Percy 2001:13041). For instance, Pope John Paul II and Martin Luther King (Junior) have been instrumental in turning back tides of communism and racism (*ibid*:13081). Among the major religions,

Christianity is one. History shows Church did play role in political movement; acting as an instrumental role in the birth of nationalism, agent of peace, reconciliatory or mediatory roles among the conflicting parties. Church's role in political movement is worldwide.

In the United States of America, the Declaration of Independence, Abolition of slavery, Civil War, Labour Rights, Anticommunism and Civil Rights Movement—all were argued in the name of God (Leege, 2001:13041). The Constitution of the United States provides the principle of secularism, however, the influence of Christianity in State politics is very much observable. During the colonization of Latin America, Christianity served as a vehicle of accommodation as well as of protest (Benavides, 1972:1764). Catholic Church played a vital role during the freedom struggle of Ireland from British colonialism. The Ireland was divided into two on the basis of Christian denomination, South for Catholics as independent nation and North for Protestants under British territory. And in Northern Ireland, religious polarization has attempted to hold out against political reconciliation (Percy, 2001:13078). Until Serbia recognized Kosovo as a sovereign State on 18 February, 2008, Serbian Orthodox Church continued to run a propaganda campaign of defamations against Albanians and the Kosovo Liberation Army (KLA). The Church continued persuading the United States and others to recognize Kosovo to be an integral part of Serbia (Hyseni, 2007).

In Africa, foreign missionary Church laid the foundation in many of political awareness and liberation struggles against the Imperial domination of Western Powers (Onaiyekan, 2008). Church leaders gave moral and financial support to the freedom fighters, at times even direction, to the development of new Nations. Here one can cite examples like Cardinal Malula in Congo Zaire, Cardinal Thiandoum and Senghor in Senegal, Cardinal Yago and Houphuet-Boigny in Ivory Coast, to mention just a few. In Zimbabwe and Apartheid South Africa, the Church worked consistently with other forces for the development of democracy and majority Black rule (*Ibid*). Following the end of Apartheid in South Africa, Church plays a vital force in securing peace and democracy (Percy, 2001:13078). Church played vital role in Angola to end military combat and political hostilities, and a return of National Union for the Total Independence of Angola (UNITA) rebels to the negotiable table for peaceful settlement with the Government of Angola. In Rwanda, Churches involved actively in the genocide politics of 1994 most brutal ethnic violence (Longman, 1997).

In the post-colonial era, active participation of Church in political movement was observable in many Asian countries. In the long struggle for independence from colonial rule, Philippine Christians were instrumental in overthrowing Spanish rule, and Korean Christians actively participated in the independent movement against Japanese (Young, 1999:163). In Vietnam, Catholic Church was a strong supporter of moves for peace during Vietnam War and of subsequent North-South reconciliation efforts after the war (Northcott, 1972:1763). In Taiwan, Presbyterian Church advocates for the Taiwanese to live in freedom, peace and justice, and not to be governed by China (Homrighausen, 1972:180). During the freedom movement of Papua New Guinea, the Church supported and involved in the struggle for political independence (*ibid*: 187). Despite of being in minority, Indonesian Christians were active in the struggle for Indonesian Independence against Dutch rule (Northcott, 1972:1763). In East Timor, Catholic Church remained a cornerstone in the struggle for East Timorese self-determination against Indonesian occupation (Lundry, 2001), and Church leaders, like Bishop Belo, support to Revolutionary Front for Independent East Timor (FRETILIN) helped in attaining their Independence. The Church provided shelter and gave support to the members of FRETILIN before the independence of East Timor in 2002.

Nationalism and the Naga Movement

Both religion and nationalism are the most potent and inspiring sources of collective identity, but also the most destructive forces for mobilizing large numbers of people and generating social conflict and change (Smith, 2001:13085). Nationalism is first and foremost, 'a state of mind', 'an act of consciousness' (Kohn, 1951:4). Nationalism is the political belief that some groups of people represent a natural community which should live under one political system, be independent of others and have the right to demand an equal standing in the World order with others (Robertson, 1985:225). It is a complex, often problematic concept for social scientists. But among existing definition of the term, one finds three critical agreements: the rise of Nationalism is *historically specific*; nationalism exemplifies an ideological movement, promoting the autonomy, unity and sovereignty of those gathered in a single territory; and nationalism evokes a *strong collective sentiment* (Cerula, 2001:10330). In the Indian or Asian (as well as African) context, nationalism came to mean independence from foreign rule and opposition to imperialism and colonial domination. Indian nationalism grew partly as a result of colonial policies and partly as a reaction to colonial policies. The nationality question in India is not a new phenomenon. It had taken root well before the existence of Indian Union itself. On the eve of the British transfer of power to India, a strong whirlwind of national movements did arise. The Naga movement for self-determination, to be an independent nation was one of them. It is one of the oldest surviving movements in Asia and India's longest-running political movement.

The word Naga is an identity or the collective name given to tribes who trace their descent from a common ancestor belonging to the Sino-Mongolian family, and speaking languages which fall under the Tibeto-Burman group. By analyzing the Naga legends, myths, stories and folksongs which were passed from generation to generation, the Naga origins can be located somewhere in South East Asia. However, the exact place of their origins is yet to ascertain. Naga territory covers an area of 1,20,000 square kilometres with a population of more than four million (Shimray, 2005:17). At present, the Nagas live in the state of Nagaland, Naga Hills of Manipur, Zemi and Rengma Naga tribes in Assam, Tirap and Changlang districts of Arunachal Pradesh, and some in Kachin state and Sagaing Division (formerly known as Naga Hills) across the border in Myanmar. The international boundary of India and Myanmar cuts their territory thereby making them a citizen of two sovereign States. There are 66 lists of Naga tribes both in India and Myanmar as suggested by the Naga Hoho, a federation of all the Naga tribes which was formed on 25th June, 1994 at Wokha, Nagaland state (Ngalung, 2010:7). The largest tribes are the Konyak, Ao, the Tangkhul and Semal Sumi.

The establishment of modern political and administrative systems, the spread of Christianity and modern education, participation of thousands of Nagas in the two World Wars led to the birth of educated middle class and thinking citizens among the Nagas. They rose above their tribal loyalties and dreamt of uniting all the Nagas. Undoubtedly, awareness of its history, cultural identity, languages and race of the people inculcated the feeling of nationalism which led to the formation of the Naga Club in 1918. Nagas' first political aspiration was made with a submission of memorandum to the Simon Commission in 1929, a memorandum to exclude the Nagas from the future 'Reform scheme' of British India and to leave them (the Nagas) as they were before the British conquered them. Some of the more advanced tribes among the Nagas submitted the memorandum and not all the Naga tribes; however, the signatories accommodate other Naga tribes in the memorandum. Responding positively to the wishes of the Naga Club, the Government of India Act of 1935 designated the Nagas as an 'excluded area' where laws applicable to the rest of British-controlled India would not operate and the Nagas could continue with their own traditional ways of life with little interference from the federal or the provincial government (Srikanth, 2005). Naga Movement gained its momentum in 1946 under the banner of the Naga National Council (NNC). The British offers 'Crown Colony' to the Nagas but the latter rejected and sought nothing less than sovereignty. Mahatma Gandhi, father of the Indian Nation, did promise the Nagas to be independent if they (Nagas) don't want to be a part of India. Accordingly, the Nagas declared themselves as independent nation on 14th August, 1947, a day ahead of India's independence. However, Nehru's approach to solve the Naga movement was different from that of Mahatma Gandhi. On the background of backwardness and size of the Nagas, and security point of view, Nehru did not recognize the Nagas to be independent.

Nehru portrayed the Indo-Naga conflict as a mere 'internal disturbance (Law and Order problem)' and Naga areas within the 'Indian borders' have been declared 'Disturbed Areas' for decades. The Nagas of Manipur like Mao, Tangkhul and others protested at Mao Gate in 1948 and sought 'No House Tax Payment' to the government of Manipur (Ngalung, 2010:30). They demanded to be with other Naga tribes and not to include their land within the territory of Manipur. Like the 2010 Mao Gate incident, the outcome of the 1948 civil disobedience movement was that some Mao Nagas were killed, and many were tortured. From 1918 to 1954, Naga political struggle was a peaceful movement; their aspirations were made through non-violence means. It was only when Nehru started using repressive measures to suppress the Naga movement by enacting several Black Acts (like Armed Forces Special Power Act), deployment and empowerment of thousands of Armed Forces in the Naga Hills with enormous power to undertake arrest and suppress the Naga National Council's leaders and people supporting the movement drove the Nagas to take up arms against the Indian State (Srikanth, 2005). These Black Acts give licence to the human rights abuses of the Indian Army. The immediate manifestation of the special power assigned to the Indian Armed Forces was that they resorted to blatant violations of human rights where civilians were the prime targets. From 1954 to 1964, 'Nagas suffered immeasurably from the Indian Armed Forces almost to the point of genocide' (Mao, 2007). The Government of India (GOI) claims that its use of Armed Forces is lawful because it is directed to secure the territorial integrity of an existing State. India justifies human rights violations of the Naga people in the name of territorial integrity and National sovereignty. However, the right to territorial integrity is not an unlimited right under International Law rather subject to a respect for human rights. Moreover, scanty News was published and the crime against humanity have been conveniently buried and forgotten by the Media. In the struggle of more than six-decades-old Naga movement, thousands of Naga militants and civilians were killed; untold numbers tortured, beaten, mishandled and humiliated by the Security Forces; scores of women raped and molested; and huge amount of resources ransacked and looted (Hazarika, 1994:101; Ao, 2002:52 & 99; Verghese, 2004:95-102). On the other side, numbers of Indian Armed Forces lost their lives in 'counter-insurgency' politics. From Nagas' first expression of their political aspiration was made in the formation of Naga Club in 1918 till date, there are numerous points of conflict between the Government of India and Naga People in resolving the political issue which resulted in a series of armed struggle, signing of Accord and Agreements, Cease-fires and Negotiation within the two sides. Peace process continues till date, but agreeable solution to both sides is yet to hammer out. Goswami pointed out that the Government of India's inability to provide 'meaningful substantive peace packages other than an annual extension of the ceasefire' is perceived by Nagas as a deliberate ploy to prolong the peace negotiations (Goswami, 2008:128-29). It is to be noted that political issue has to be solved politically and not through economic packages.

Conflict and Justification

The pioneer among the American Baptist missionaries was Rev. Miles Bronson (1838) who worked among the Nagas. But it was E.W. Clark (1876) and William Pettigrew (1896) who began systematic conversion work. Many scholars writing on Naga maintain that Christianity modernized the Nagas and elevated their thinking and seems to have contributed to creating a common Naga Identity (Das, 2008:124). Today, 90 per cent of the Naga populations are Christians with more than 10,000 Naga Churches (Chiru, 2007:3). Small section of the Naga people continue practicing their traditional religion, and some villages converted into Buddhism especially Nagas in Myanmar. Among the many Christian denominations, Baptists are the predominant denomination comprising 80 per cent (approx.) of the total population. Since majority of Nagas are Christian by faith, the Church plays an important role in Naga politics. Whatever the Church says tends to become more authoritative and they (Nagas) are bound to follow it (Ao, 2002:187). The Church leaders were among the first Nagas who imparted education, and the first preachers, teachers and leaders of the Nagas. This makes them more influential in their society. Naga Leaders like Th. Muivah believed that the greatest gift of God to the Nagas is their land, but some 'church leaders like Tuisem A Shishak wanted to give away to the Indians' (Muivah, 2010). One Naga researcher reported that at one point of time 'I feel like living in a theocratic state, everything seems controlled by Church' in Nagaland state. From 1960s onwards, Church leaders' involvement in Naga politics was very much observable. One Naga writer remarked that the Church has become the most 'powerful social and political institution' in Naga society (Chasie, 1999:81). In any crisis due to political uncertainty or armed conflicts, active role of Church leaders have been found to bring normalcy in the society (Zhimomi, 2004:131).

The Government of India and Naga militants have points of conflict, so also between Naga militants and Church Leaders on the Naga political issue. The Church is in support of a Nation of the Nagas (Singh, 2004:187), but they condemn using violence as a means to achieve the goal (Nuh, 1996:109). Contrarywise, the Naga militants rule out the 'illusion of saving of Nagalim' through peaceful means, so long as the Government of India continue using brute force to torture and kill the Nagas (NSCN Manifesto, 2007:33). The conflict over 'Means' is the bone of contention between Church leaders and Naga militants. Even among the Naga intellectuals and civilians, there are differences over the 'Means'. During the early period of the struggle, the Naga National Council (NNC) under A.Z. Phizo found Church leaders' gesture inconvenient and warned it to 'keep aloof from politics', consequently, Church leaders denounced the actions of the NNC as 'not authorized by the people's consent' (Chiru, 2007:152). For the first time, a conflict occurred between the two sides in the history of Naga politics.

To restore peace and facilitate talks between the Naga militants and the Government of India, initiation was taken by the Nagaland Peace Mission, which came into existence with the efforts of Nagaland Baptist Church Council. Nagaland State came into being on 1st December, 1963, which was the by-product of the struggle to restore peace and harmony in the Naga society initiated by the Church leaders (*ibid*:138-39). The term 'Nagaland' itself as incorporated under the Indian Union was intended by the Government of India to create confusion among the Nagas, while in fact the term is 'incorrect' (Ward, 1993:7). It is to be noted that the term 'Nagaland' is used for the first time by the Nagas which is incorporated in the memorandum submitted to the Simon Commission in 1929 (Horam, 1998:105). 'Nagaland' can mean the lands belonging to the whole Nagas living in different states, regions, or countries (Horam, 1998:12). In order to avoid confusion, the NSCN-IM called the land of the Nagas as 'Nagalim' which means the land of the Nagas, derived from some Naga dialects. The Aos call *Lima* for land, Changs and Sangtams call *Lim* for land (Atem, 2010). On the other side, 'Nagaland' means the whole land of the Nagas and not only present Nagaland state for the NNC, NSCN-K and NSCN-KK.

The Church leaders are believed to have played the 'most negative role' from the time Th. Muivah made contact with the Chinese in 1967 (Maxwell, 1980:11). The Church leader warns the danger posed by Communism; highlighting Communist hostility to the Church and the totalitarian nature of the State (Rao, 1986:88-9; Shimray, 2005:88-92), considering the Naga militants who went to China as 'communists'. It was during this period when the Church leaders like Rev. Longri Ao was openly preaching and warning the Naga Christians not to give assistance to the Naga militants for fear of communism. Whereas, the Naga militants repudiated the accusation that they were communists (Shimray, 2005:91), and claim that they were the first to build Church in China after the Chinese Revolution (Gwaizan, 1981:8). It was during this period that the Church leaders treated the Naga militants as 'citizen treated to lepers' in the *Old Testament of the Bible* (Atem, 2010). There was, no doubt, absence of proper networking and communication between the Church leaders and Naga militants especially among the key leaders, which resulted in creating confusion between the two. They couldn't meet openly and formally as the Naga militants were hunted by the Armed Forces of India in almost all the land of the Nagas. However, it is to be noted that the Church leaders' activities were not only confined in religious affairs but many a times in politics.

In the mid-seventies, Church leaders backed some Naga militants to have Peace Talk with the Government of India (GOI), and (thus) the final outcome of the Peace Talks was the signing of Shillong Accord in 1975. The Church leaders 'meticulously campaigned for' the signing of this accord in order to bring normalcy, peace and to end the human rights violations by the Armed Forces of India. However, this was vehemently opposed by the key Naga militant leaders who called it as 'Accord of treason' and 'ignominious sell-out made in the history of Naga people' (GPRN, 1980:4). The Church leaders vehemently opposed the principles of communism always fearing that the Naga militants may sow the seed of communism in the land of Nagas. This could be seen even after the Accord as the Church leaders became quite vocal against Nagas seeking Chinese assistance (Shimray, 2005:93 & 129). Instead of bringing peace and solving the Naga political movement, it further divides the Nagas and factionalized the Naga militant organization. In 1988, brutal massacre—more than 140 of Muivah's Cadres, primarily Tangkhuls—took place in a pre-emptive strike by Khaplang's Cadres and Burmese troops against Muivah's Cadres. The alleged 'double standard politics' of the Government is greatly responsible for this pre-emptive strike. The Government of India used some Church leaders to serve their purpose. This incident resulted in the vertical split of NSCN into two factions which was 'caused' through Rev. Chingan Konyak who acted as go between Government of India and NSCN in 1988 (Tajenyuba Ao, 1993:304). At present, the moral and 'national principles' of some Naga militants are questioned by the Naga people (Nuh, 2002:97). Also, some Naga Churches and leaders by and large have departed away from Biblical truth (Nuh, 2001:37). However, this does not necessarily mean that all Naga militants and Church leaders are involved. Many a times, scholars failed to distinguish this, but rather equalize the individual with the organization or institution.

Towards Understanding and Reconciliation

With the passage of time, transparency and networking between the Church leaders and Naga militants has become cordial. At the close of 20th century, the Church leaders involvement in bringing peace and reconciliation among the various Naga factions are very much observable. The Church leaders programmed to meet the leaders of various factions, some other political and communal leaders at Atlanta in 1997 which was hosted by the Baptist Peace Fellowship of North America led by Ken Sehested and Daniel Buttry. Some leaders failed to attend the Atlanta Meet as that was not a conducive moment. However, the talks that culminated in a jointly agreed-upon statement calling for a cease-fire, Naga unity and the pursuit of peace. A delegation of Naga Church leaders, human rights activists, leaders of various civic organizations and others launched a 'Journey of Conscience' at Delhi in 2004 which was participated by many Indian activists and organizations. Individuals, such as Rev. Wati Aier, from among the Church leadership have acted courageously and working for a genuine solution to the Naga situation, and for the reconciliation among the various factions under the banner of Forum for Naga Reconciliation (FNR). Many Church leaders and civil organizations shuttled the factional leaders. Through their efforts, the 'Covenant of Reconciliation' was signed by Isak Chishi Swu, S.S. Khaplang and S. Singya. In September 2009 representatives of the NNC, NSCN-K and NSCN-IM attended the meeting of the Joint Working Group organized by the FNR at Chiang Mai, Thailand. During this meet, 'Declaration of Commitment' was signed by V.S. Atem,

Zhopra Vero and Wangtin Naga representing the NSCN-IM, NNC and NSCN-K respectively. The signatories resolved to facilitate the meeting of a Summit at the highest level in affirmation of the 'Covenant of Reconciliation'. It is true that mass-based organizations and Churches of the Nagas now have a more conducive context in which to raise their voices and act.

Conclusion

The history of Naga politics shows that the relation between the Church leaders and the Naga militants was greatly influenced by the leadership interests and less by the Christian principles and 'national principles' respectively. At some point of time, there was a struggle for power between Church leaders and Naga militants as one could see in the formation of Nagaland state, Shillong Accord and aftermath. In most of these historical events, influence of the Government of India on Church leaders is very much observable. The Church leaders are partly responsible for factionalizing the Naga militant organization which, consequently, divides the Naga population. At the same time, the leadership crisis among the Naga militants is equally responsible for factionalism. It is not Christianity but the Church leaders and followers who degraded the values of the Christian religion. Xavier Mao rightly pointed out that religious leaders should emphasize 'more on the Christian values and the good Naga traditional values like love, compassion, and sacrifice, concern for others, courage, honesty and hospitality through their own lives more than the preaching.' At the same time, Naga militants need to reconsider on their activities reflecting on their 'national principles' and find political solution at the earliest, which in fact requires sincerity from the GoI. More importantly, political issue has to be addressed politically and not economically, even though the latter is vital for the solution. It is just a part of the whole. Today, the Church leaders are engaged in reconciling all the factions of Naga militant organizations. Neutrality among the reconciliatory agent is of utmost importance to every reconciliation movement. However, for the sake of neutrality and to bring reconciliation, the historical facts and events of the Nagas cannot be undermined. Therefore, careful and minute considerations in each move reflecting on the historical facts are very much necessary.

REFERENCES

Interview

Atem, V.S. (Personal interview)
Muivah, Th. (Personal interview)

Secondary Sources

Ao, Lanunungsang A. 2002. *From Phizo to Muivah: The Naga National Question in North East India*. New Delhi: Mittal Publications.

Ao, Tajenyuba, 1993. *The British Occupation of Naga Country*. Mokokchung: Naga Literature Society.

Baruah, Sanjib, 2003. 'Confronting Constructionism: Ending India's Naga War', in *Journal of Peace Research*, Sage Publication, New Delhi, Volume 40, Number 3, May 2003.

Benavides, G., 1972. 'Christianity in Central and South America' in David L. Sills (ed.), *International Encyclopedia of the Social Sciences*, Vol. 3, London: The Macmillan Company and The Free Press.

Bendangangshi, 1993. *Glimpses of Naga History*. Mokokchung: Suyim Press.

Cerula, K.A. 2001. 'Nationalism and Expressive forms' in Neil S. Smelser & Paul B. Baltes (eds.), *International Encyclopedia of the Social and Behavioural Sciences*, Vol. 15, Oxford: Elsevier Science Ltd.

Chasie, Charles, 1999. *The Naga Imbroglio: A Personal Perspective*. Kohima: Standard Printers and Publishers.

Chiru, Samson Shekho, 2007. *American Baptist Mission: Integrating Agent of Nagas into Indian Union*. New Delhi: Sunrise Publications.

Das, Pushpita and Namrata Goswami (eds.), 2008. *India's North East: New Vista for Peace*. New Delhi: Manas Publications.

Ebner, Paul, 2008. *The Role of the Church in South Africa's Negotiated Revolution, Perspectives on International and Multicultural Affairs*, Vol. 1, Issue 1, http://www.2.davidson.edulacademics/acad_depts/rusk/primal Vol. 1.
Issue 1 /safrica_revolution. (accessed on August 13, 2009).

Goswami, Namrata, 2008. 'The Naga Rebel Groups' Narratives of Dissent: A Critique' in Pushpita Das & Namrata Goswami (eds.), *India's northeast: New Vistas for Peace*, New Delhi: Manas Publications.

GPRN, 1980. NSCN *Manifesto*. Oking, January 31, 1980.

_______ 1985. *Polarization*. Oking, February 7, 1985.

Gwaizan, Mowu, 1981. *A Brief Testimony of Nagaland for Christ*. Nagaland: Published by the Author.

Hazarika, Sanjay, 1994. *Stranger of the Mist: Tales of War and Peace from India's North East*. New Delhi: Penguin Books India Ltd.

Horam, M. 1988. *Naga Insurgency: The Last Thirty Years*. New Delhi: Cosmo Publications.

Horam, Rinkahao, 1998. *The Genesis of the Naga Political Movement*. Imphal: Published by Mrs. Singanila Horam, Tangkhul Avenue.

Hyseni, Shkruamga Mehdi, 2007. *Political-National 'Symphony and Cacophony' of the Serbian Orthodox Church vs. Kosovo's Independence*, December 2007, http://www.unitedalbania.org.(accessed on August 13, 2009).

Iralu, Kaka D., 2005. 'The Fifty Four Year Indo-Naga Conflict' in Monirul Hussain (ed.) *Coming Out of Violence: Essays on Ethnicity, Conflict Resolution and Peace Process in North East India*. New Delhi: Regency Publication.

Kohn, Hans, 1951. *The Idea of Nationalism*. New York: Macmillan Co.

Leege, D.C., 2001. 'Religion and Politics: United States' in Neil J. Smelser and Paul B. Baltes (eds.), *International Encyclopedia of the Social and Behavioural Sciences*. Vol.19, Oxford: Elsevier Science Ltd.

Longman, Timothy, 1997. *Christian Churches and Genocide in Rwanda*. Revision of paper originally prepared for Conference on Genocide, Religion and Modernity, United States Holocaust Memorial Museum, May 11-13, 1997, http://faculty.vassur.edultilongmalchurch&Genocide.html. (accessed on August 13, 2009).

Lundry, Chris, 2001. *From Passivity to Political Resource: The Catholic Church and Nationalism in East Timor* (abridged version). http://www.etan.org/etreligious/2001aJpolresrce.htm. (accessed on August 20, 2009).

Mao, Xavier Pfokhrehe, 2007. 'Naga Insurgency: Solution or Revival or Decay?' in NPGSCC's *Silver Jubilee Souvenir*, NEHU, Shillong: Naga Post-Graduate Students Coordinate Committee (NPGSCC), October 2007.

Maxwell, Neville, 1980. *India, the Nagas and the North East*. London: Minority House.

Ngalung, Yaronsho, 2010. *Integration of Naga Areas: A Prerequisite to Indo-Naga Political Solution*. Ukhrul: Published by the author.

Northcott, M. 1972. 'Christianity in Asia' in David L Sills (ed.) *International Encyclopedia of the Social Sciences*. Vol. 3, London: The Macmillan Company and The Free Press.

NSCN, 2007. *Free Nagalim Manifesto* (third edition). March 20, 2007.

Nuh, V.K., 2002. *My Native Country: The Land of the Nagas*. New Delhi: Spectrum Publications.

_______, 2002. *Nagaland Church and Politics* (Reprinted). Kohima: Novelty Printing Press.

_______, 2001. *Struggle for Identity in North East India: A Theological Response*. New Delhi: Spectrum Publications.

Onaiyekan, John, 2008. *The Church Work for Peace and Reconciliation in Africa* (A talk by John Onaiyekan, Archbishop of Abuja-Nigeria)

Indiana-USA: University of Notre Dame, South Bend, April 15, 2008, hptt://nd.edul—cpn/papers-2008CPN/Catholic%2OPeacebuilding 20%Onaiyekan.pdf (accessed on September 30, 2009).

Percy, M. 2001. 'Religion: Mobilization and Power' in Neil J. Smelser and Paul B. Baltes (eds.) *International Encyclopedia of the Social and Behavioural Sciences*. Vol. 19, Oxford: Elsevier Science Ltd.

Rao, O.M., 1986. *Longri Ao: A Biography*. Gauhati: Christian Literature Centre.

Robertson, David, 1985. *Dictionary of Politics*. London: Penguin Publication.

Shimray, A.S. Atai, 2005. *Let Freedom Ring: Story of Naga Nationalism*. New Delhi: Promilla and Co. Publishers.

Shimray, U.A., 2007. *Naga Population and Integration Movement: Documentation*. New Delhi: Mittal Publications.

Singh, Chandrika, 2004. *Naga Politics: A Critical Account*. New Delhi: Mittal Publications.

Smith, A.D., 2001. 'Religion: Nationalism and Identity' in Neil J. Smelser and Paul B. Baltes (eds.) *International Encyclopedia of the Social and Behavioural Sciences*. Vol. 19, Oxford: Elsevier Science Ltd.

Srikanth, H. and C. J. Thomas, 2005. 'Naga Resistance Movement and the Peace Process in North East India'. *Peace and Democracy in South Asia*. Volume 1, Issue 2.

Vashum, R. 2001. *Indo-Naga Conflict: Problem and Resolution*. New Delhi: Indian Social Institute.

________, 2000. *Nagas' Right of Self-Determination: An Anthropological-Historical Perspective*. New Delhi: Mittal Publications.

Verghese, B.G., 2004. *India's North East Resurgence: Ethnicity, Insurgency, Governance and Development* (Second Revised Edition). New Delhi: Konark Publishers Pvt. Ltd.

Wallensteen, Peter, 2004. *Understanding Conflict Resolution: War, Peace and the Global System* (Reprinted). New Delhi: Sage Publications.

Ward, David, 1993. *The Nagas Right to Survival*. Naga Vigil Group: London.

Young, Serinity (ed.), 1999. *Encyclopedia of Women and World Religion*. Vol. 1, New York: Macmillan Reference, USA.

Zhimomi, Kuhoi K., 2004. *Politics and Militancy in Nagaland*. New Delhi: Deep & Deep Publications Pvt. Ltd.

12

Formation of NSCN (IM)

Manifesto and Support Base in the International Forum

T. Ninghorla Zimik

The Naga National Council (NNC) which was the first organization to express and articulate the Naga political aspirations was formed in 1946. The Nagas were invited to join the Union of India when it was formed for the first time in the history of Nagas in 1950 but the Nagas outrightly rejected the proposal. Thus, the Naga people informed the Indian Government, the U.N. and those countries that had their embassies in Delhi on 24th January, 1950 that "the Nagas do not accept the Indian Constitution". On 1st January, 1951 the NNC informed the Indian State that the Naga people wanted to hold voluntary plebiscite and invited India to send observers. The Indian State did not respond. On 5 May, 1951, the plebiscite began in Kohima and 99.90 per cent of the Naga populace voted in favour of remaining independent. With the establishment of the State of Nagaland, military operations against the NNC and the Naga people continued with renewed vigour and spite.

In 1975, the State of Nagaland was placed under "President's Rule". This was followed by the declaration of the "National Emergency" all-over the States of India from 1975 to 1977. Taking advantage of this precarious political scenario, the Indian State launched a continuous series of military operations and pressure with threats and undemocratic means. It was under these extreme compelling circumstances with no formal international support of any kind that NNC members belonging to the Federal

Government of Nagaland under duress, signed the Shillong Accord on November 11, 1975 to accept the Indian Constitution and surrender their arms and in due course formulate other issue for settlement. The Indian Armed Forces and intelligence agencies warned against any criticism against the Accord. India also warned that the arms deposit were to be completed by January 25, 1975, but the deposited arms were much less than what was expected. By mid-June 1976, hundreds of Naga villages were placed under curfews imposed by the Indian Government as military operations resumed against those who opposed the Accord. The intention behind the Accord had the classic ingredients for keeping the resistance in check.

Until the signing of the Shillong Accord in 1976, the Naga National Council (NNC) remained as the sole political organization to represent the Naga people and voice their aspirations. However, with the unmandated signing of the Shillong Accord within the members of the organization, some fundamental issues arose questioning the manner in which the NNC dealt with the crisis and its subsequent role in representing and realizing Naga rights. By the time Shillong Accord was signed, both Isak Swu and Tb. Muivah were in China.

Before Th. Muivah set off to China, he strongly cautioned the national workers that "danger of defeat is inevitable before long" and warned them stating that "our people completely failed to see the writing on the wall. Fortunately, I was able to forewarn the national workers in my area of the possible happening of a great failure within a year or so and so when that come they should stand their ground, hold their gun fast, eat whatever will be available even grass but never surrender." Muivah went to China again with more than 200 cadres starting in the month of September 1974. The justification of the Accordists was that the situation was so tense that they had no option but to accept the imposition but the issue raised by the non-Accordists was one of condemnation.

After they returned from China in the month of February 1976, they condemned the Shillong Accord and established their base area in the eastern side starting from Khianmiungan area. Eventually, they could extend their military base virtually to all Eastern Nagalim. Though the Accord brought setbacks, it did not block the way of the Nagas instead they saw the rise of the younger generation. The Tangkhul area which was not very strong started witnessing surging waves of nationalism. It was an awakening of great magnitude. Six Leaders of NNC like Isak Chishi Swu, Th. Muivah and S.S. Khaplang and other NNC leaders rejected the Accord. They provided avenues and opportunities for other top NNC leaders to clarify their position and officially denounce the Accord. When this failed, they were compelled to disassociate themselves from NNC. After a long silence and the lack of clarity from the NNC, emerging conditions necessitated the resurgence of a new political organization to continue the Naga resistance movement. They continued to conduct the national affairs under the official name of the NNC for three years. In 1978, they organized a meeting of the NNC rebels in Burma (Myanmar) and rejected the leadership of A.Z. Phizo, the President of the NNC. In January 1980, along with S.S. Khaplang, a Hemi Naga, they formed the National Socialist Council of Nagaland. Isak Chishi Swu was elected as its Chairman, S.S. Khaplang Vice-Chairman and Th. Muivah as General Secretary. Subsequently, the Government of the People's Republic of Nagalim (GPRN) was formed on 21st March, 1980.

Manifesto of NSCN

The manifesto of the new Council of the Naga People whose ideology is mainly based on cultural ethos of the traditional Naga Society reads: "To us, the sovereign existence of our country, the salvation of our people in Christ are eternal and unquestionable. It is because life has meaning and that is in freedom alone. Indeed our Nagaland shall refuse to perish together with any leadership or organization that has failed and betrayed her cause, that has no promise of future for her people. Time moves on and we have to move along although the Naga National Council does not seek to redeem Nagaland. Therefore in this irreconcilable world our National Socialist Council declares:

(a) National Existence

We stand for the unquestionable sovereign right of the Naga peoples over every inch of Nagaland wherever it may be and admit of no other existence whatever.

(b) Political Institution

We stand for the principle of people's supremacy, that is, the dictatorship of the people through the National Socialist Council and the practice of democracy within the organization until the goal is achieved and as long as it is deemed necessary.

(c) Economic System

We stand for socialism. Because it is the only social and economic system that does away with exploitation and ensures fair equality to all the people.

(d) Religion

We stand for the faith in God and the salvation of mankind in Jesus, the Christ alone, that is "Nagaland for Christ". However, the individual freedom of religion shall be safeguarded and the imposition of this faith on others is strictly forbidden.

(e) Means

We rule out the illusion of saving Nagaland, through peaceful means. It is arms and arms alone that will save our nation and ensure freedom to the people. However, if India and Burma sincerely realize the folly of the use of brute force and stop killing and torturing the Nagas then we shall not fire a single shot as we did for a decade before the start of our violent resistance.

(f) Self-Reliance and the Policy of United Front

We stand for the practice of the principle of self-reliance and for the policy of United Front with all the forces that can be united with.

Thus it was made convincingly plain and to one and all that NSCN stands for sovereign independent existence and political liberation of Nagalim, socialism of national brand for her economic emancipation and above all, faith in Jesus Christ for her spiritual salvation. Muivah spent ten years in China but always said "our eternal salvation lies with Jesus Christ alone — We did not go to China to exchange Christ for a piece of arms."

In an exclusive interview with Naga leaders by Deepk Dewan (N.E. Sun in 1997), who put a question to Isak Swu, "you call yourself the national council of Nagaland. What is the Socialist content of your programme ?" Isak Swu stated: "our socialism is the oldest institution in the world. Even before Marxism-Leninism came into being, we have been practicing it. And we had both private and community ownership. The poor people are benefited because of the community land they have. We take care of the poor and the orphans. Our democracy is based on our traditional socialism. We did not have a proper term to call it by, so we called it national socialism." On the question of Christian socialism he answered "we call it Christian socialism because it is akin to that. We take care of the poor and the helpless..." "The political ideology of the NSCN (IM) is socialism with the power of Christ rather than Marxism-Leninism. NSCN motto is "Nagaland for Christ"."

Between 1985 and 1988, New Delhi sent several intermediaries to start dialogue within the framework of the Constitution of India. There was information from Chingang Konyak, that the Government of India wanted to hold talks with NSCN within the framework of the Constitution of India, which was a deliberate back out from the previous unconditional approach of Mrs. Indira Gandhi. This information was sent to S.S. Khaplang for joint consultation but he did not turn up. As the nature of the matter did not warrant delay, they dispatched a reply to Mr. Chingang, a pastor, stating clearly that NSCN would not hold talks with India whatever on the betrayed terms within the framework of the Constitution of India. He should not, therefore, take the risk of coming to them for unconditional talk. The copy of the reply was given to each authority. In the rneantime, holding of an emergency meeting was necessitated because of a proposal to send out a group to outside to be headed by Chairman Isak. To that effect, enough circulation were dispatched and since S.S. Khaplang's presence was greatly felt necessary, they sent men and letters repeatedly. They all reached him but of no avail. The number of members who attended the emergency meeting was far more than the quorum stipulated. Most of the top members from both civil and military were present excepting Khaplang and others. In the meeting the main points of discussion were:

(1) Alee Commands;
(2) The Government and the party seals; and
(3) The explanation to be given on the stand of the National Socialist Council in the event of actual political talk with India.

After lengthy deliberation, the house agreed that the foreign Command headed by Chairman Isak be sent before the start of February 1988. Leadership was called upon to give a concrete explanation on the NSCN stand. In view of that General Secretary Th. Muivah explained at length the firm and clear-cut stand of the NSCN. He recalled repeatedly the decision of the house taken in 1984 at Iphai that NSCN would hold talk with India only if the talk be on equal terms. In other words, NSCN would under no circumstances talk with India within the framework of the Constitution. In the process of the explanation, their reply to pastor Chingang was also clearly made known to the house. Things were clear-cut and there was practically no room for misunderstanding. The house then offered a prayer and adjourned *sine die*.

But some two weeks later, a report reached CHQ that Lt. Colonel Kango, the fighting commander had run away to Konyak region collecting arms and Konyak boys. It was a serious case provoking the authorities and all to anger. However, to play it cool, army HQs were advised not to take immediate step against it. In the meantime they also discovered a secret communication network and at the same time many fabricated allegations and propaganda were mongering around. To their amazement eight unfounded allegations were charged against Isak Swu and Th. Muivah. Some of the allegations put forward were:

(1) Chairman Isak together with other 29 had been flown by helicopters to New Delhi to work out the terms of settlement within the Indian Union.
(2) Chairman Isak, Secretary Muivah and Konser Hanong were ready to accept uncle Suisa's proposal that is, to have the Indo-Naga issue settled within Indian Union.
(3) General Secretary Muivah was determined to do away with all the Konyak and Pangmi national workers to seize all arms to surrender them to the Indian Union etc.

Khaplang party justified the allegation that preparation to talk with the Indian Government to settle the Indo-Naga issue within the Indian Union was clearly spoken in the emergency meeting. Isak, Muivah party strongly refuted the allegation and gave their clarification that what they discussed and deliberated were widely circulated among all the Kilonsers and there cannot be any doubt about it. "It was also read out in the Assembly Session. We are sure it can be available from every Kilonser's office. What wrong then have we done that dastardly backbiting Khaplang had to raise a hue and cry that he had to make an issue of it. Even the Government of India may be asked for validity of the blatant charges. We challenge for all time to come and we mean what we say." "They felt the compulsion of the moment and challenged one another and pledged a new that they would be firm to the last man for the ideals for which the Manifesto of the National Socialist Council had been brought into being. They would not yield whatever to Burma, India and to the internal evil forces……. Yet they never abandoned the faith they repose in the open discussions, Secretary put forward the proposal that the prevailing problems arising from the allegations be heard out in the congregation of all the national workers and the village elders in the base area through open discussions and swearing by God's Holy name. Everyone gladly agreed to it and a fasting prayer to the effect was offered the following day. Then through a letter Messrs Khaplang and Kwikhip were told to refrain themselves from being violent. We waited at least for a reply to the letter we had written. Moreover, the approaches made by our friends UNLF and ULFA for peaceful understanding deserved a response of a sort. But very sorry, the interim council HQs. was encircled and attacked with volley of bullets and bombs." It was on the 30th April at 5.30 a.m. 1988 that both Khaplang and Burmese troops launched the bloody coup. The coup was carried out after seizing all the arms and ammunition. More than 200 Naga revolutionary patriots were murdered.

However, about 230 of them mostly, women and children including Chairman Isak Swu and General Secretary Th. Muivah survived the abortive coup. Their stories of escape was miraculous and suffering and hardship was beyond human endurance.

In the event of the crisis and bloody coup, an emergency national workers' conference was convened on 20th August, 1988 at operation salvation headquarters as there was leadership crisis in the Eastern part of Nagaland. Altogether 427 full-fledged NSCN members representing different regional unit and commands attended the crucial meeting where the house unanimously resolved and declared:

(a) Unwavering allegiance to the principle of the National Socialist Council of Nagaland enshrined in its manifesto for sovereign Christian socialist country.
(b) Undivided faith in the collective leadership of Messrs. Isac Swu and Th. Muivah in the struggle for self-determination.
(c) Lastly, the conference also resolved that it will ceaselessly work for the restoration of the true image of the National Socialist Council of Nagaland and expressed its earnest desire and hope for an immediate reconciliation in the leadership through democratic means.

S.S. Khaplang was then expelled from the NSCN on November 7, 1989. He then established his own organization known by the same name NSCN. To distinguish the two groups, journalists have often referred to them by their leaders initials as NSCN (K), NSCN (IM). The NSCN (K) has its support base mainly among the Hemi Nagas of Burma as well as the Konyaks and the Aos etc. Ever since the break up of the organization, the two factions are functioning as a separate wings of organization. Many Naga Church leaders, HOHOs, NGOs, Prayer Groups etc. have given their maximum effort to get them reconciled but of no avail. Of late, Forum for Naga reconciliation is working strenuously to shun violence and bring reconciliation among the different factions of national workers and civil society. For this purpose, various Naga Peace meetings were held in Chiang Mai Thailand participated by various Naga Organizations including American Baptist Churches and the British and Canadian Quakers. The Forum, despite the difficulties, affirmed to continue pursuing peace and reconciliation amongst all sections of the people. Through the tireless efforts of FNR, the spate of factional killings have been reduced to a considerable degree.

NSCN Support Base in International Forums/Organisations

After the abortive coup by S.S. Khaplang and party in 1988, the NSCN turned over a new leaf in the history of Nagalim's struggle for liberation. The collective leadership along with some other members left Nagalim for foreign countries. The leaders availed opportunities to meet the International figures who were willing to help the causes of the oppressed people. Teams of national leaders were sent out on diplomatic mission in four groups beginning from 1989: (1) European countries and United Nations Conferences, (2) Rh. Raising and Angelus Shimrah to United States of America, (3) K. Hurei and party, and (4) Brig. Ningkhan and party to some part of Asian Countries. They launched intensive lobbies with different dignitaries on political situation in Nagalim. They could get warm response and encouragement from leaders of various countries and forums. Through their tireless efforts they could gain materials and political supports from many friendly countries, peoples and nations.

A historic landmark was achieved when the NSCN got admission to the Unrepresented Nations and People's Organization (UNPO) on January 23, 1993. The Chairman of the UNPO Mr. Erkin Altekin announced the acceptance of the membership of Nagalim in the UNPO in the Assembly Hall of the 3rd UNPO General Assembly at the Hague on January 23, 1993 at 10:11 p.m. From that day onward the flag of Nagalim was unfurled and seen flying with flags of other nations at the UNPO headquarters in the Netherland. Again the Fourth General Assembly of the UNPO held from January 20-26, 1995 at the Hague passed a historic resolution (No. 5) with regard to the struggle of the Naga People for Liberation from the invasional forces. Among other points in the Resolution, it "strongly condemns the Indian and Myanmar Governments and their militaries for their invasion and continued occupation of Nagalim and for their rampant violations of human rights of the Naga People. "The UNPO vows to continue its support for Nagalim and the Naga people". The UNPO has become a strong and effective instrument for liberation of the oppressed people. Fearing the association of the NSCN with the UNPO, thereafter the cumulative result of the association, the Government of India tried to dislodge it from the UNPO by branding the NSCN as a "Terrorist organization" but the UNPO stood solidly behind the

NSCN and rejected Government of India's plea for dislodging the NSCN from the UNPO.

In pursuance of the UN declaration of the year 1993 as the "International year of Indigenous People", the NSCN along with the NGOs in Nagalim, actively participated in all the UN working group consultation meetings on indigenous peoples at Geneva, Switzerland etc. In all these forums, Chairman Isak Chishi Swu on behalf of Nagalim, addressed to the satisfaction of the members present. During such meetings, the Naga Representatives could get ample opportunities to interact and understand with the international communities. The NSCN could also garner support from Indigenous Peoples and other communities.

KWIA, which is a powerful and highly respected Non-Governmental Human Rights organization based in Belgium is one of the strongest support groups for the oppressed and Indigenous Peoples all-over the world. It is also a strong supporter of the cause of the Naga people. The KWIA declaration on Nagalim on July 30, 1993 in Geneva is historic: "The Naga people as a whole has the Right to determine its own future, its own political institutions. We respect and support the Naga resistance by all legal means, including armed resistances, as authorized by International law."

The Society for Threatened Peoples (STP) based in Germany and International Human Rights Association of American Minorities have also been supporting and helping the NSCN in its international lobbying providing necessary information and the like. With the help of the society of STP (as required by UN Rule), the NSCN could make a number of verbal statements at different sessions of the United Nations' Commission on Human Rights (UNCHR) and Sub-Committee on Prevention of Discrimination and Prevention of Minorities.

The NSCN achieved a very important breakthrough in its International Campaign for Liberation of Nagalim when a written statement on "The Human Right Situation in Nagalim" could be submitted directly to the Secretary General of the United Nations, and its copies were circulated in accordance with ECO SOC Resolution 1296 (XLIV). This was the first time the UN officially accepted a written statement from Nagalim on "Naga Cause".

Another significant breakthrough was achieved when the UN Commission on Human Rights granted the NSCN to speak during its 54th Session from March 16—April 27, 1998. As usual, Government of India attempted to prevent the NSCN from participating in the UN meeting. The UN officials turned down its plea. Chairman Isak Swu has made several speeches in the UN sub-commission meetings.

NSCN also tried to establish good relationships with the neighbouring countries. Deepak Dewan interviewed Muivah in September 2000 in N.E. SUN and asked: which are the other countries you're visited to inform about the Indo-Naga Peace Process ? To his question Muivah answered: "All the neighbouring countries. We know who they are, we trust them and have to keep them informed about what we do. So is the case with Pakistan." Muivah and his men stayed ten years in China. In his autobiography "A short Account of my younger days", he has recorded that "The Chinese really took care of us. They also tried to learn the actual condition of our land in order to be realistic in their teaching to our men. They treated us with special care throughout our stay there. Their love and concern for us in our difficult time was really great. We are so much indebted to the Chinese. We shall remember them with respect and love. On my farewell speech I said: we shall pay back what you've done for us but in terms of victory. It must also be mentioned to the greatness of the Chinese leadership and Liberation Army." In another interview Th. Muivah stated: "The greater question when it comes to China is that our relations will not be to the detriment of India. India should not be apprehensive... At the expense of India we shall never seek relations with China".

It is also noteworthy of record that when Th. Muivah was lodged in Bangkok Central Jail, many individuals and organizations around the World appealed and extended their sincere efforts for his safe release. In this respect the NSCN (IM) Chairman expressed the organization's deepest gratitude for their outstanding efforts and sacrifices in securing the release of its general secretary Th. Muivah from Thai Jail on September 13, 2000. The NSCN (IM) Chairman in a statement said "we would particularly like to express our indebtedness to our individual friends from Australia, Canada, Germany, Holland, India, Italy, Japan, Philippines, Thailand, South Korea, Switzerland and United States and other organizations including United Nations Commission on Human Rights, United Nations High

Commissioner for Refugees, European Parliament, Unrepresented Nations and Peoples Organizations, the Netherlands, Congress of United States Committee on International Relations, Churches in the United States, Sommer Haven, U.S.A. DoCip Switzerland, Society for Threatened Peoples, Germany, Baptist Peace Fellowship, USA, Documentation Centre of Threatened People, Italy, Transnational Radical Party, Europe, International Federation for the Protection of Ethnic, Religious, Linguistic and other Minorities, USA, International Working Group, The Quakers, International Rehab Hope Fund Inc, Movement Against Racism, Friendship Among Peoples' Association of World Citizens, World Federation of Democratic Youth, East Timor Human Rights Centre, Churches in Japan, Churches in South Korea, Indonesia Human Rights Campaign, Interfaith International, International Educational Development, International Campaign for Tibet, International Work Group for Indigenous Affairs, Denmark, Council of Khalistan, USA, Iraqi Turkmen, CDPM Comissao, Direito Povo Maubere, Agoraficaa Senegal, UNA, United Kingdom, Christ to the Orient, the Philippines, Universal Alliance, Council of Indigenous Peoples in the Netherlands, Churches in the Philippines, Asian Baptist Peace Network, Australia Union for Civil Liberty, Thailand, Foundation for the Future of Scania, Representative of the Republic of Chechnya to the UNO, Asian Buddhist Conference for Peace, Churches in Australia, Forum Asia, Thailand, Asia Indigenous People Pact, Justice and Peace Commission Thailand, Asian Forum for Human Rights and Development, Thailand Law Society of Thailand, Asia Human Rights Commission, Hong Kong, Burma Lawyers Council, South Asia Forum for Human Rights Commission Nepal and various organizations from India. The above voices and appeal of the people around the World signifies that Naga issue is widely internationalized as Rh. Raising Kilo Kilonser wrote: "It is on the strength of International support base/group in various countries that the Indian Government could not overlook the case of Nagas any longer."

As of now the Government of India is drowsily dragging the peace process in a snail pace. So far more than 60 rounds of talks have been taken up without showing any sign of progress in these eleven long years. People have lost faith in the peace-process and consider it as yet another dilly-dallying tactics of Government of

India as it used to be in the long bloody history of Indo-Naga conflicts. Many North East insurgent groups are reluctant to enter into any peace dialogue taking the precedence of NSCN (IM). A serious indebt and judicious workable approach should be initiated in order to bring lasting solutions. Government of India should start diagnosing the disease of the North East in general and each group in particular and given the right medication according to the diagnosis. It is also a wake up call to Government of India as to why mushrooming of insurgencies are on the rise instead of declining in spite of massive deployment of army and paramilitary forces. We can call North East India as flower garden of insurgencies blooming in varied hues and colours. The world is ever changing and 'might as right' holds no more relevant. Winning the hearts through genuine love is the mantra of turning the black into white, hatred to love and this mantra will pull down the wall of division.

North East should also acknowledge the greatness of India as it is an emerging power in the world. Now India is slowly giving attention and turning towards North East after long years of negligence as it is the power house of energy; granary of natural resources, art and culture, land of magnificent beauty which has a big scope for Eco-tourism being the gateway to South East Asia.

Regarding the Naga issue of North East, it should be viewed and taken seriously as it is the mother of all insurgencies of the region. This hard earned peace process should be materialized and bring to fruition. The longing of the people, i.e. peace and prosperity should be given top priority. The challenging role of Tankhul women and civil society in the recent Shirui stand off between Assam Rifles and NSCN (IM) is a clear cut demonstration of people's love for peace and non-violence. Braving the chilly winter nights for more than two weeks, the women of Shirui village and the surrounding villages guarded the area by standing in between the two parties in case of any violent escalation between the heavily armed Assam Rifles and ever ready young NSCN (IM) who were holed up in the camp by cutting off all the lifeline and the camp fenced around by electrified barbed wire. The situation was very tense and volatile. The very fact of women singing and praying for heavenly intervention throughout the day and night for the solution of the crisis without violence touched the hearts of both the state and non-state actors and they won the war by demonstrating motherly love and sacrifice as Tangkhul Phukreilas of yester years who stopped severest bloody battles and inter-village war. The empowering of Tangkhul women to stop war or conflicts was the highest prerogatives given to women in the traditional Tangkhul Naga Society and this tradition is still continuing in tune with the changing situation of the time.

To conclude, it is suggested to both Government of India and NSCN (IM) to understand and respect each other and maintain the hard earned peace process. Both the parties should adopt a concerted effort to work out an amicable and acceptable lasting solution. In this respect India should be sincere and not betray the confidence of the Naga populace. Give peace a chance is the cry of the Naga people and North East as a whole.

REFERENCES

25 Years of NSCN & GPRN (1980-2005), p. 6.

A Brief Account of Nagaland—FGN, 2000.

A Rejoinder to the Indian Propaganda stunt, Th. Muivah—GPRN.

BBC Hard Talk with Tb. Muivah, April 2005.

Free Nagaland Manifesto—NSCN Second edition, 1993, p. 39.

Interview with Naga Leaders—Bharat Bhusan, p. 87.

Kaka D. Iralu—*The Blood and the Tears.*

M. Horam, *Naga Insurgency—The Last Thirty years*, 1988.

Naga Homeland in Danger—GPRN, 2007.

Nagas - Their Pilgrimage for Self-existence and Quest for Dignity and Peace, February 2006, GPRN, p. 16.

Personal Interviews.

Souvenir: *Wung Tangkhul Region* NSCN-GPRN Goes Silver (1980-2005), p. 11.

The Legal Status of Naga Armed Resistance, published by GPRN, 8 January, 2001, p. 8.

The Legal Status of Naga National Armed Resistance, GPRN, 2001.

13

Analyzing Extremism

Extremist Programmes and Organisational Processes in North East India

Biswajit Mohapatra

Extremism as a term, going by our common perception, has often been used invariably, or almost invariably, used pejoratively to describe the actions or ideologies of the so-called individuals or groups existing outside the established or perceived political centre of a society; or otherwise which is perceived to violate the common moral standards. While extremism is generally contrasted with moderation, and the extremists with that of moderates, people use this term to label a group rather than by a group labelling itself. The group rather than labelling themselves extremist, often portray themselves as militants since they claim to be believing in militant action.

The problem of a clear understanding of what can be meant by the term "extremist" gets more accentuated when it is used to describe groups and individuals who claim to have become radicalized, in some way or the other, in contrast to the usage of the word "extremist" as is sometimes used by groups in their portrayal of themselves.

The term "extremist" is also often marked to have been used to categorise those who use or avidly advocate use of "violence" against the will of "society at large" as being intolerant or opposed to the prevailing practices and policies and also as a marker to isolate the groups or individuals who also advocate or use "violence" to enforce the will of the existing government or that of the majority constituency existing within the society. Robert F. Kennedy said, "What is objectionable? What is dangerous about extremists is not that they are extreme, but that they are intolerant. The evil is not what they say about their cause, but what they say about their opponents."

On the other side those who are described as such as above as extremist do not in general easily admit that what they practice in actual or advocate, constitutes "violence". Rather they instead describe their activities as "acts of resistance" or "militant action" or that of "the use of force".

In the light of the above, the notion that there is a philosophy which can be described as "extremism" is viewed by some social scientists with suspicion. According to Jerome Himmelstein held "At best this characterization tells us nothing substantive about the people it labels; at worst it paints a false picture."[1]

Further according to others, the very act of labelling a person, group or action as "extremist" is sometimes used as a technique to further a clear-cut, perceived political goal—often resorted to especially by governments committed to defend the *status quo*, or the actions of the actors believed to be "political centrists".

Defining an Extremist

It's often the case that Libertarians are often labelled with the accusation "You are an extremist." By calling them such what is meant is that as a libertarian, he holds or maintains political and economic beliefs that can be said to be located at the extreme or outside the fringes of the society. The term is sometimes also used to cast an insult or to derogate the person.

However, the word "extremist" is also a relative term. That is, whether one's extreme can be said to be heavily dependent mostly, on a particular time and place in a situation where he has chosen to position himself.

Most people living in any society are born and hence live by the society's specific set of political and economic programmes as they exist, e.g. welfare, public schooling, public spending, economic regulations and government policies.

This philosophy behind all the abovesaid programmes tends to lay down the manner in which individuals are expected to conduct their peaceful affairs and also subjects them to control and regulation by their respective government. The core element behind this philosophy stands out to be that government alone is sovereign and as such supreme and that mere individuals, with their rational choices and desires, are however subordinate and hence inferior.

People are required to submit all their economic activities to political oversight and regulation in the interests of the larger society. What is sought to be emphasized and of great importance is that the sovereign should ultimately decide who to get what.

What is, however, well known is that the libertarian philosophy advocates a political and economic philosophy which is in total opposition to the philosophy that is sought to be superimposed on any liberal society today. The core element of the libertarian philosophy simply states that people should be free to do whatever they want in life, so long as it's peaceful. Thus, libertarians maintain that government's role should be limited rather than as expansive as it is today.

According to Libertarians, people have their right to live their lives anyway they choose, not excluding the right to enter into mutually beneficial transactions with others, so long as their conduct is peaceful. In other words, according to the libertarian philosophy the peaceful choices that people make with their lives and fortunes are not proper to be subjected to the majority vote system.

Many times, the immediate reaction of a person hearing about such libertarian demands voiced by such people is taken as if these libertarians are advocating communism, socialism, or fascism. This becomes much more evident if we are to honestly and deeply believe that our way of life these days are based on freedom and free enterprise as is the attributes of any democratic society and when we are now being confronted by some such libertarians or groups demanding for espousal of an opposite way of life, then it is perfectly natural for any person to conclude that what is being advocated by the libertarians is certainly the opposite of freedom and free enterprise, i.e. communism, socialism, or fascism.

Hence, it is clear that extremism is certainly used in a relative manner as, whether something or someone is an extremist is determined by the type of society with its elaborate framework of policies, in which one tends to live at a particular time.

For example, when we look back into the National Socialist Germany in the 1930s and early 1940s, the regime which ruled

Germany, the Nazi government headed by Adolf Hitler, is held out by most people as being extremist.

If we look at our present day societies, including the Indian society, citizens are seem to be showing a propensity to support their own government's policies and consider only the bad things that other governments or groups opposed to them, do as extremist. In this context countering of these violent extremist ideology gains urgency in the public sphere.

In the middle of 20th century, in the celebrated works of two political scientists, viz. Eric Hoffer and Arthur Schlesinger Jr. wherein they have extensively dealt with the problem of political extremism. In *The True Believer* and *The Passionate State of Mind*, Eric Hoffer has sought to analyze the psychology and sociology of the people who join fanatical mass movements, while Arthur Schlesinger in *The Vital Centre*, has identified, "the supposed centre of politics within which mainstream political discourse takes place in the situation and the importance of the drawing of limits to determine what would be considered to be falling outside of this acceptability."[2]

As such not only both Communism and Fascism were described as "extremist" movements, but also those groups like Nation Of Islam and even the movement for nuclear disarmament which held views outside of the "mainstream" though they did not at all advocate the use of physical force for achieving their objectives were also labelled as extremists.

Extremist politics is the politics of despair.[3] When we look into our history, the movement of political extremism can be said to have consisted of three different kinds of meshed conditions: conditions of ideology, conditions of history, and conditions of popular attitude. Such extremist movements anywhere have been seen to have been born out of the causes of disaffection present in the respective societies. Since such extremist movements have always been movements of disaffection, these movements easily begin when certain groups of people feel that they are about to be, deprived of something important or groups whose rising aspirations lead them to feel that they have always been deprived of something important which they have always had or owned in their society. In majority of cases such deprivation has many a times been accompanied by a process of political dislocation. Further, their feelings of alienation is complicated when they assume that the traditional political structure or structures of their self-governance with which these groups have been associated no longer seem to be serving their needs or are being replaced by a different structure altogether. It has also been observed that extremist movements are not primarily the product of extremists. The critical mass in extremist movements are not necessarily composed of evil-minded types called "extremists" but rather of ordinary people been caught in certain selective kinds of stressful and rather disturbing situations.

The North-Eastern Situation

In order to understand analytically as to why extremism or as many call it terrorism is prevalent in this region one is required to take into account the changes that have occurred all these years in the form of Population Displacement, Political Disorganization, *Population Dynamics, Political Dynamics,* Status Preservatism, Low Democratic Restraint and Cultural Baggage etc.

The basic ideology of extremism as can be seen here is as encapsulated in a so called model of monism. Hence, the extremist actions as manifested in our neighbourhood involves the violation of others' constitutional rights as a citizen, through sustained acts of violence aimed at innocent people and advocacy for the destruction of the very political process, which allows them to co-exist.

We all know that the democratic political process refers primarily to democratic political pluralism: an "open democratic place" for coexistence of ideas, speech, and consonant political action. This kind of monism followed by various extremist groups has tantamounted to the closing down of the democratic space, whether by a massive majority brought under submission through the power of the gun or by a pre-emptive minority composed of their own extremists.

Within a short span of time after independence this region has been witnessed a succession of social changes affecting or threatening displacement. There has been a shift of power from community to elites along with the rising regional disparity. In addition to the large-scale migration within the country, massive waves of immigration has also taken place. Further, as economic development has been initiated by successive governments as a matter of policy of both promoting an all inclusive development and to end the isolation of this region, one can see a many-staged shift from slow development to fast paced developments.

As a consequence of all these developments, the predominant positions of various regional, religious, economic, ethnic, and racial groups have also continually been shaken and sharply diminished.

In such an unenviable scenario the extremist groups are marked to have undergone programmatic and organisational processes of change as they have picked up on social problem situations and crisis processes and have been able to exploit them to the utmost with their rosy promises of a future to the people different from the present as can be seen in their utmost belief in the leftwing ideologies of equality, economic prosperity and a homeland based on self-determination which will assure each person access to society's—which, of course, have not come true as yet.

They have been able to strengthen themselves as well-knit groups through the processes of renewal in accordance with the changes in their social acceptance, the crystallization of specific social and cultural environments, the changes in the forms, methods and argumentation lines of their self-presentation, their political beliefs according to their respective ethnic communities.

In quite a number of cases even after utter failure to live up to their expectation and aspirations to bring about the intended changes in the society, these extremist groups have managed to survive through a process of regrouping and of differentiation. Their relevance has been proved by their enhanced capability to participate in anti-government operations as fighting the paramilitary forces or respectively by influencing government formation in the vicinity, aided by the international forces inimical to our country.

The existence of such right-wing extremist groups can also be seen in their innovative ways of adapting themselves to newly formed specific social environments upon which they can rely and then carry on their acts.

They have cleverly positioned themselves within existing society and its political camps as the society is grappling with the phenomena of paradigmatic change from economic and social state to the competitive state.

The proliferation of the *locational nationalism* (Christoph

Butterwege) and the economisation of all areas of life have also provided for a social climate to which these right-wing extremist groups hook on very well. They claim that the only way to solve the problems of the society by way of nationalism as opposed to the demand for a strong state and inclusion. In that endeavour, they address themselves both to those, who are intent on asserting themselves in the national competition and to secure their own perquisites that way as well as to those who are unsettled by unemployment and precarisation of work and daily life. Competition and social and economic profit maximisation emerges as the central principles of actions of the extremists rather than any benevolent claims which are made by them on their behalf.

It is revealed from a study of data relating to civilian fatalities as a result of social and political violence in the country over the period September 1, 1999 – August 31, 2001, that over 33 per cent were accounted for by a range of insurgencies and terrorist movements in India's North East—and these were overwhelmingly concentrated in a small number of districts in four of the seven States in this region.[4]

It is well known that separatism constitutes a primary demand of many of the groups that are active in India's North East. However, many North East groups have not clearly defined their separatist goals so far. There has also been a major proliferation of militant groups in over the years, with 108 groups active in the region, though some appear to be either insignificant gangs and some now dormant.

Amongst all the groups, the United Liberation Front of Asom (ULFA) which pleads for the secession of Assam and the National Socialist Council of Nagalim (Isak-Muivah) (NSCN-IM) leader of the longest insurgency in the region, seeking Naga independence stand out prominently. Their influence in the region is still overwhelming despite a decline in the number of violent acts. They are known to be carrying out widespread networks of extortion, smuggling besides other criminal activities and also being in control substantial overground business operations. While the NSCN-IM is now continuously engaged in peace negotiations with the Union Government under a cease-fire agreement that has been effective since August 1997, the ULFA has consistently rejected possibilities of a negotiated settlement. It is reported widely in the media that ULFA and the NSCN-IM have also continued to extend their spheres of influence in the region through intermittent low-grade violence and by training and arming a large number of other terrorist and proxy groups at the behest of ISI.

The activities of such groups in the region goes beyond the term normally understood as extremism since the actions have proved to be disruptive, secessionist and self-motivated personal gains rather than the social gains they claim to be at their back of mind.

NOTES

1. Himmelstein, Jerome L., 1988. *All But Sleeping with the Enemy: Studying the Radical Right Up Close* ASA, San Francisco.
2. Schlesinger, Arthur, 1949. *The Vital Centre: The Politics of Freedom.* Various editions, first published.
3. Seymour Martin Lipset, 1970. *The Politics of Unreason: Right Wing Extremism in America, 1790-l970,* Earl Raab; Harper & Row, p. 554.
4. Gill, K.P.S., 2004. *Islamist Extremists and Terrorism in South Asia, Institute for Conflict Management,* New Delhi.

14

Extremism in North East India

A Conceptual Analysis

Kundan Hazarika

Extremism has become a recurring phenomenon in the North East in the last few decades. Scholars, both from the region as well as from outside, have been seriously trying to address divergent aspects of the problem. However, the term extremism is often used loosely to refer to the insurgent groups operating in the region. In other words, there is not much concern regarding the theoretical aspect of the term extremism, if it can be defined properly from a North-eastern perspective. A look at the works of the scholars regarding the North East in the area of Peace and Conflict Resolution reveals that a number of terms like extremism, insurgency, separatism, militancy and even terrorism are used simultaneously to refer to almost similar phenomena.[1] Hence, it is necessary to clarify these confusions regarding the use of the term extremism so as to put it on better theoretical premises, which may eventually lead to a better understanding of the discourse of extremism.

In common usage, the term extremism moves around two kinds of usages. The first one is the deviance from political norms or in other words, political repression. From that point of view, the political system of any country whose traditional system includes political repression can be called extremist. The second usage is regarding the tendency to violate democratic procedures. in this sense, extremism describes the violation of the democratic political process which stands for a free flow of ideas, speech and constant political action. So, ideologically extremism stands on monism. It is opposite to pluralism which allows the coexistence of different political entities, ethnic groups and ideas.[2] Extremism being an advocacy of extreme measures implies deviating from prevailing political norms. In a country where democratic procedures are accepted norms, extremism means departure from modes of democratic functioning, going beyond the limit of the established institutions and their moral and ethical bases and as the institutions are not static and they do undergo modifications and changes with the passage of time; the concept of extremism also changes with the changes in the society.[3] Scruton maintains that taking a political idea to its limits, regardless of 'unfortunate' repercussions, impracticalities, arguments, and feelings to the contrary, and with the intention not only to confront, but also to eliminate, opposition amounts to extremism. That would imply adoption of means to political ends which disregard accepted standards of conduct, in particular which would be viewed as showing disregard for the life, liberty and human rights of others.[4] Extremism then might refer to a view that purports extreme change of any established system be it economic, political or social. Extremism would also stand for political radicalism of any form or variety such as of the left or the right. If extremism means going beyond the limits of normative procedures which define the democratic political process, many of these procedural norms are themselves constantly redefined.[5] Walter J. Raymond defines extremism as "The view that purports extreme change of the economic, political and social system (or any part of it). In the popular usage, extremism stands for political radicalism of any form or variety such as of the left or the right (e.g. communism, Nazism, anarchism, etc.). On the extreme left, the guerilla communism of the Chinese, Vietnamese and Combodian kind (one that is characterized by an irregular, unconventional, insurgency type partisan military activity) proved to be an effective means of gaining state power. On the extreme right, particularly in the United States, the struggle for the preservation of the *status quo* is mainly ideological and of a non-insurgency type...."[6]

Historically, extremist movements are movements of disaffection. Occurring in periods of incipient change, they are employed by groups who feel that they have just been, or are about to be, deprived of something important, or to groups whose rising aspirations lead them to feel that they have always been deprived of something important they now want. Such deprivation is accompanied by political dislocation.[7]

Right wing extremism seems to be a very common phenomenon in many of the Western countries. On several occasions, the term extremism is used to refer to certain political parties which are known as "extremist parties" or "right wing parties" in various western countries.[8] Theorists and analysts of party systems have warned that support for extremist political parties poses serious threat to democracy.[9] There are two visions in this regard, i.e. divergent issue positions and severe discontent with the political system. In the first instance, extremism seems to mean widely-divergent positions on policy issues or on the nature of the regime. The extremist party represents a demand for major transformation of the society, either towards some future vision or back to an idealized past. Such demands diverge from the general, current policy consensus. In this sense, extremist parties are those parties promoting clearly articulated issue proposals that are at odds with those promoted by most other parties. The alternative vision of "extremism" focuses on expression of severe discontent with the authorities, perhaps with the regime itself. Such discontent or alienation presents serious problems. Because, distrust and frustration leads to bargaining and ultimately it creates the propensity towards angry or obstructive conflict behaviour.[10]

In the Indian scene some discussion of extremism exists in the form of commentaries on left-wing extremism, i.e. the Naxalite Movement.[11] Extremism in North East India has drawn the attention of a large number of scholars. Many of them support the 'colonial hinterland' theory as a cause for the rise of extremism. Tilottma Misra[12] shows that Assam has become a colonial hinterland. In fact, this has become a major thesis of many extremist groups in the North East in propagating their cause.[13] This thesis was further developed by Baruah[14] when he contextualized "elites in a colonial hinterland". Baruah comments that it is but natural for the educated elites in Assam to stand against the exploitative nature of the ruling class in India and also oppose the people, with big brotherly attitude towards the local inhabitants, come to the state from mainland India. Udayon Misra[15] credits ULFA of being the first insurgent outfit of the North East which focused effectively on the colonial thesis. Misra[16] regards underdevelopment and relative deprivation syndrome as the major factors contributing to the sense of alienation and ultimately leading to insurgency. S.K. Chaube[17] holds that the mainstream and its agents in India appear to be the 'internal colonisers' in the less fortunate regions. Amalendu Misra[18] seems to follow the same line when he says that hegemonic control of the resources by a particular community and unequal distribution of wealth feed all the separatist movements in India. Samir Kumar Das shows ULFA's argument that India has only replaced the 'colonial rule' of Great Britain in Assam[19]; and that the internal colonialism that Assam has been subjected to is made in the context of India's capitalist socio-economic structure.[20] Colonial hinterland thesis thus remains a major argument in the study of extremism in the region. Sajal Nag's[21] view that the regional and secessionist tendencies of the North East and elsewhere had its origin in the dominance and recognition of the language, culture and political aspirations of the advanced nationalities at the cost of smaller ones when the latter's ethnic area was included in the other's provinces seems to be a minority view in the literature. But is there a difference between cultural identity in terms of a nationality and the potential allegiance to the State of India? Baruah tries to differentiate the concepts of 'Nation' and 'State', which are often used as a common term, i.e. 'Nation State'.[22] Monirul Hussain[23] in this regard argues that the big Indian State has failed to understand its own smaller communities and their hinterlands which leads to alienation and frustration and ultimately it is expressed through conflicts. However, in this context the distinction between the Indian State and Indian Nationalism needs to be taken into account. Though many of the smaller nationalities have accepted the reality of the Indian State, the expansionist trend of Indian Nationalism and the attempt at mixing together Indian Nationalism and Indian State have resulted in the mobilisation of smaller nationalities in a great way.[24] Baruah shows the connection between the rise of ethnic and communal feelings and the rise of extremist movements in this regard.[25] Misra[26] warns that conflict situations are bound to arise whenever attempts are made by the Indian ruling elite to overrule the diversity of a particular community or people and impose homogeneous set of values. B.B. Kumar[27] maintains that it is the British who sowed the seeds of separatism and secessionism in the North-eastern region. Their policy of gradual segregation of the tribals and non-tribals, hills and the plains was mainly responsible for the creation of a feeling of distrust and deprivation that ultimately led to such tendencies. J.B. Bhattacharjee[28] also agrees that colonial rule had strengthened the barriers by its segregating policies. Samir Kumar Das also argues that rather than being hegemonic, the Indian State is a non-hegemonic state, a repressive one.[29] Scholars like Sanjib Baruah[30], Udayon Misra[31] have also discussed about ULFA's support base and causes of the insurgent movements. Jaideep Saikia[32] and Ajay Sahani[33] have also discussed various aspects of ULFA, its working and prospects of peace in Assam.

Such studies of the scholars of the North East reveal that, more often than not the scholars are interested in analyzing the causes for the rise of extremism, evolution of extremism, contemporary status of extremism, possible solutions to it and its consequences. But, the terms such as insurgency, secessionism, separatism, militancy and extremism have been almost mixed together and one chooses to use anyone of them according to convenience. Insurgent, separatist and secessionist are three related terms. Insurgency is an extra-constitutional, compositively progressive and variegated struggle launched against the incumbent authority by the consciously mobilized sections of indigenous masses for the fulfilment of certain conceptual goals, manifesting emancipation.[34] Separatism is resistance by a political entity to further incorporation or subordination within the larger political authority of which it is already a member.[35] Secessionism, in contrast, is a narrower and more specific term referring to a demand for formal withdrawal from a central political authority by a member unit or units on the basis of a claim to independent sovereign status.[36] Separatist movements can become secessionist in course of time, and secessionist movements can revert to merely separatist movements. A secessionist movement by definition refers to claims and struggles to achieve sovereignty of its own in the form of independent statehood. Secession represents an instance of disintegration, wherein political actors in one or more sub-systems withdraw their loyalties, expectations, and political activities from a jurisdictional centre and focus them on a centre of their own.[37]

From that point of view, from a north-eastern perspective, the scope of the term extremism becomes broad enough to include the actions of all secessionist, separatist or insurgent groups and also actions of peoples which are not violent in nature but somehow do not fall within the range of the methods permitted to be employed by the Constitution of India. Therefore, though in common parlance extremism is associated with violence, yet we can define extremism as such views or actions of a group of people with a political end; which are violent or non-violent in nature but which stand inconsistent with the prevailing norms that fix the limits of democratic code of conduct or which do not fall within the established limits of political practices of a country. Such limits are often constitutional in nature. In this way, the term extremism can be used as an umbrella term putting together all the similar terms which mainly refer to the insurgent organizations but it can also include any other kind of action not necessarily initiated by insurgent organizations. Rather, they are initiated by organizations which generally function within the limits fixed by the constitution; but sometimes involved in some non-violent actions taking place outside that limit. Many of the actions of AASU in Assam or the KSU in Meghalaya can fall into this category and in such conditions their actions can also be regarded as extremist since it implies political repression and conduct not permitted by the Constitution and "normal" political code of conduct. Extremism in this sense remains an ideology that supports and promotes such extremist politics.

NOTES

1. The same phenomenon is used in various senses; see the use of the term extremism in Apurba K. Barua (2005) "Communities and Democracy: A North East Indian Perspective". *North East India Studies.* Vol 1.1 No.1 June. Hiren Gohain. (1996) "Extremist Challenge and Indian State: Case of Assam. *Economic and Political Weekly*. Vol. 31, No. 31 Aug. 3. see its other usages in Girin Phukan "Terrorism in North East India and its External Linkages" in Ashok Kumar Roy & S.K. Agnihotri (Eds) (2007) *Terrorism and Peace Initiatives in North East India,* Om Publications, New Delhi; Ashok Kumar Roy, B.J. Deb (Eds) (2007) *Terrorism and Human Rights in North East India,* Om Publications, New Delhi; Tarapot Phanjoubam (1996) *Insurgency in North-Eastern India,* Vikas Publishing House, New Delhi; B. Pakem (Ed.) (1997) *Insurgency in North-East India,* Omsons Publications, New

Delhi; Sajal Nag. (1999) *Nationalism, Separatism and Secessionism.* Rawat Publications, Jaipur and New Delhi. Sajal Nag (2002) *Contesting Marginalities: Ethnicity, Insurgency and Sub Nationalism in North East India.* Manohar, New Delhi.

2. Seymour Martin Lipset and Earl Raab. (1970) *The Politics of Unreason: Right Wing Extremism in America 1790-1970,* New York: Harper and Row, p. 3.
3. Amiya K. Samanta. (1984) *Left Extremist Movements in West Bengal: An Experiment in Armed Agrarian Struggle.* Calcutta: Firma KLM Private Limited, p. 1.
4. Roger Scruton. (1982) *A Dictionary of Political Thought.* London and Basingstroke: Macmillan, p. 164.
5. Lipset *op. cit.,* pp. 4-5.
6. Walter J. *Raymond Dictionary of Politics,* Lawrenceville Brunswick Publishing Company, 1978, 6th ed., pp. 206-07.
7. William Roy McPherson. (1967) *Parallels in Extremist Ideology.* Ph.D. Thesis, Department of Social Relations, Harvard University, cited in *ibid,* pp. 17-24.
8. See Michael O'Neil Belgium: "Language, Ethnicity and Nationality", Roger Eatwell "The Rebirth of the 'Extreme Right' in Western Europe?", Kurt Richard Luther "Austria: A Democracy under Threat from the Freedom Party?" Uwe Backes and Cas Mudde "Germany: Extremism without Successful Parties" James L. Newell "Italy: The Extreme Right Comes in from the Cold", Christopher T. Husbands "Switzerland: Right-Wing" and Elisabeth L. Carter "Proportional Representation and the Fortunes of Right-Wing Extremist Parties" *West European Politics*, Vol. 25, No. 3 July, 2002.
9. G. Bingham Powell, Jr. "Extremist Parties and Political Turmoil: Two Puzzles", *American Journal of Political Science,* Vol. 30, No. 2, May 1996, p. 357.
10. *Ibid.,* pp. 358-59.
11. See Samanta *op. cit*; Satyabrata Rai Choudhuri. (1977) *Leftist Movements in India: 1917-1947.* Calcutta: Minerva Associates; Rabindra Ray. (1988) *Naxalites and their Ideology.* Delhi: Oxford University Press; Sachchidanand Pandey. (1985) *Naxal Violence: A Socio-Political Study.* Delhi: Chanakya Publications; Sankar Ghosh. (1975) *The Naxalite Movement: A Maoist Experiment.* Calcutta: Firma K.L. Mukhopodhay; Biplab Dasgupta. (1974) *Naxalite Movement.* Bombay: Allied; Amrik Singh Nimbran. (1992) *Poverty, Land and Violence: An analytical study of Naxalism in Bihar.* Patna: Lawman's Publications; Sumanta Banerjee. (1980) *In the Wake of Naxalbari: A History of the Naxalite Movement in India.* Calcutta: Subarnarekha; Vrajendra Raj Mehta. (1978) *Beyond Marxism: towards an alternative perspective.* New Delhi: Manohar; P.V. Ramana. "Naxalism: Trends

and Govt. Response." *Dialogue*, Vol. 8. No. 2. Oct-Dec. 2006. pp. 58-69. Ved Marwah. "India's Internal Security Challenges." *Strategic Analysis*, Vol. 27. No. 4, Oct-Dec. 2003, p. 512; also see for a detailed journalistic approach on left-wing extremism, *Frontline*, Vol. 22, Issue 21, October 8-21, 2005.

12. See Tilottama Misra (1980) "Assam: A Colonial Hinterland", *Economic and Political Weekly*, Vol. 15, No. 32, August 9, pp. 1357-64
13. This is a thesis strongly propagated by ULFA. For a detailed discussion see Samir Kumar Das. (1994) *ULFA: United Liberation Front of Assam: A Political Analysis*. Delhi: Ajanta Publications.
14. See A.K. Baruah, "Elites in a Colonial Hinterland" in B.L. Abbi (Ed.) (1984) *North East Region: Problems and Prospects of Development*, Chandigarh: Centre for Research in Rural and Industrial Development, pp. 322-28.
15. Udayon Misra. (2000) *The Periphery Strikes Back. Challenges to the Nation-State in Assam and Nagaland*. Shimla: Indian Institute of Advanced Study, Rashtrapati Nivas. p. 144.
16. *Ibid.*, p. 157.
17. S.K. Chaube, "Insurgency in North East India: A Heretical View" in Pakem *op. cit*, p. 30.
18. Amalendu Misra, "The Politics of Secessionist Conflict Management in India". *Contemporary Security Policy*, Vol. 22, No.2, August 2001, pp. 49-68.
19. Das *op. cit*. 29.
20. *Ibid.*, p. 34.
21. Sajal Nag (1999) *Nationalism, Separatism and Secessionism*. Jaipur and New Delhi: Rawat Publications, p. 26.
22. A.K. Baruah (1991). *Socal Tensions in Assam. Middle Class Politics*. Guwahati: Purbanchal Prakash, p. 9.
23. Monirul Hussain, "Building Peace: Locating the Actors and their Roles" in Imdad Hussain (Ed.) *The Guwahati Declaration and the Road to Peace in Assam*, New Delhi: Akansha Publishing House, 2005, p.107.
24. Apurba K. Baruah "Roots of Conflict" in *ibid*, p. 35.
25. Apurba K. Baruah "Communities and Democracy: A North East Indian Perspective." *North East India Studies*. Vol. 1, No. 1, June 2005, p. 14.
26. Misra *op. cit.*, p. 155.
27. B.B. Kumar, "Ethnicity and Insurgency in India's North East". *Dialouge*, Vol. 8. No. 2, Oct.-Dec. 2006, p. 159.
28. J.B. Bhattacharjee, "Understanding Conflicts: Towards a resolution" in Hussain *op. cit.*, p. 19.
29. Das *op. cit.*, pp. 9-10.
30. See Sanjib Baruah. "The State and Separatist Militancy in Assam: Winning a Battle and Loosing the War?" *Asian Survey*, Vol. 34, No. 10, Oct. 1994, pp. 863 & 877; also see Sanjib Barua, 1999. *India Against*

Itself Assam and the Politics of Nationality. Philadelphia: University of Pennsylvania Press, pp. 146-47.

31. Misra *op. cit*, p. 147.
32. Jaideep Saikia. "Autumn in Springtime: The ULFA battles for survival". *Faultlines*. Vol. 7 in http://satp.org/satporgtp/publications/faultlines/volume7/Fault7/JaideepSF.htm.
33. Ajay Sahani and J. George. "Security and Development in India's Northeast: An Alternative Perspective". *Faultlines*. Vol. 4 in http://satp.org/satporgtp/publications/faultlines/volume4/Fault4-JG&ASf1.htm (accessed on July 10, 2008).
34. V.K. Anand. (1981) *Insurgency and Counterinsurgency: A Study of Modern Guerrilla Warfare*. New Delhi: Deep and Deep Publications, cited in R.N. Prasad. "Retrogression of Insurgency: A Conceptual Analysis" in B. Pakem. (Ed.) (1997) *Insurgency in North East India*, New Delhi: Omsons Publications, pp. 60-61.
35. Peter Lyon. "Separatism and Secessionism in the Malaysian Realm, 1948-65", *The Politics of Separatism*, Collected Seminar Papers, No. 19, Institute of Commonwealth Studies, University of London, p. 69, cited in John R. Wood, "Secession: A Comparative Analytical Framework", *Canadian Journal of Political Science*, Vol. 14, No.1, March 1981, p. 110.
36. *Ibid*.
37. Wood *loc.cit*., pp. 110-11.

15

The State Response to Violence in Manipur

L. Seityabati Devi

Violence may be defined roughly as the illegal employment of methods of physical coercion for personal or group ends. It must be distinguished from force, or power, which is a purely physical concept having direction and intensity, which has legal sanction and which expresses itself in the imposition of physical constraints as well as in the use of less conspicuous but more effective social pressures, such as discriminatory economic, cultural and administrative measures. The use of physical coercion by duly constituted government, either as a method of defence or as a means of consolidating its rule, collecting taxes and the like raises no particular problem of social ethics—once the sovereignty of the government is accepted—but the debate goes on the expediency. Physical coercion or the threat of physical coercion is in the very nature of state rule; there can be difference only upon its occasion and degree. The really troublesome issues over the use and justification of violence arise out of the problems faced by a politically subordinate group, whether minority or not, which seeks to capture political power or complete the acceptance of some specific measure. On certain occasions these issues have taken acute form, especially among those groups which have justified their revolt against the existing government on the ground that it had exercised terrorism against its own citizens. A recurrent theme which runs through the literature of social reform, especially that of pre-revolutionary Russia, concerns itself with the spiritual predicaments which flow from the attempt to meet violence with greater violence. If violent action against man is wrong, is it any less wrong to use violent action against the men who practice it ? Approached from the moral angle the paradox cannot be resolved except by the formal statement that where devotion to the values of peace and spiritual serenity is higher than devotion to life itself and all the other values which life makes possible, the use of violence against violence cannot be sanctioned; where other values are considered as intrinsically desirable as serenity or blessedness, the use of violence may be extenuated as the necessary, even if painful, means of achieving them.

Practically all movements of social revolt which have proved to be successful have been compelled to use violence at some point in the process of acquiring power.[1] With the progress of human civilization different forms of violence occurred from time to time. In a democratic society, the existing government is the sole authority to control such types of violence. The existing government introduced different forms of Acts, and pursued different policies for the control of violence and the society. The persons who indulged in violence are firmly dealt with by the machineries and law enforcing agencies of the government.

Violence emerged as a strong force in North East India especially in Manipur during the last three decades. There are different types of violence caused by Policies of government from time to time. At the same time, there is also violence caused by the conflict among ethnic groups.

Ethnic Violence

Present Manipur is a land of ethnic conflicts on social, economic, cultural and political issues. These conflicts are to be managed in such a manner that the parties evolved in the conflicts are neither loser or gainer. If there are conflicts, there should always be ways to manage and resolve. The initiative for management and resolution may originate from the government, voluntary organisations and individuals. All conflicts concerning the individuals, groups, communities can be managed and resolved in a creative manner guided by the spirit of general interest. The politics of the North East India has been highly ethicized because of the awakening of ethno-cultural consciousness and assertion of ethnic identities in the last part of 20th and beginning of 21st century. Manipur has been under the grip of the problem of ethnic conflict, after 1990s which crippled the state development in all aspects.

Naga-Kuki Conflict, 1992-1996

The violent ethnic conflict was happened between the Naga and the Kuki groups during 1992-1996. This conflict continued for about five years, resulting in the death of many persons including men, women and children, burning of houses, displacement of many persons belonging to both ethnic groups.

The violence continued unabated leading to gutting of altogether 5724 houses out of which 3110 belonged to Kukis and 2614 belonged to Nagas. In addition to this around 15,000 people were internally displaced and 1000 people were killed. Action taken by the Government — Neither the State Government nor the Central Government has so far instituted any enquiry Commission to understand the causes for evolving policies for the lasting solution to such clashes. No venture on social planning will succeed if it is based on common/sensical notions and mere assumptions in relations to needs, problems and aspirations of the people. The Governor recommended the imposition of President's Rule on the ground that the continuation of the existing ministry would provide an impetus to the extremist activities, fuelling the Kuki-Naga clash and further incapacitating the administration and law enforcement agencies.

Meitei and Meitei Pangal Conflict, 1993

The Valley of Manipur also witnessed conflict between the Meitei and Meitei Pangals (Muslim) in May 3, 1993. The conflict was managed and resolved within a short period of time as it was caused by a misunderstanding of buying and selling of arms. This conflict resulted in the death of 96 Muslims and 4 Meitei. In Meitei and Meitei Pangal Conflict, state response show that, one hundred and one cases were registered by the police and 423 persons arrested in connection with the incident. Fortunately, it ended abruptly, though healing of wounds took a bit long, and both communities are living harmoniously now as before.

Kuki and Paite Conflict, 1997-98

The Kuki and the Paite conflict took place in 1997-98 in Churachandpur district of Manipur. In the conflict 562 persons died; 39 were missing, 263 got injured and 6626 houses were gutted. All sections of the society tried to resolve the conflict.[2] On March 4, 1998, the Government of Manipur formed a High Level Committee headed by the Chief Minister W. Nipamacha Singh to find out ways and means to stop the ethnic clash between the Kuki and the Zomi and to restore peace and communal harmony. Memorandum of understanding was signed on March 26, 1998 between Zomi Council and Kuki Inpi Churachandpur. Both the groups agreed on ten point agreements and decided that all forms of violence including burning of houses, kidnapping, killing, extortion, fabrication of false rumous and even using of harsh words against each other shall be stopped forthwith.

As a follow-up action of MOU, a joint meeting of ZC-KIC was held at DC's residence on March 29, 1998 and passed another ten point resolution which among other things provided for separate and joint peace campaign. On April 2, 1998, the convener of Cabinet Sub-Committee of the State High Level Committee convened a joint meeting and passed the resolution to sort out the issues between the Kuki and Zomi communities. As instruction by the State Government (vide MOU dated 26-3-98) to work together for bringing out a final solution to the conflict in Churachandpur, the ZC and KIC met repeatedly and campaigned widely in the District for peace.

Thus with sincere and tireless effort of the people and the government led by W. Nipamacha, the then Chief Minister of Manipur and other organisations like Meitei Society, Churachandpur, AMUCO, Meira Paibi groups, Church leaders were able to convince the two groups Kuki and Paite to end their conflict peacefully. As a result, the conflict was resolved as the leaders of the two groups signed the final Peace Accord on October 1, 1998 in presence of governmental and non-governmental representatives. In the aftermath of the conflict, the number of clashes has virtually receded significantly but the damage done on the pattern of human habitation needs to be compensated. Almost 40 per cent of the affected persons were given *ex-gratia* and compensation by the Government.

Violence and Armed Groups

To curtail different underground organizations, the Government of India and the State Government introduced different Acts and Bills in the name of the maintenance of law and order. The Armed Forces Special Power Act, 1958 was imposed in 1980. The Ministry of Home Affairs declared several underground organizations as unlawful organizations and their functioning was interpreted as the acts of insurgency and terrorism that upset the unity and integrity of the country. This Act was further extended by Central Government on 14 December, 2005 (AR News, Imphal).[3]

During the last five decades, the security forces who had Special Powers to contain insurgency had not been able to do so. On the other hand, on the pretext of protecting the people, the Indian security forces have been constantly violating basic rights of the people including the right to life enshrined in the Constitution of India as well as the International covenants of the United Nations to which India is a signatory. In the name of counter-insurgency, the Indian State unleashes the brutal force of its security agencies on the innocent population of the state. The untold miseries include molestation, rape, killing front ranking innocent people like artists, sports persons and National bravery award winning children in fake encounters. The year 1980 has a black legacy in the history of Manipur. It was on 26 April, 1980 when at Langjing Patsoi Khunou, that the armed insurgent groups attacked the CRPF and took away the arms. In retaliation the CRPF conducted search operation in the area and tortured the innocent civilians. Manipur witnessed gross violation of human rights by the armed forces on March 14, 1984 at the volleyball ground of Heirangoithong, Imphal in a shooting killing 13 spectators and injuring 39 persons during a volleyball match.[4]

On January 7, 1995, the undergrounds attacked CRPF personnel posted at Regional Institute of Medical Science. A CRPF man was killed and the forces in retaliation shot dead 15 civilians including a medical student from Arunachal Pradesh, five Auto Rickshaw Drivers and one Rickshaw puller and nine civilians. On October 3, 1999, some unknown militants ambushed a combined team of 81 CRPF and 35 CRPF at Tonsem Lamkhai in Thoubal District and killed seven CRPF personnel on the spot. Minutes after the encounter the CRPF personnel forcefully stopped a bus carrying some polling personnel at the ambushed site and started beating, kicking, hitting the civilian people in the bus. They were lined up and shot dead. The killing of ten civilians at Tousem Lamkhai outraged the people who demanded a judicial inquiry into the incidence. Different women and civil organizations of different localities organized public meetings to arouse public opinion against such atrocities committed by the arm forces. They registered strong protest against frequent killing of civilians in the name of tracking down armed insurgents and tried to exert public pressure on the Government to withdraw the Armed Forces Special Power Act, 1958 from Manipur. The public also condemned the activities of the underground organizations. The frequent killings of civilians in insurgency related incidents created public distrust towards the security forces whose services were needed to protect the innocent civilians.

On November 2, 2000, a patrol party of Assam Rifles was returning from Nambol in Bishnupur district. When the para military forces reached Malom area near Imphal airport at around 3.30 p.m., some personnel were injured by a powerful bomb planted by some militants on the road side. The Assam Rifles personnel opened fire in different directions, killing altogether ten persons including one women and her two nephews waiting at the bus stand nearby. This incident came to be known as "Malom killings". Protesting against the killings, Irom Sharmila, a 32 years old woman went on fast-unto-death from November 4, 2000 and demanded immediate withdrawal of the AFSPA, 1958 from the state. In another incident, eight innocent civilians were killed by 117 Bn. Jat Regt. at Tabalong, Tamenglong district by exercising excess power under the Act, 1958 on December 28, 2000.

Over and above, there were issues like custodial deaths, fake encounter, rape and torture in the custody. Th. Monorama was arrested from her house at late night by showing an arrest memo to her family member on July 10, 2004 by the Assam Rifles. She was given charge of being an active cadre of the banned PLA, one of the dozen or so militant organisations active in the State, and was killed when she tried to escape from custody. Next morning she was found dead on the road side of Ngariyan Mapao Maring village about 4 kms away from Irilbung Police Station. This killing led to a mass movement in Manipur, for the repeal of the AFSPA, 1958.[5]

Meanwhile, the killing has drawn flak from the general public as well from various social, civil and students' organizations and women and local Meira Paibi groups. While in most cases of spiralling violence, the general public watch helplessly, occasionally when a large number of civilians are senselessly murdered the general public get outraged. Some such well documented cases are the Heirangoithong Massacre (1984) in which 13 spectators of a volleyball match were arbitrarity killed by the CRPF; the Oinam Massacre of (1987) where 15 villagers were arbitrarity murdered by the Assam Rifles, the RMC Hospital Massacre (1996) where 9 civilians including a medical student were killed inside the hospital premises by the CRPF; the Tonsem Lamkhai (1999) incident where 10 civilians including state Government employees on election duties were arbitrarily killed by CRPF. In order to damp down the public outcry the Government of Manipur usually, but not always, institutes Judicial Inquiries under the Commission of Inquiry Act, 1952 to ascertain the facts of the incidents. But due to lack of co-operation from the armed forces and recently due to active intervention against such inquiries by the armed forces, the inquiry reports could never be made public.

Violence Created by Social Movement

Cease-Fire issue—Protection of the territorial integrity of the state of Manipur is one of the most important duties of the present generation. But there was a great shock when the Government of India signed a peace talk with the NSCN (IM) in 1997 which could potentially disturb the territorial boundary of Manipur because the cease-fire between Government of India and NSCN (IM) extended to all the Naga inhabited areas. While people in Manipur supported the peace initiative in Nagaland, they had apprehensions in their mind. And on 4 August, 1997 more than five lakh people organized a rally throughout the state capital to show solidarity against any attempt to divide Manipur's territorial integrity. The rally was organised by the All Manipur United Clubs Organisation (AMUCO), a body of several organizations. The AMSU also played a major role in organizing the rally. The AMUCO sponsored rally sent a clear message that the people of Manipur will not allow disintegration of the state "at all cost".[6]

A five point cease-fire agreement was signed between the Government of India and the National Socialist Council of Nagaland (NSCN, IM) on June 14, 2001 in Bangkok (Thailand). In fact, NSCN (IM) has been consistently putting forward to the Government of India to recognize Naga inhabited areas of Manipur, Assam and Arunachal Pradesh as parts of Nagalim (coined in 1998). The outfit also pressurised Government of India "to make an official declaration, that the cease-fire coverage encompasses all the Naga areas, because it is the agreement between NSCN (IM) and the Government of India".[7] This had happened despite the reported assurances and categorical commitments made by the Prime Minister, the Home Minister and other dignitaries to the effect that the area of cease-fire shall be confined in territories of Nagaland.

In fact, article (1) of the Agreement, viz., "without territorial limits" threatens the territorial integrity of the Manipur state. Consequent upon the extension of cease-fire to Manipur a General strike was called by the AMSU and AMUCO, AMKIL, NIPCO and UPF and IPSA and various other organisations for 72 hours from mid-night of 15th June to 18th June, 2001. On 18th June, a group of people of Manipur unprecedentedly resorted to massive violence and burnt down various important buildings including Manipur Legislative Assembly Building and Secretariat, Chief Minister's Secretariat, several MLAs Bungalows and Office of Political Parties etc. In the mass uprising, CRPF personnels fired upon the agitating people indiscriminately with live bullets killing 14 persons and injuring many others. In the subsequent events, people of Manipur from all walks of life including students, social workers, women organisations, eminent sport persons, writers, senior citizens etc. came out on street, neglecting their normal duties and defying prohibitory order on the apprehension that the extension of cease-fire will affect the territorial integrity of the state, having more than 2000 years of old history.

On 27 July, 2001, the centre indicated that it might decide to restrict the cease-fire with NSCN (IM) to Nagaland and not extend it to other North Eastern States.[8] The then Prime Minister Atal Bihari Vajpayee told a meeting of Chief Ministers of North Eastern States that the words 'without territorial limit' in the agreement reached between the Centre and the NSCN (IM) on June 14 would be deleted and the *status quo ante* of June 14 would be restored.[9]

AFSPA 1958—The Armed Forces Special Power Act, 1958 has been the bone of contention for a long time. This Act giving security forces the powers to search, arrest and even kill any person on mere suspicion is operational in Manipur. Under the Act, no action can be undertaken against the security force personnel without the prior sanction of the Central Government.

The ongoing agitation was stirred by the alleged rape and custodial death of a 33 years old Thangjam Manorama, after she was picked up by personnels of the Assam Rifle engaged in counter-insurgency operation in the state, on the night of July 10, 2004. Family members alleged that Manorama's brother was brutally beaten and she herself was tortured by the Army personnel before taking her away. Surprisingly, the Assam Rifles team gave an arrest memo to the family before taking her away. The 24 hour general strike, called by Apunba Lup conglomeration 32 social bodies spearheading the agitation against the killing of Manorama severally affected life at the twin valley districts with all business establishment, remaining closed. Meanwhile, the killing has drawn flak from the general public as well as various social, civil and students organisations and local Meira Paibi groups.[10]

Meanwhile, an indefinite curfew was imposed in and around Imphal East and West District from 11 a.m. on July 15, 2004 after which women staged a nude *dharna* here, in protest of the killing of Manorama Devi by the elderly women who were in the age group of 50-65 years. They took off their clothes and shouted slogans like—'come rape us and kill us'—in front of the Assam Rifles (AR) Western Gate in the heart of Imphal city. The movement, spearheaded by 32 social organisations under the banner of 'Apunba Lup' spiralled into a 'Civil disobedience' movement which become violent after a student leader Pebam Chittaranjan immolated himself on Independence day in 2004. The suicide note of P. Chittaranjan stated "It is better to self-immolate than die at the hands of security forces under this Act with this conviction I am marching ahead of the people as a human torch".[11]

The students organisations had declared closure of educational institutions since they were of the view that their was no meaning in attending classes where human rights were trampled with impunity. With great pressure from the MLAs from different constituencies and also by different student organisations and women and civil organisations, O. Ibobi Singh, the Chief Minister of Manipur lifted AFSPA from Imphal East and West on 2004. On August 12, 2004, the Manipur government withdrew the controversial AFSPA from seven Assembly constituencies in Imphal East and West area. It decided to lift the Act from the Municipal area having ten per cent of the total population of about 12 lakh people. The decision was taken in view of the popular agitation against it after the killing of Manorama Devi. But Irom Sharmila is still going on with her hunger strike because she thinks that the people of districts are also very much suffering from this problem.[12]

With regard to the killing of Th. Monarama Devi in July 2004, on June 23, 2005, the Guwahati High Court directed Manipur State Government to hand over the report of justice (retd.) C. Upendra Singh Commission to the Union Ministry of Home Affairs for necessary action against those indicated in the inquiry report without loss of time. No action was however taken.[13] A dithering Chief Minister O. Ibobi government withdrew the disturbed area status in a 20 square kilometre area falling in seven Assembly Segments in Imphal Municipal limits, in order to render the AFSPA ineffective there. However, the delayed decision, despite the fact that it was against the wishes of the UPA government at the centre, failed to address the public anger. Following the long struggle, the Prime Minister of India handed over Kangla to civilian authority on 20th November, 2004, after 113 years of military use.[14]

The demand of Sharmila was supported by the Retd. Justice Jeevan Reedy Committee Report which recommended to repeal the Act altogether. Justice Jeevan Reedy's report was submitted to the Government of India on June 6, 2005 with the recommendation of repealing the AFSPA, 1958 after long discussions, visits, meetings, presentations by different sections of the region. This report was not made public by the Government of India even after one year of the submission. It was made public by the *Hindu* newspaper (*Hindu*, Oct. 2008). It is followed by the Second Administrative Reforms Commission (ARC) which also recommended repealing of the controversial Armed Forces Special Powers Act (AFSPA), 1958, saying that its scrapping would remove the feeling of discrimination and alienation among the people of the North-eastern States. (*Hindu*, June 26, 2007).[15]

Violence Against Women

If there is any conflict or problem, the most affected are the weaker and backward groups of people. In Manipur, women are becoming the target of both underground and overground armed groups. The most serious problem of the present day Manipuri society is that the women become the worst victims of insurgency and violence. Women are abused, battered, molested, raped, murdered and forced to commit suicide.

On March 4, 1974. the reported rape of Miss Rose in Manipur by the Military came to light. An officer of the Border Security Force repeatedly raped her. Rose committed suicide out of shame while the perpetrator went scot free, due to lack of sufficient evidence. On April 26, 1980 at Langjing Patsoi Khunou, the arm insurgent groups attacked the CRPF and took away the arms. In retaliation, the CRPF conducted search operation in area and tortured, harassed and raped women and one woman called Bino, who was hiding with her small son in the paddy store, was killed.

In 1986 Neelam Panchabheiya was raped and killed. During that time a student action committee was formed along with President of Manipur Students' Council. The committee submitted a memorandum to the Governor and the Chief Minister on 19 April, 1986 to hand over the case to CBI or to institute a judicial enquiry. The problems of violence against women is still going on in Manipur.[16]

On August 27, 1989, R.K. Tamphasana was gang raped and murdered. The students and civil organisations submitted a memorandum to the Chief Minister on 5 September to investigate the case properly and punish the criminal. Many other social organisations including the informal associations of Meira Paibi, were also pressing the government of Manipur of this effect.[17]

On May 4, 1996, Ksh. Prabhahini of Kwakeithel Soibam Leikai in Imphal was shot dead by Assam Rifles personnel of 30th Battalion during a search operation. In August of the same year, the armed personnel also raped Smt. Ahanjaobi Devi of Takyetpat in front of her family members. In January 1999, two sisters Laishram Bimola (32 years) and Laishram Manishang Devi (29 years) of Pukhao Ahallup Awang Leikai Imphal East were picked up by the CRPF on charges of giving shelter to the underground activists. They were stripped off and were inhumanly beaten by iron rods and stick on their hips, buttocks, thighs, callus and feet in the army camp of Pangei Imphal.[18]

Smt. Ahanjaobi Devi, a married woman was raped in front of her son and husband by two army personnels. The public outrage and the intensity of the movement practically forced to the Army Authority to initiate court martial proceedings. The two Army personnels were found guilty and punished for the crime in 1997. The demand of the people were not fulfilled only by giving punishment to those army personnels, they demanded some compensation. The Gauhati High Court directed the State Government to pay rupees two lakhs as a compensation.[19] On June 27, 1998, Mrs. Naorem Ongbi Thoinu of Kakching was raped by 5/5 Gurkha Rifles. Many such rape cases by the army go unreported due to fear of social stigma and state inaction towards the culprits of the armed forces. Ch. Jamini Devi an 11 years old girl was taken to custody by 32nd Assam Rifles stationed at Yairipok on the charges that she was the girl friend of an underground activist. She was interrogated at the army camp. The recorded version of the girl's statement was broadcast at a public meeting convened by the commander of the Assam Rifles post. Two days later, on April 2, 1999, the girl committed suicide, being unable to bear the public humiliation.

On October 4, 2003, another case of rape of Miss Nandeibam Sangita, Uchathol Jiribam by 12 Grenadier Rifles was reported.[20] In the ongoing armed conflict situation in Manipur killings and counter-killings is a daily phenomenon. For many decades the local newspapers have been ceaselessly reporting stories of the military hunting down the "insurgents", the "liberators" ambushing the "occupation army", the Army troops taking out their wrath on the "suspects" and torturing them sometimes to death.

Conclusion

Violence was used for decades by both the State agencies as well as the numerous non-state actors in pursuing their respective agenda in Manipur in such a way that the very concept of violence has come to be accepted as a way of life. Situation has come to such a pass that today, senseless killings, either by State agencies or non-state actors no longer outrage the sensibilities of the people. On the other hand, it has also become something of a trend for the public to take the law into their own hands and go on a spree of violence, even to the extent of causing death. This in a sense reflects the utter failure of the government to instil faith and confidence of the public on the system that is associated with it. What is alarmingly disturbing is the growing culture of both state and non-state actors to justify the violence they unleash by coming out with one statement or the other. The non-state actors use violence overtly and justify it with their own reasonings while the state agencies use violence overtly but justify it covertly, though the effect is the same. With such cultural paralyses the sense of the public and incidents and events which would have elicited strong responses from the public are being increasingly passed off as something inevitable, something which the people of Manipur have resigned themselves to. The result is, therefore, before all to see. It is a free for all where anyone with a gun can settle scores. It is a situation in which unidentified callers can ring someone up and demand that such and such conditions should be met if they do not want to suffer the worst. When the government is trying to give support and protection to the masses in connection with violent issues, they are also facing difficulties due to the prevailing social tensions.

State agencies use violence and fear and justify it on the ground that they are doing it for the cause of the 'Nation'. Nothing perhaps illustrates this better than the Armed Forces Special Power Act and the frequent reports of encounters in which one or two suspected militants are killed. Non-state actors on the other hand justify the violence they unleash to cleanse the rot within the society or to punish traitors or anti-social elements. In the process the principle of natural justice is confined to the dust bin and anyone with power, real guns and fire power, can act as the police, the judge and the executioner as well. So much violence, too many deaths, too many hand grenades, too frequent blockades and bandhs frequent sit-in-protest demonstrations have vitiated the expectations the people of Manipur in their endeavour towards progress.

New hopes and aspirations are still being built up in the minds of the people. Let all the concerned stakeholders including community-based organizations, students organizations, civil society organizations, armed groups which are in favour of suspension of operations with the government, so also armed underground organizations, the Manipur Police Commandos, the Assam Rifles and other Central forces — start thinking of finding ways and means of launching the kind of conflict resolution which should not disturb normal life of the general public. Let all parties concerned make it a necessary rule to avoid using force that may give rise to violence.

The Government is taking the burden of difficulties by sharing moral, physical and monetary problems of the people due to the violent activities coming from angles. There are number of cases which are not clear to the public about the steps taken up by the government. But those cases shaken the heart of the masses like the kidnapping and murder of Baby Lungnila Elizabeth on November 2003, two Senapati Kids Hrini Hurbert and Muhini Martin on December 2006 and Sub-editor Rishikanta on November 2008, still remains unsolved. The terror attack at ISKCON, 2007, Namthanlong, Ragailong Bomb Blast, October 2008 still remains unsolved. Over and above, the issue of killing of Dr. Th. Kishan, SDO of Kosum Khullen and two subordinate staffs Y. Token and A. Rajen on February 17, 2009, with extreme degree of brutality and cruelty using stones, blunt weapons and spades remains unsolved.

The Government of Manipur reacted in a knee-jerk manner with a CBI inquiry and promised of a Government job each to the next of kin of the deceased officials and *ex-gratia* compensation of rupees ten lakh and rupees five lakh, in accordance with the status of the deceased officials.

NOTES

1. Edwin R.A. Seligman's: *Encyclopedia of the Social Sciences,* Cosmo Publication, New Delhi, 2006, p. 264.
2. Devi, Ksh. Bimola, *Social and Political Conflicts in Manipur and its resolutions,* key note address, organised by SSRA, MU.
3. Phanoubam Tarapot, *Bleeding Manipur,* Anand Publication Pvt. Ltd., New Delhi, 2004, p. 204.
4. *Ibid.*
5. *Ibid.*
6. *Ibid.*
7. *The Poknapham,* Imphal, June 27, 2001.
8. *The Sangai Express,* Imphal, June 31, 2001.
9. *North East Window:* Pardip Phanjoubam, August 30, 2004, p. 10.
10. *Frontline,* India's National Magazine, September 10, 2004, p.10.

11. N. Urmila, The Student Movement in Manipur—A Case of AMSU 1965-1992 unpublished Ph.D. Thesis submitted to M.U.
12. Human Right Alert in Manipur, 2008.
13. *North East,* October 15, 2004.
14. S.S. Hanjabam, *The Meitei Upsurge in Manipur,* Published online, January 17, 2008.
15. N. Urmila, The Student Movement in Manipur—A Case of AMSU 1965-1992, unpublished Ph.D. Thesis submitted to M.U.
16. *Frontline,* September 10, 2004. Human Right Alert in Manipur, 2008.
17. Devi Ksh. Bimola, Women and Human Rights in Conflict situation in Manipur, in *Human Rights and Women of NE India,* Women Studies Centre, Dibrugarh University.
18. *The Poknapham,* Imphal, August 13, 2008.
19. Devi Ksh. Bimola, Women and Human Rights in Conflict situation in Manipur, in *Human Rights and Women of NE India,* Women Studies Centre, Dibrugarh University.

REFERENCES

Asok Kumar Ray, B.J. Deb (ed), *Terrorism and Human Rights in North East India,* Om Publication, New Delhi, 2007.

B. Pakem (ed) *Insurgency in North East India,* Omson Publication, New Delhi, 1997.

Phanjoubam Tarapot, *Insurgency Movement in NE India,* New Delhi, 1994.

Ram Ahuja, *Social Problems in India,* Rawal Publication, Jaipur, 1992.

Th. Binarani: Social and Political Change in Manipur, 1947-87. Unpublished Ph.D. Thesis, submitted to M.U.

The Hindu, New Delhi, October 8, 2006.

The Sangai Express (editorial) Imphal, January 12, 2009.

The Sangai Express (editorial) Imphal, January 3, 2009.

Times of India, November 6, 2005.

16

Extremism and Human Rights in Manipur

Th. Binarani Devi

Post-independent political system of North East India in general and Manipur in particular is regularly threatened by destabilization. People not feel sign of economic satisfaction. Agriculture is the main occupation of the people of North-East India but the region witnesses a deficit in food production. The land relation is chaotic. Although since 1951 many well meaning land reform measures have been enacted, they have not been implemented with seriousness. The region has fallen behind the rest of the country in terms of every yardstick of development in the field of oil, natural gas, eco-tourism, tea, herbal medicine etc. which are the unrecognized potentials of this region. The economic policies contributed to regional disparities. As a result, there has been a decline in the working population. The New Economic Policy adopted by the Government of India in 1991 had the objective of integrating the Indian economy with the global economy. The major objective of this policy is to raise the global competitiveness of Indian products by effecting cost and price efficiency and thereby create global demand for Indian products. At this time of upsurge of market forces all-round integration of markets across the countries got facilitated by the radical advancement of information and communication technology. This facilitated the process of globalization. Till now, the New Economic Policy had marginal impact on the people of North East India. This is due to economic backwardness of the region with the semi-feudal anarchy in land relations which is the basic anchor of the economy of the region. But in urban areas, new wants and new aspirations among the middle class are being created. An active consumerist culture is coming up in urban societies. Modernization has to a large extent impacted the traditional economic activities in the state. Traditional occupations in handloom and handicrafts are not expanding. This caused rise in unemployed women labour force and marginalization of the women labour in the villages. Such unemployed women labour army finds their place in the dingy lanes of Imphal, Churachandpur, Ukhrul and Moreh towns; in the pavements of market towns, in the kitchens of the middle class, in sand quarries and construction work-sites, clinics and parlors; in hotels and even in brothels. Such state of womanhood in the state of Manipur goes against the history of self-esteem, pride and self-dignity.[1] As a result, the traditional skills of women of North East in the field of agriculture clashed with new technology which permeated the emerging fields and small scale industries. New land owning classes are emerging. The average men and women are pushed to the margin.[2] The problem of unemployment in the North East India has been increasing in its intensity. The North East region of India is known for its social and economic backwardness as well as never ending story of social and political instability and poor political delivery system. There is a great need for a participatory human development, the investment in human beings themselves by means of education and training, i.e. human capital is quite necessary. Again in the field of human capital accumulation, youth constitute the latent resource of human resource development. At the stage of youth we can impart, train, nurture skills and help them to maintain good health. Unfortunately, substantial section of the youth does not get the opportunity to go for training or better higher education. Even those who do get the training and education do not get proper employment. Today the trend of unemployed youth signals a major crisis in the human resource development. The crisis sometimes responds negative human capital investment.[3] The number of unemployed youth registered in the employment exchange crossed over six lakh in March 2009 in Manipur. The negative responses arising as a result directly make erosion in the human capital. Such erosion in the human capital is caused by drug abuse, addiction of alcohol, tobacco and infection through HIV virus. Lack of employment opportunities contributed to the growth of hopelessness and frustration among the youth of the region leading to militancy in them. They feel alienated from the rest of the country and this is particularly true for those who live in the periphery and having transboarder kinship. Some groups no doubt speak in terms of right to self-determination, meaning thereby right of secession from the country. Some of the militant groups speak vaguely of socialist preference of the new order they dream of and some of them do not indicate any idealistic commitment.[4]

Different scholars are giving different opinions regarding the causes for extremism and insurgency, but one of the main causes in Manipur is growing unemployment of the educated youth and the economic backwardness of the region especially after the merger of Manipur to the Indian Union. Psychologists observed that when certain situations come into direct confrontations with the established norms of behaviour, it creates alienation and discontent. This alienation grows from economic, political, cultural and ethnological inequalities. It makes individuals feel worthless, meaningless and estranged. The socio-political environment of India and her attitude towards the people of North East India is one of the main causes of alienation and insecurity in the minds and hearts of the people of the region.[5] These tendencies reflect perceived inadequacies of sub-regional political systems that lead to the emergence of different overground and underground movements in the region. The origin of such movements is not recent contemporary movements of any society, in the sphere of economy, politics or culture, are inspired by conscious national motives and urges, irrespective of whether they are organized to defend and develop the freedom and culture of respective nation or to mitigate or suppress the freedom or culture of other nations. The irreconcilability over the years has incubated the process of extremism by the groups in this region, often challenging the sovereignty of India. Theoretically, the nature of extremism is political, but practically, acts of violence are the main methodology subscribed to, and targeted towards socio-political and economic changes of the whole society. During the British imperialist era, the militant nationalists or the extremists drew inspiration from the India's past, invoked the great episodes in the history of the

Indian people, and tried to infuse national pride and self-respect among them. The militant nationalists were distinguished for the great qualities of immense self-sacrifice and suffering for the cause of freedom. They constituted the first batch of martyrs in the nationalist movement. Their very programme brought them into conflict with the government. They experienced imprisonment and deportations and suffered privations.[6] Today, extremism has most commonly become identified with individuals or groups attempting to overthrow existing political institutions, often substituting violent acts like kidnapping, assassinations, bombings and hijackings for legitimate political activities. Extremism has become the detested thing for the civilized nation. The statecraft of colonial interventions and the whole idea of mainstreaming frontier space have created resentment among native communities. Similarly, ethnic identities, constructions of the 'others' is gaining new meaning as autonomy movements have succeeded in instigating federal state in the region. Insurgency in this context has to be understood as a contest over nationalism and a struggle to sustain the plurality of social forms and community life. The ethno-political and ethno-nationalistic demands foster as well as rearticulate the web of political culture that has been formalized by colonial forms of governance, based on power, privilege, and patronage in the highlands and foothills of North East India. Post-colonial North East India as a political, geographical and cultural entity present these contests over identities as pure acts of 'developed mentalities' thus negating the cultural and historical context in which these communities were organized and imagined towards the idea of India.

Extremism in Manipur

The post-colonial Indian states are built on contradictory principles of sovereign nation states, political obligations of the citizens and institutionalized force. In relation to North East India the continual exposition of the institutionalized force on the part of the state has raised the fundamental question on the irreconcilable needs of territorial integrity and national security on the one hand and the need of adhering to the basic canons of human rights on the other. Consequently, a situation in which the imperatives of rule of law and the inevitability of the reign of terror challenged each other has occurred. Whereas such extremism in the North Eastern Region generally and especially in Manipur posed a challenge to the ruling elites, both the rhetoric of mainstream and systemic integration-needed for consolidation of the nation-state were also challenged. On the other hand the issues of human rights arose out of the emerging trends. The state forces under such circumstances built its repressive image and such repression targeted not only to the extremists but the civil populace too, who also struggle for a just and equitable social existence.

The Government of India employs Armed Forces Special Power Act and many other draconian laws as devices to institutionalize violence against the people with an aim to build legitimacy of the state activities. It is worth stating that the desperate resort to naked use of force only indicates the erosion of legitimacy of the Indian government. As we know, force is necessary to extract obedience from the masses only when there exist a crisis of legitimacy. This infers that the open resistance of the people in the recent past against the government demonstrated a crisis of allegiance, which the people of Manipur owe towards the established system. The frequent resort to brute force underscores the very fact that Indian response in Manipur is sustained through perpetration of violence against the natives in the absence of popular base among the masses.

After merger with the Indian Union, Manipur has witnessed the emergence of various dissenting nationalist groups launching a systematic and sustained militant campaign against the Indian Government to claim their sovereign nationhood. But, the responses of the Indian Government to such indigenous reactions came in terms of enacting numerous black laws and deployment of armed forces resulting in militarization of Manipur. The logical consequence of such a conflict-situation is the violation of human rights and civil liberties on a wide scale. Now-a-days, the notion of national security, law and order, national integration etc. have become powerful justificatory doctrines of state violence against the civil population. The Indian state resorts to repressive measures in the name of protecting national sovereignty and territorial integrity. Thus, the atrocities committed by the governmental forces towards the people of Manipur secured legitimacy through state sponsored legislations. The conflict situation prevailing in Manipur is not a law and order issue as depicted by the state machineries.

It remains conspicuous that the resistance movement spearheaded by the dissenting nationalist groups has gained a great momentum despite stringent military operation launched by the Indian Army and paramilitary forces under the immunity granted by the Government of India and its legislations.

The people of Manipur as represented by the Armed Nationalist Groups or Extremists strongly questioned the legal validity and democratic basis of Manipur's Integration with India. It now becomes obvious that there has not been any legality and constitutional validity as per the provisions of International Law and the Manipur State Constitution Act, 1947. Besides, all the provisions of the agreements were in the nature of personal agreements between the Dominion of India and the Maharaja as a person and not as a head of state. It also does not give any reference to any state machinery as Manipur had a responsible Government before the agreement.

Manipur was a princely state for about two thousand years. Unfortunately, Manipur lost her independence in the Anglo-Manipuri war of 1891 and became a part (though not annexed) of the British Empire. But with the passing of the Indian Independence Act, 1947, Manipur for the first time in its history adopted a democratically elected Legislative Assembly with the Maharaja as a titular head of the state. The society in Manipur during the period 1947 to 1949 remained stable. The social order was mainly based on Hinduism. Most of the educated class got employment in government jobs enjoying higher status in the society.[7] The Standstill Agreement did not infringe upon the sovereignty of Manipur as nothing in the agreement included the acceptance of any future Constitution of India. When India got Independence in 1947, the suzerainty of the British Crown and the rulers of the Indian States ceased to exist. Consequently, Manipur became a new entity legally and technically free from the British Parliament and the British India. The nature of the functioning of the political authority exercised by the Chief Commissioner had given a negative impact on the peaceful and stable social order of Manipur. The concentration of political power in the hands of the Chief Commissioner who acted on behalf of the President of India had created dissatisfaction in the minds of the people of Manipur. The members of the Advisory Council, as the name indicates, were only advisers to the Chief Commissioner.

The later was not bound to accept the advice given by the advisers. The people of Manipur had started movements demanding higher political status of Manipur.[8] But the response of the Government of India was slow and minimum which they have learnt from the British colonizers. And again the repressive measures were so serious which even the Britishers did not employ. Consequently, a number of armed nationalist groups sprang up and revolted against the Government of India.

Issues of Human Rights

For achieving their objectives and targets armed nationalists or insurgent groups commit violent action. They resort to guerrilla warfare and easily disappear in the jungle or in the crowded urban areas after attacks on the police and the military forces including the high officials, looting arms and ammunitions and extorting money etc. As opposed to this act the counter insurgency measures let loose by the government through deployment of Army and paramilitary forces, often meet with counter-productive result. At each stage human rights are violated at varying degrees. In some situations, perpetual presence of police or paramilitary forces is necessary for peacekeeping mandate of the government. But as violence begets violence, it threatens civil liberty. The right to life, liberty and security of persons and equality before the law are the essence of Human Rights mentioned in the UDHR.

Human rights violation accounting in the state of Manipur during the last twenty five to thirty years has gone to the extreme. During this period there have been innumerable told and untold incidents of violation of human rights. The violations included arrest, detention, disappearances, custodial torture and killing, atrocities, rape and sexual violence to women and so on by the armed forces in the name of controlling the extremism committed by the armed nationalist groups in state. The draconian Acts including AFSPA are imposed in the state which violate every canon of democracy and human rights. Growing militarization of the society make civil life miserable. Instead of aiding the civil power as stipulated in the Act, the armed forces make civilians equal targets of state violence in the name of containing underground organizations.

Extra Judicial Killings by Security Forces (Children and Civilian victims)

1. Th. Netaji of Kakwa: February 28, 1996.
2. Kangjam Ojit, Iroisemba: September 25, 1997.
3. Y. Iboyaima Ukabi of Awang Potsangbam: March 19, 2002.
4. Th. Dhirendra of Naorem Leikai: April 6, 2002.
5. Md. Jane Alam of Hatta: August 1, 2002.
6. Thangtinsein Kipgen and Limbertlen: August 2008.

Through wholesale counter terrorism of the state perpetually threaten the basic principle of political life shatters right to movement of the citizens, and their right to life and liberty. The counter-insurgency is indiscriminate, and affects the civic zones badly. On the other hand, the militant terrorists in order to disseminate terrorism implicate the entire civil society and tend to universalize terrorism through their acts in public places. This causes casualties not only to the state forces but also to the civil populace. Thus, the state and the insurgents alike had pressed the civil society and reduced civic rights.

Some Major Incidents of Gross Human Rights Violations in Manipur

1. Heirangoithong Massacre: March 14, 1984.
2. Operation Blue Bird at Oinam: July 10, 1987.
3. Tera Bazar Massacre; March 25, 1993.
4. RMC Massacre: January 7, 1995.
5. Tonsem Lamkhai Killing: October 4, 1998.
6. Malom Massacre: November 2, 2000.
7. The GreatJune Uprising: June 18, 2001.
8. Leplen Mass Torture: 2002.
9. Pangei Bazar Firing: April 9, 2002.
10. Sharajeevan Bomb Blast, Paona Bazar, October 2007.
11. Ragailong Bomb Blast, October 2008.

The social and psychological cost of insurgency and counter-insurgency cannot be measured through quantitative terms as they increase anxiety, unpredictability of life and liberty and fragile peace feature of the state. There are innumerable cases of disappearance of the youth and involuntary migration of the youth community from the state.

Disappearance and Killings

1. Loken & Lokendro of Basikhong: September 23, 1980.
2. C. Poul & C. Daniel of Ukhrul: March 10, 1982.
3. L. Bijoikumar of Thangmeiband: June 5-6, 1996.
4. Mr. Mahaimi of Ukhrul: 1995.
5. Y. Sanamacha of Angtha: February 12-13, 1998.
6. Boyai of Kwakeithel: 1998.
7. Koijalal Paite: 1997
8. Md. Tayeb Au of Kairang: July 25, 1995.
9. Baby Luiningla: November 2003.
10. K. Rishikanta: November 2008.

In Manipur, gender based violence encompasses a wide range of human rights violation, including sexual abuse of children, rape, domestic violence, sexual assault and harassment, trafficking of women and girls and several harmful traditional practices. Any of these abuses can leave deep psychological scars, damage the health of women and girls in general, including their reproductive and sexual health, and in some instances, result in death. Violence against women has been recognized as 'the most pervasive yet least recognized human rights abuse in the world.' Accordingly, the Vienna Human Rights Conference and the Fourth World Conference on Women gave priority to this issue which jeopardizes women's lives, bodies, psychological integrity and freedom. Violence against women and girls constitute the single most prevalent and universal violation of human rights. The United Nations, in keeping with the spirit of the UN Declaration of Human Rights, work in many ways to eliminate this morally unacceptable scourge. UN Conference on Human Rights, the 1979 Convention on the Elimination of All Forms of Discrimination Against Women (CEDAW), the Beijing Declaration, the United Nations Development Fund for Women (UNIFEM) etc. are some of the instruments that would address the issue of gender violence. Despite regard for the principle of non-discrimination in the enjoyment of rights contained in the UDHR, ICCPR, ICESCR, and other human rights instruments, women were not treated equally at the global level.[9] CEDAW acknowledged that discrimination against women violates the principles of equality of rights and respect for human dignity, and is an obstacle to the participation of women, on equal terms with men, in the political, social, economic and cultural life of their countries. This in turn, affects the development of family and society as a whole. In the armed conflict situation in Manipur many people are killed and kidnapped. Many newly married and unmarried women are forced to commit suicide to save themselves against rape and social abuse by the security forces. With the increase of state violence in the state particularly against the youth and women, the women community in Manipur staged unrobed protest march against custodial rape and killing of Ms. Manorama by the Assam Rifles personnel on 11th July, 2004. The demonstrators carried the honour of their community on their bodies and demonstrated that by raping them the army would defile the entire community.[10]

Rape Cases Committed by Security Personnel and Killing

1. Miss Rose of Ukhrul: March 4, 1974.
2. Mrs. Ahanjaobi: 1996.
3. Mrs. Pramo of Moirang: 1998.
4. Mrs. Mercy of Lamdan: 2000.
5. Mrs. Bina of Luwangsangbam Matai Village: 2001.
6. Miss N. Sanjita of Jiribam: October 5, 2003.
7. Laisram Bimola Devi and Laisram Manisang Devi, Pukhao Ahalup Awang Leikai: 1999.
8. Ch. Jamini Devi, Yairipok: 1999.
9. Thangjam Manorama Devi: 2004.

The other dimension of human rights violation arises from the factional fights among the underground organizations that often take the toll of human rights. Manipur also witnessed the violations of human rights among members of the different underground organizations. Though working and struggling together for the common cause and common ideology, the members of the underground organizations killed each other whenever any disagreement or factional interest developed affecting the factional forces within the organization.[11] There is distrust and disagreement within the factional forces within the underground organizations like NSCN (IM) and NSCN (K), and the different Kuki underground organizations in Manipur. Besides violation of human rights by the militant organizations themselves one cannot lose sight of ambushing by the army in the public place, encounter between the state and non-state actor, planting explosives and many other acts of this nature ending valuable lives of many civilians. Apart from huge human cost of the insurgency and counter-insurgency in the state, the magnitude of social cost in terms of fear psychosis, melancholy, financial extortion has a erious human rights concern. On 1st September, 2007, the then Union Home Minister, Sivraj Patil gave the Status Report in connection with the violence and terror in North East India. According to his statement, the rate of violence was highest in Assam among the North East States followed by Manipur, Nagaland and Tripura. In terms of the number of victims, his statement was quite right. But after a clear analysis with reference to the total number of population, the rate of percentage of violence up to June 30, 2007 in Manipur was higher than Assam according to the Status Report.[12]

Terror Attacks and Killings in North East India

Name of State	*Total no. of population*	*Killed*			
		Civilian	*Security personnels*	*Total*	*Per cent*
Assam	26655528	156	15	171	0.00064
Manipur	2293896	72	25	97	0.0004229

There is a perception gap between government and the people of the region which should be bridged without delay by constant interaction between the two. North East India has become a victim of easy money poured by the Central Government which has affected the moral and social fabric of the people instead of assuring sustained development. There is an urgent need for adopting a dynamic approach requiring a new orientation in policy perception remembering that the people are the most important resource of the country. We need to create a climate in North East India so that every citizen of the region feels assured that his or her language, culture and distinct identity is secured in India. For this, the crucial requirement is creation of conditions for meaningful community participation at every level through greater decentralization of power, political and economic, ensuring equitable distribution and sustainable use of productive resources and raising capability and skills of the people of the region. The suggestion is for a better coordinated development strategy for North East India and a strong and transparent political will to instil a sense of participation in the minds of the people of the hills and the valleys.

NOTES

1. Th. Binarani Devi, Women's Movement in Conflict Situation of Manipur in Asok Kumar Ray and S.B. Chakraborty (ed), *Society, Politics and Development in North East India,* Concept Publishing Company Pvt. Ltd., 2008, p. 113.
2. R.B. Dutta, North East India in the context of New Economic Policy, in Ray B. Dutta, Dev Bimal J., Sengupta Kiya,(ed), *Globalisation and North East India,* Concept Publishing Company Pvt. Ltd., New Delhi, 2004.
3. Th. Binarani Devi, India's Look East Policy and Youths of Manipur, in Ray B. Dutta, Dev Bimal J., Sengupta Kiya, *Globalisation and North East India,* Concept Publishing Company Pvt. Ltd., New Delhi, 2008, pp. 320-21.
4. Pakem B., *Insurgency in North East India,* Omson Publications, New Delhi, 1997, p. V.
5. Th. Binarani Devi, Insurgency and Human Rights in Manipur, in B.J. Dev and Asok Kumar Rai (ed) *Terrorism and Human Rights in North East India,* Om Publications, New Delhi 2007, p. 118.
6. Desai A.R., *Social Background of Indian Nationalism,* Popular Prakashan, Bombay, 1986, p. 333.
7. Ksh. Bimola Devi, Society and Politics in Manipur, in Asok Kumar Ray and S.B. Chakraborty (ed.), *Society, Politics and Development in North East India,* Concept Publishing Company Pvt. Ltd., New Delhi, p. 103.
8. *Ibid.,* pp. 103-04.
9. Human Rights Documentation Centre, *Introducing Human Rights, South Asia,* Oxford University Press, New Delhi, p. 155.
10. Th. Binarani Devi, in Asok Kumar Ray and S.B. Chakraborty (ed), *Society, Politics and Development in North East India,* Concept Publishing Company Pvt. Ltd., New Delhi, 2008, pp. 110-11.
11. Ksh. Bimola Devi, Violation of Human Rights and Peace Initiative in Manipur, in B.J. Dev and Asok Kumar Rai (ed) *Terrorism and Human Rights in North East India,* Om Publications, New Delhi, 2007, pp. 112-13.
12. *Poknapham* (Manipuri Local Daily), Dt. 2-9-2007, p. 1.

17

Terrorism in Assam

An Analysis of Economic and Political Factors

Jagadish Ch. Sarma

The word 'terrorism' has its roots in French expression 'terrorise', which gained currency during the revolutionary period in French between 1795 and 1798. It is not at all easy to evolve an universal definition of terrorism. Terrorism has been generally recognized as a special method of struggle to obtain specific political results. Terrorism as a form of political violence has raised its ugly head in India particularly in Assam. Political thinkers, intellectuals and religious leaders have been trying to draw out various strategies to fight against terrorism. Serious study of the phenomenon of terrorism needs to be undertaken not only by the government agencies but also by all peace loving people.

In India, terrorist activities were started since 1902 with the formation of 'Anushilan Samiti' and subsequently 'Juganthar Party' in Bengal. During the independence struggle, some nationalists, frustrated by the failure of political struggle turned to revolutionary terrorism. They felt that the British must be physically expelled from India. They resorted to use of violence against unpopular British Officials. Governors and Viceroys. Certain newspapers like 'Sandhvu' and 'Ynganlar' in Bengal and 'Kapi' in Maharashtra began to advocate revolutionary terrorism after 1905. Soon many secret societies of terrorist youth came into existence. The most famous of these was the 'Anushilan Samiti'. The terrorists also established centres of activity abroad. The "Ghadar" party was constituted in 1913 by revolutionaries in USA and Canada. Except for a couple of acts terrorism did not achieve much. It gradually petered out. The first phase of terrorism in free India started in Telengana in 1947 and spread to West Bengal. According to A.K. Tripathi, it was a purely communist terrorism. The second phase terrorism in independent India appeared in 1967 in the form of Naxalite violence and continued up to 1972 and even today. Their terrorism spread over West Bengal, Andhra Pradesh, Kerala, Bihar, Orissa, Tripura and Punjab. However, since the eighties, in Assam, terrorism and violence has been a common headline of our daily newspapers. Formed in 1979, the ULFA led by some frustrated youths have been demanding to liberate Assam from India. Similar formula have been followed by NDFB/BLT among Bodos, KNV/ UPDS/KPF among Karbis and DHD among Dimasas to create separate homeland. Assam is inhabited by several tribes who have ethnic and cultural links with the inhabitants of China, Tibet and Burma. As most of these groups came in waves of different periods of history, the ethnic and cultural identity of the region has blossomed into a wide multiplicity of colours. Each group is keen and determined to preserve its separate identity. Some ethnic groups selected terror activities to fulfil their purpose. Despite these social factors, there are some economic and political factors which needs to be examined.

In the 1930s, Jawaharlal Nehru described India under the British rule as a "servile state with its splendid strength caged up, hardly daring to breath freely, governed by strangers from a far, her people poor beyond compare, shortlived and incapable of resisting diseases and epidemic." On being sworn in as India's first Prime Minister in 1947, Nehru called for "the ending of poverty and ignorance and disease and inequality of opportunity."

Since then, India as well as Assam has had more than six decades of plans and programmes to promote development and eradicate poverty. What has been achieved?

In Assam (as per Statistical Handbook, Assam, 2002), 87 per cent people live in villages of which 74 per cent people solely depend on agriculture. Assam has a total agricultural land of 31,61,000 hectares. Per capita agricultural land 0.14 ha (0.98 Bighas), per capita food production 134 kg (all-India 204 kg). Only 14 per cent land is irrigated, 60 per cent agricultural holdings have land less than 5 Bighas. The per capita income of 95.4 per cent families is Rs. 380 or less. Poverty, food shortage and government/callous attitude are the main hurdles for slow agro-economic growth in the state. Assam's population share is 2.65 per cent but the share of agricultural production is only 1.75 per cent. Huge number of youth in rural areas are left without any work to do. As per Economic Survey Assam, 2007-08, the number of job-seekers on the Live Register of Employment Exchanges has stood at 12 lakh in 2006.

As per results of 61st Round of NSSO during the year 2004-05, the number of unemployed per 1000 persons by broad usual activity in Assam were 26 persons in rural areas against 10 persons at all-India level. Similarly, the unemployed per 1000 persons in urban areas in the state were 72 persons against 19 persons in all-India indicating thereby the greater dimension of unemployment in the state in comparison to the position in the country as a whole. It has also been reported by the Economic Survey, Assam, 2007-08 that Assam's Below Poverty Line (BPL) population has fallen to 19.7 per cent in 2004-05 compared to 36.09 per cent in 1999-2000 and 40.6 per cent in 1993-94 as against all-India figures for the same are 27.50 per cent in 2004-05, 26.10 per cent in 1999-2000 and 35.97 per cent in 1993-94 respectively. But still BPL population in Assam (19.7%) are higher than some selected states of India like Andhra Pradesh (15.8%), Gujarat (16.8%), Himachal Pradesh (10.0%), Jammu and Kashmir (6%), Kerala (15.0%) and Punjab (8.4%).

Moreover, Assam is also lagging behind almost in all the human development indicators in comparison to all-India level. As per HDR, 1999 the average life expectancy at birth was 54.9 years as against 62.6 years in all-India level. Middle school enrollment ratio was 53.4 as against 55.0 of all-India level. Under five mortality rate in Assam was 141 per 1000 live birth, doctor in primary health care per 10,000 population was 0.29 and hospital per 10,000 population was 5.6. The corresponding figures of all-India level were 125, 0.36 and 7.0 respectively.

Thus, the pace of economic development in Assam is slow. Poverty, inequality and unemployment have been the common phenomenon. The unemployed youths are highly frustrated and this kind of people are more easily attracted towards these subversive activities.

The most important political cause of sub-national violence in Assam is the language controversy. In India from the time of inauguration of the Constitution, the rulers both of the central and state levels have thought about the problem of language and they have not been able to apply the scientific approach. In the case of Assam, for example, no steps were taken to restore the rightful place of the Assamese language. In the same way nothing was done for the use of such indigenous languages as Bodo, Karbi, Mishing, Dimasa, Tiwa etc. as media of instruction for the students of those language groups. This aroused discontent in the minds of people who speak these languages. For six years since the commencement of the Constitution, Article 350 helped the people speaking languages mentioned in the Eighth Schedule, Article, 350A and 350B were added only in 1956, but Bodos, Mishings Karbis, Dimasa etc. were not helped. It was only in 1956 that the Government arranged the publication of the first Bodo primer written by Mr. Bandhuram Kachari. Mr. B.P. Chaliha, then Chief Minister of Assam ultimately decided to introduce Bodo language in the primary schools of Kokrajhar sub-division as a medium of instruction and since May 18, 1963, the Bodo students in this sub-division have been able to learn through the medium of Bodo in the primary stage. At the same time, they have been able to learn Assamese as an associate language. But the Government was not serious about the publication of Bodo text-books. In regard to the Mishing, Dimasa, Tiwa and the Karbi languages also the Assam Government did not take timely action. Only very recently attempts have been made to rectify past mistakes. The Mishing students now can learn through their own medium in the primary stage. The promotion of the Karbi language in the Karbi-Anglong District is the responsibility of the Krhi Anglong District Council. The number of Karbi books so far published is very small.

Thus, insurgency and turmoil occurring in Assarn is rooted in economic and political deprivation. In conclusion we may say that terrorism is not a disease which can be cured by medicine. It is a man-made problem. So it may be solved through friendly accommodative and courageous attitude. It can be checked by concerted development, legislative measures and political dialogues. A sustained effort should be made to contain balanced economic development to deal with poverty, inequality and unemployment. Generation of employment through labour intensive technique is necessary. Everyone in the state has a role to play in reducing crimes and upholding law and orders. The identification of the problems of various ethnic groups and issues of identity can help in understanding the psychology of the terrorists. Re-arrangement of administrative institutions involving decentralization of power is the need of the hour. Assamese should be adopted only as a link language and not as an official language in the Sixth Schedule areas. We may also need a National Terrorism Prevention and Management Commission to continuously monitor the development, co-ordinate the implementation and recommended preventive action.

REFERENCES

Anastasi, A. (1958): *Differential Psychology*.

Basic Statistics of NER, 2002.

Bhuyan, B.C. *Political Development of the North East*, Vol. 1, 1989.

Choudhury, Dr. P.C., *The History of the Civilisation of the People of Assam*, 1966.

India Towards Population and Development Goals, 1997.

Mannan Abdul, Strategy for Development of Rural Economy and Employment in India (A Seminar Paper).

Sarma J.C. and Bhattcharjee Dhira, The Psychodynamics of Terrorism and Violence in India Today (A Seminar Paper).

The Economic Survey, Assam, 2007-08.

The Frontline (June 1987, May 1990 and March 1989 issue).

The Human Development Report, 1999.

The India Today (February 1988, April 1990, April 1991, March 1992 issue).

The Statistical Handbook, Assam, 2002.

Tripathi, A.K. and De Barun, *Freedom Struggle*.

18

Extremism in the North East

Problems and Solutions

Xavier P. Mao

The English word extremism means the views or opinions that fall outside the normal range. In politics, extremism stands for very strong and abnormal views. In what follows, I wish to critically examine the brand of political extremism that has been prevailing in North-Eastern part of the country for the past many years. The reasons for political extremism are many and varied from state to state and within existing states of the North East India. The first call for sovereign, independent nation state was given by the Nagas led by their late leader A.Z. Phizo. That was followed by Mizos led by their late leader Laldenga. Subsequently, various other ethnic groups of the North East also started raising similar demands although their reasons are different. Many of these organizations started using extremism or terrorism as a means or method to achieve their goals or objectives. Some of these outfits or insurgents, however, started using violence or terrorism as the very objective itself, and not as a method.

The Nagas had given the clarion call for a complete sovereign, independent state even during pre-independent India. A.Z. Phizo categorically stated that Nagaland (all the inhabited Naga areas) was never part of India, historically, culturally, racially and ethnically, and Nagas are not Indians. As a matter of fact, the Nagas and most of the tribes from North East were not part of ancient and medieval India except during the British Rule. These tribal groups have the same cultural, linguistic, ethnic and racial boundaries with the South-East Asia and East Asia people. Phizo met a number of Indian leaders like M.K. Gandhi, Jawaharlal Nehru, Subhas Chandra Bose, Rajagopalachari for the purpose. Gradually, the secessionist movement spread to other parts of North East like Mizoram, Manipur, Tripura, Assam and Arunachal Pradesh. Some people in North East India even started saying that they were with India but not as Indians. Since an influential section of the tribals are of Mongoloid origin, they are most of the time mistaken with the south-east Asian and east Asian people by the rest of Indians. Their food habit and life-style are very different from the rest of India. After being converted to Christianity and Hinduism they have given up their indigenous tribal religions. Thus, they suffer an identity crisis. They claim that they are Nagas, Mizos, Meiteis, Khasis, Bodos, Garos etc. but have given up their tribal religions. At a deeper level there is a crisis. Of course, this is true that they have not completely given up their respective tribal way of life. When it is pointed out that religion is an integral component of culture and by completely replacing their original religions by new religions, they have lost substantially their culture too, they have no definite answer. Perhaps, this state of affairs coupled with minority psychology that is the fear of being completely assimilated with the majority, continues to create stir and turmoil in their unconscious and subconscious mind. The first general election of 1952 was completely boycotted by the Nagas. Even the second general election of 1957 was also partially boycotted by the Nagas. In due course of time, the Government of India in 1959 decided to create a separate statehood for Nagaland and eventually Nagaland became a separate full-fledged state in 1963. Subsequently in the early seventies, a number of separate states were created in the North East like Meghalaya, Tripura and Manipur. The Government of India partially solved the political crisis that emerged in North East India through the creation of new states and entering into dialogues and talks and signed accords, with insurgent leaders. In consequence, Mizoram was given statehood in 1987 and Laldenga became the Chief Minister of the state. Subsequently, even Arunachal Pradesh was given statehood. Nagaland, Mizoram, Manipur and Arunachal Pradesh were given Central Universities and Assam got two Central Universities and one I.I.T. Further, ten per cent of the national budget is earmarked for the North-Eastern states and if unspent it automatically goes to the non-lapsable fund. In other words, seen in this light, the North-eastern states are being treated as most favoured states unlike their fellow counterparts in Myanmar and Bangladesh.

At the same time, in spite of all the benefits extended to North-Eastern states, the persistent struggle for sovereignty is very much alive among the Naga insurgents. In the case of other North-Eastern states, occasionally there happens to be outburst of extremism and terrorism. One may be allowed to say in this connection that in some cases, this is the function of a handful of misguided youth. At the same time, instigation and encouragement of India's neighbours and other powerful countries in this regard cannot be ruled out at all. From time to time, some self-styled intellectuals of the region have been consciously fuelling the fire of extremism. In early eighties, a Professor from the region published a paper entitled "My Language and Yours" in *Man in India,* wherein he argued that language is the soul of man. He illustrated the point in the following manner. If somebody's mother tongue, say is Assamese his soul becomes Assamese and if a Bengali, for instance, learns Assamese and read, write and speak it fluently yet he cannot understand it completely because his soul is primarily a Bengali soul. Therefore, he concludes that two linguistic communities cannot live together because their souls are different. This is a kind of neo-Nazism that the Professor concerned was trying to propagate. After some years the same Professor presented a paper in International Socrates' Day, wherein he argued that his identity is that he is a 'y' tribes man. The Professor forgot that a person has multiple and various types of identities. Such identities are racial, ethnic, religious, linguistic and cultural. To pick up one identity and declare it as the sole identity of a person is a gross mistake.

Now time has come for North-Eastern people to have a serious reflection and realistic assessment of their societies. For whatever reasons, they are now an integral part of Indian republic, with almost full participation in the Indian electoral system the demand for secession at this point of history is perhaps impossible or unwise. Firstly, India as a nation-state has emerged as a very powerful player in the world today. Secondly, the various insurgent groups of the region have not shown any spirit of self-sacrifice and service to their societies or to humanity in general. On the contrary, what we witness is the endemic instability for the worse.

Even the insurgent groups which have initial legitimate demands have degenerated into anti-social gangs, devoid of any moral content or ideology. This is clearly illustrated through political fragmentation and endemic factional killings motivated by raw greed and taking violence as an end in itself and not merely as a means.

Further, there is no imposition of any alien language, culture or religion on the North-Eastern people. They are treated on par with citizens from other parts of the country. Policy of reservation and other special treatment have given to them a booster. It may not be out of place that because of policy of reservation many tribals from North East are there on the faculty of many universities in other parts of India. If there is suspicions, apprehension and doubt against the Indian state in this respect, it is misplaced. The North-Eastern people particularly the youth must rise to the occasion and make best use of the various benefits extended to them by the Government of India, sometimes at the cost of others. They should actively participate in the process of building their societies and work hard particularly in developing their language and culture.

The extremists should realize that the Indian state has gradually become democratic and secular in this regard. The only thing is that they do not wish to give away one inch of land to others. But greater autonomy, equal say in important decision making process and other desirable political, social and economic reforms can be debated for a better tomorrow. Modern state and citizenship is purely contractual and the Indian state is no exception to it. Democracy is gradually beginning to strike its roots in India. To become a member or citizen of Indian republic does not mean to sell away one's identity, dignity, honour and respectability. Therefore, give up senseless extremism and terrorism and to participate in the process of development and progress should be the motto of the youth in the North East. The dream that China, Pakistan or even the United States of America will come forward to liberate them in their endeavour to become sovereign nation state while they themselves are busy fighting for their own rapacious, greedy selfish interests with the consequence of moral chaos is perhaps too farfetched. They must remember and realize that ten per cent of national budget is earmarked and spent on only five per cent of people and ninety per cent is being spent on (95%) ninety five per cent only. Such plain truths and obvious facts must be brought to the notice of misguided North-Eastern youth who still keep on indulging in acts of extortion, violence, extremism and terrorism.

Recourse to extremism and violence may be taken as a means of upholding justice and for defending a just cause and legitimate claim. Also, as the history has repeatedly shown, violence may be used in support of evil. Moreover, violence may become an end in itself serving merely the animal instincts or an expression of frustration, despair, oppression, suppression and thereby sacrificing the noble side of human nature. Very few people would object violence when used to defend and support a just cause. Violence has acquired its justification from the defence of such legitimate claims. But many a time it sinks into the abyss by defending amoral and immoral causes, modifying itself as an end in itself. These are the time tested lessons. Therefore, the excessive emphasis placed on violence and bloody armed struggle to achieve political independence without moral and spiritual content has its dangerous counter-productive effect as we eloquently witness the activities of the various insurgent outfits of the North East. Because even many great thinkers and saints have clearly stated that virtue and violence can never be friends.

The future of humankind rests with achieving enlightenment and cultivating compassionate love as the ultimate value to which all of us should try to adhere in all aspects of our life. All instrumentalities of social action should be based on the principle of compassionate love progressively limiting violence and replacing it by altruism, self-sacrifice and love for common good and welfare. The way of greed, insecurity, uncertainty, hatred and mutual distrust and self-centredness must give way to 'care' reconciliation, love, freedom and understanding.

19

India's North East

Political Instability, Conflict and Regional Disparities

P.K. Ryngnga

Introduction

India's North East is one of South Asia's hottest trouble spots, not simply because the region has as many as thirty armed insurgent organizations[1] operating and fighting the Indian state, but because trans-border linkages that these groups have, and strategic alliances among them, have acted as force multipliers and have made the conflict dynamics all the more intricate. With the demands of these insurgent groups ranging from secession to autonomy and the right to self-determination, and a plethora of ethnic groups clamouring for special rights and the protection of their distinct identity, the region is bound to be a turbulent one.

Moreover, the location of the region itself is part of the reason why it has always been a hot bed of militancy with trans-border ramifications. This region of 2,63,000 sq. km[2] shares highly porous and sensitive frontiers with China in the North, Myanmar in the East, Bangladesh in the South West and Bhutan to the North West. This region's strategic location is underlined by the fact that it shares an international border of 4500 km long with its four South Asian neighbours and ironically it is connected to the Indian mainland by a tenuous 22 km long land corridor passing through

Siliguri in the eastern States of West Bengal, approximately described as the 'Chicken's Neck'.

The distinct feature of the region in itself speaks volume that unwrapped the region to be so strategically important and vulnerable to external leverages. Some of the region's personality can be outlined below:

Location: The North-eastern region of India is strategically located and is characterised by socio-political instability and economic backwardness, isolation and inaccessibility continue to exert a considerable influence in the geo-political aspect of socio-political and economic interactions and relations within and in between the constituent units in the region. The region is constantly threatened with escalation of tension and conflict involving the local and regional parameters and dimension. The resultant problems have continued to dominate all transaction in the regional landscape. This is despite the fact that the region with sizable natural resources has experienced more than five decades of planned development.

Socio-Economic Problems: The region has also experienced scores of problems emanating from the continuous inflow of migrants, land alienation, lack of industrial infrastrucure etc. These have, cumulatively, negated the efforts towards sustained development and as a consequence towards maintaining stability in the region. The State, the participants and the actors, have all been caught in a struggle for dominance, where multiple nature of fissiparous tendencies have consistently divided and sub-divided the polity and the territory. These, then, suggest that there exist higher levels of incompatibilities between the statists and the planned transition on the one hand, and on the other, between the socio-political priorities and requirements of the territory.

Inter-State Distinctiveness: Rigorous environment and varying locational attributes fostered physical, economic and socio-cultural isolation that came within the sphere of influence of the neighbouring countries. Arunachal Himalaya and the Eastern Hills-Mountains came within the sphere of influence of Tibet (China) and Myanmar Western Mizoram, Tripura and Meghalaya Plateau within Bangladesh orbit; and Assam Valley within Bihar-Bengal orbit. These encouraged the respective territorial formations to develop social and political distinctiveness. This enabled them to mobilize and propagate against any form of centralization and expressed themselves in terms of autonomy or separation and independence. Separate territorial compartments in which various social formations found themselves in, encouraged them to develop separate ideological perspectives and political organizations to back their demands for separate existence. This led to intransigence among the inhabitants, particularly of hill and mountain section and restricted the scale and scope of accommodation in the region.

Rearranged Administrative Structure: Systematization and rearrangement of administrative structure in the region was a post-Independence phenomenon. Administration was extended to the remotest parts of the region and brought all the inhabitants within the development stability parameters. This extension was viewed with the hesitation and was interpreted in terms of continuation of political outlook and consequently economic and social domination along with fears penetrated in cultural absorption. The resultant responses of the various social formations and their respective pressure groups suggested the existence of alternatives (traditional) centres of power and influence. This became the focal point of mobilization.

Political Dimensions in the Region since Pre-Independence

Since colonial period, the region's responses to change were more or less proportional to degree of impact the change had brought upon the groups and sub-groups whose territories were gradually, in distinct phases, incorporated into British India. There was a proportionality of responses that went a long way in shaping the ideological perspective of separation—a theme that became increasingly common with various population groups and sub-groups when they mobilized themselves. Objectives and priorities became abundantly clear when dual administrative system—one for the plains and valleys and the other for the highland section, was adopted by the colonial administrators. The approach of the State was progressively equalizing the inhabitants and their territories as well as marginalizing the aggressive intents that encouraged destabilization of the state. This in turn accentuated fissures and differences both within and between groups, to move first developing a common platform and later to divide and sub-divide into active pressure groups. In other words, it can be said that the levelling impact of the state enhanced the levels of competition within the groups that had for long lived in a state of dynamic equilibrium and as a group, were involved in a constant struggle with available resources.

However, the post-1947 situations projected an entirely different equation altogether. The constituent units—population elements revived the themes for reversing the territorial-administrative process and once more assume their earlier pre-colonial status. But the state's welfare measures (though limited), works of various agencies had introduced several changes that affected the traditional societies of the region. These were in terms of relationships within as well as between the groups and in doing so had established the irreversibility of change in the politico-geographical processes that drastically transformed the region. The movements towards separation and the formation of several discontented groups in the region, therefore, suggest reasons that go well beyond their present stance and lies perhaps in their respective territories or aspects that closely influenced their concerned territories.[3]

Forms of political change, then, were mostly transitional in character. Elements failed to solve their respective legitimacy problems/issues and became vulnerable. In most cases, such instances were dependent upon resources or availability of resources either generated within the respective territories or provided by the regional/national core. However, it was the geopolitical significance of the location of the territories that provided their respective inhabitants with adequate leverage to negotiate. Again, such availability of resources were necessary for change, development and modernization but were normally utilized to strengthen the respective political administrative base. Development issues though salient, remained the dominant theme. As a result, many of the issues that encouraged mobilization of the inhabitants have remained centred around the questions of allocation of power and allocation of resources, running concurrently.[4]

In the regional configuration, the state's interaction pattern exhibits significant variations and changes. Expanding but complex interdependencies are frequently overshadowed by geographical and historical inertia. This, in turn called for reinforcements of integration processes. The states also exhibit difficulties in managing their respective political economies and associated policies. This reflects constant internal pressure for more effective direction. Regional and sub-regional patterns of integration concern themselves with smaller dependencies that gradually evolving in the respective state's landscape. The imperative towards cooperation are weak and tenuous and were overshadowed by disputes and disparities.

In terms of continuing instability, economic backwardness has become a serious hindrance to sustain sub-regional and regional cooperation in the development of the various territorial compartments. This together constituted the states and finally, the regional mosaic. In such a situation, a question on integration assumes particular importance and call for measures that will not only minimize the degrees of effectiveness of political instability, but induce greater development or positive cooperation within and between the states of the region. Politico-geographical processes have encouraged maintenance of both individual identities of the various territories and collectively the regional distinctiveness mechanisms.

Therefore, politico-geographical change in the region has to substantially affect the structure, function, value and the societal involvement in the growth and development of the various territorial components. The changes in some instances were abrupt and encouraged destabilization. This has been frequently reinforced by poor/weak performances. Dimensions and speed of such transformation and changes varied and were less controlled or ordered.

The political change has its background in the subordination of the various territories to the Imperial power, influence of the missionaries and the associated agencies and Post-Independence developments. It, in fact, introduced significant alterations in the regional polity (in terms of coherence and purpose). Thus, efforts towards integration became weak and tenuous. Conflicts of interests and overlapping of functions made the consensus difficult. Most significant changes in the sub-regional and broader regional levels in last five decades in the North East have been the assertion of traditional loyalties and ethnic affinities; while legitimizing the movements geared towards resolutions of the issues with separatist contents. The states in the region are, therefore, caught in a paradox, where the emergent elites tended to be more parochial and frequently resorted to mobilization of popular sentiments to further their individual group causes at the cost of wider regional levels.

A prolonged instability has unmistakably altered the spatial arrangements of political geographical processes; so that no population group could demand exclusive rights over specific territory. Within the framework of the Constitution, there were alternatives that provided individual populations to establish their position and identity. This set off the interaction process. This aspect gradually allowed for antagonism in the group's perspective to emerge and created opportunities as well. Consequent dilemma, of either withholding the group's effort or encouraging them towards self-determination, has definite connotations for stability.

Further, the immigrants who now form a substantial percentage of the regional population, had initially entered the region as workforce for the secondary and tertiary activities, initiated by the Colonial power in the region. Later, they settled in and around their place of work. Goalpara and Cachar became the core area for the entry of these immigrants and from these cores, the immigrants moved into other parts of the region. In doing so, they gradually began to upset the delicate socio-political balance of the inhabitants. Since 1947, these immigrant elements in the regional population have become the cause of several crisis situations in the region.[5]

However, the situation clearly indicated the functioning of tension parameters that was directly/indirectly aided and betted by the region's geography and history. These parameters were:

- natives *versus* natives
- natives *versus* outsiders

It soon became part of the politico-economic development crisis and centred around resources (particularly land, its system of allocation and transfers), and political participation and representation in the decision-making bodies.

Of course, there is no denial that the socio-political movements that shook the states like Nagaland, Mizoram, Manipur, Meghalaya or for that matter, Assam, did not consider all alternatives but emphasized territorial separation in different stages. For instance, the Assam Valley experienced conflict of interest, political tension and in an imbroglio situation from 1979 to 1985 which today has transformed itself into the ULFA problem. This further is been accentuated by the fact that most of the insurgent outfits have joined hands and are attempting to direct a combined movement. One such effort is the formation of the Indo-Burma Revolutionary Front. Besides, other significant population minorities in the Valley like the Bodos have also launched movements to gain recognition and legitimacy of their demands. Thus, indirectly seeking devolution of power and possibly the application of federal concepts at lower regional scales.

Regional Development and Lewis of Disparities in North East India

The long struggle, mistrust, political tension, and conflict of interest in the region not only disturb peace, tranquillity, and stability but it has greatly impacted the region in development aspects since regional development is the result of interest between various economic and socio-institutional factors.

Compared to other regions in India, development in North East is relatively slow. Till date it still occupies the bottom most position in almost every aspects of development. It has high concentration of tribal population with their different traditional laws and order to the extent that no outsiders can purchase land in the region which in turn opens little scope for outsiders (non-tribal) to venture and invest in the region.[6] Consequently, there is little capital formation and little exposure to relatively more developed region of the country. Moreover, during the British period, the infrastructure that was developed to buttress the colonial interests continue to survive and to accentuate distortions in the nature of development over time and space. The question of viability of fast development (particularly industrialization) is still a far cry. Development in its wider connotations is often subject to misinterpretation. The author is of the opinion that the term 'development' in the region becomes more meaningful when equality, coherence, and reciprocity at the sub-regional and regional scale are maintained at all levels of transactions. But if this sequence is subject to the influence and interaction just within a particular ethnic group and not between ethnic groups then the resultant development can be perceived as ambiguous. It will remain weak and tenuous. In the process, the links between states will tend to get further weakened and this will also enhance the tendency of dissatisfaction and less self-determination among the population groups and subgroups. It is, therefore, understood that why the many different communities in the region reject the overtures to join the mainstream so as to bring social, economic and political development but rather resort to movements. Regional Development may perhaps be ameliorated by discouraging parochial considerations and extra-territorial influence.

It is also worth mentioning here that there are differences in natural resources, topography, density of population in all regions of India, but in the case of North East, it is extremely incongruent. Lack of development in basic infrastructure, difference in the level of living, cultural and linguistic differences[7] etc. have added affliction to regional development that also encouraged social tensions, violence and separatist attitude. Due to increased attention and resources devoted in the region to law and order issues, the development of the region is deteriorating day by day. The step-motherly treatment of the mainland India to the North East region in the past decades strongly left the communities to resort more to different movements and retaliation. Although different provisions have been made in the Constitution of India to bring socio-economic progress, all these went in vain and the people were offered nothing but disappointment, more hardship, more exploitation and more distributing injustice.[8]

The presence of sub-regional disparities is so distinctive in the region particularly in socio-cultural aspects.[9] The states that experiences more of conflict, insurgency and political unrest, are the ones that demonstrated a decline or a curve shows a downward trend in development patterns such as—educational set up, employment opportunities, low income and investment etc. This point to the fact that there is a positive relationship between political instability, unrest and development *per se.*

Conclusion

From the ongoing discussion, it is clear that the combined internal (political tension, conflict of interest among groups and sub-groups) and external forces (step-motherly treatment by the mainland) have left the region in turmoil, instability, and imbroglio situation. The war cry is heard from place to place. In Assam, the rumpus was over the issue of "foreigners" and the wall-posters there screamed, "Indians go back". Killings, kidnappings, and destruction of government properties became the order of the day in Assam. In Mizoram, where the outlawed Mizo National Front (MNF) had taken up arms to achieve its goal of "independence Mizoram" now agitating to oust the "outsiders". In strife torn Meghalaya the ultras day in and day out chanted 'Khasi by blood, Indian by accident'[10] in the post-1947 era and in the recent past the slogan 'Meghalaya for Meghalaya' tribals runs deep. In Nagaland, the hostile Nagas carried on insurgent movement for secession from the Indian Union at regular interval.

The present scenario on regional disparities in the region has, however, narrowed down. With the coming of the United Party Alliances (UPA) government to power in the centre, the region has somehow received attention particularly with the pronounced "Look East Policy" so as to attract and encourage domestic/foreign direct investment in the field of tourism. The tension, conflict and imbroglio situation day by day has reduced significantly although no one can rule out the still ongoing struggle in the region.

REFERENCES

1. The Indian Ministry of Home Affairs' Annual Report for 2002-03 lists 24 active insurgent groups in the north-eastern States (there are several dormant ones). In its chapter titled 'Security Scenario in the North East', the report states: "The most serious militant affected states/areas, viz., the whole of Manipur, Nagaland and Assam, Tirap and Chimglang districts of Arunachal Pradesh and a 20 km belt in the states having common border with Assam have been declared as 'disturbed areas' under the Armed Forces (Special Powers) Act, 1958 as amended in 1972."
2. Located at Longitude 89.46 degree E to 97.30 degree E and Latitude 21.57 degree N to 29.30 degree N.
3. Chaube, S.K. (1967), *Hill Politics in the North East*, New Delhi, p. 4.
4. Gopalakrishnan, R. (1996), *Insurgent North Eastern Region of India*, Vikas Publishing House Pvt. Ltd., New Delhi, ix-x.
5. *Ibid*, xii.
6. Ryngnga, P.K., (2003) Levels of Development in the hills of North East India in Mahapatra & Pathak (ed), *Economic Liberalization and*

Regional Disparities in India, Special focus on the North Eastern Region, Star Publishing House, Shillong, pp. 143-144.

7. Misra, R.P. (*et al.*) (1976), *Regional Development Planning in India: A new Strategy*, Vikas Publishing House Pvt. Ltd., New Delhi, p. 15.
8. Dutta, P.C. (2003), Regional Disparity and its Consequences in North Eastern Region of India, in Mahapatra & Pathak (ed), *Economic Liberalization and Regional Disparities in India, Special focus on the North Eastern Region*, Star Publishing House, Shillong, p. 187.
9. Dubey, S.M. (ed) (1980), *North East Region: A Sociological Study*, Concept Publishing Company (P) Ltd., New Delhi, p. 46.
10. 'Khasi Students Union (1995), *The Silent War. A Study of the Influx Imbroglia in Meghalaya*, Shillong, p. 3.

20

Some Aspects of Extremism and its Consequences in Assam

P.C. Dutta

"The soul of man (whose life or motion is perpetual contemplation or thought) is the mistress of two potent rivals, the one reason, the other passion, that are in continual suit; and according as she gives up her will to these or either of them, is the felicity or misery which man partakes in this mortal life." —*James Harrington*

The individuals who hold positions that are more radical than those of most of the people involved in a conflict can be called "extremists". Persistent experiences of oppression, insecurity, or humiliation may lead individuals and groups to adopt conflict strategies that seem appropriate in their dire circumstances. Again, political leaders capitalize on these adverse conditions and reward extremism in order to gain power for themselves. There are also instances where extremist actions are an effective strategy for gaining and maintaining power in a hierarchical environment where resources are scarce and there is an ongoing struggle for power. In short, individuals adopt extreme positions because extremism is effective. It can call attention to one's cause, damage one's opponent, and unite one's group against a common enemy.

Today, there is a need for a reassessment of concepts such as human rights, democracy, and the free-market economy. One cause for extremism is the serious economic and political problems. Extremism and terrorism can also sometimes be a reaction to extremism. It is true that all terrorists are extremists but not all extremists, are terrorists. In a country like Turkey, where the majority of the people are Muslim, extremists can achieve their political goals in most instances through democratic means if the government fails to apply necessary administrative responses. Therefore, governments have to prevent these elements from infiltrating into the governmental structure by detecting the moment when a threat to public peace and constitutional order surfaces, and dealing with it instantly.

Right at the beginning of the 21st century, two of the most shocking events in recent history, took place. The first was the destruction of over 2,000 year old ancient statues of giant Buddhas—the tallest standing Buddhas in the world. The second incident was the destruction of the twin towers of the World Trade Centre in New York City of the United States of America. A few years before these shocking incidents, the world witnessed another shocking massacre in the Republic of Bosnia-Herzegovina, where conflict between the three main ethnic groups, the Serbs, Croats, and Muslims, resulted in genocide committed by the Orthodox Christian Serbs against the Muslims in Bosnia.

The world continues to experience these traumatic happenings associated with religion now and then in different parts. The question that occurs is about the true nature and the purpose of religion. No religion, to the best of our knowledge, supports violence, tolerates inhumanity and prescribes destruction of homes and hearth. But yet the sad reality is that all the destruction, killings and inhuman happenings are being carried out, in the name of religion, in different parts of the world. The terrorist activities are proving to be a major threat before mankind.

Once again in the 21st century itself, a number of terrorist incidents have taken place in our country where many lives were lost and properties were destroyed. These incidents too were associated with religion. A good number of highly shocking and disturbing occurrences were in our country itself. We have witnessed a series of bomb blasts spread over different parts of the country, leaving behind a trail of deaths, misery, and terror.

Pakistan's president and prime minister, Asif Ali Zardari, strongly condemned the series of bomb blasts that occurred in Assam of NER on October 30, 2008 when Indian authorities suspect Islamist groups were behind coordinated bomb blasts in the troubled state of Assam that killed at least 77 people and wounded more than 320 in 12 serial blasts (*Arab Times*, Saturday, November 1, 2008). He remarked "Terrorism and extremism need to be eradicated in all its forms and manifestations." Britain has strongly condemned the serial blasts in Assam by describing it as a "terrible reminder of the threat from violent extremism". US ambassador David Mulford said in a statement by describing it as "acts of terrorism" the multiple blasts in state of Assam. "It is not improbable that dynamic of terrorism in Assam and in North East may have changed and that demands a change of template in counter-insurgency operations. The borders have been sealed, Para-military forces deployed but it seems it will be a long time that the state will recover from its worst ever terror attack." Police suspected that the separatist United Liberation Front of Assam (ULFA) had a role behind this. Blasts in Assam have usually been blamed on separatists. 18 bombs went off within an hour. Ten of the explosions happened in busy areas in Guwahati, while others in major towns.

Most Indian security analysts were of the opinion that the Harkatul-jihad-e-Islami (Huji), Bangladesh—the Islamist militant group based in Bangladesh—provided logistical support to ULFA could have sought to avenge attacks on Muslim settlers by indigenous tribes that killed at least 47 people last month (September 2008).*

At least 184 people were killed and around 714 injured, many seriously, as seven powerful blasts ripped through packed train cars and on stations at Mumbai on July 11, 2006 in the worst terror attack in India in over a decade. Again, "As many as 80 people were killed and 240 injured in the Indian city of Mumbai in grenade and gun attacks on 26 November, 2008, with five-star hotels among the sites targeted."

It is extremely important to address the reasons behind extremism, due to its strong association with the issues of stability and economic development. This is because progress in technology and informatics made the smooth movement of capital between countries possible at a record speed.

Norris and Inglehart (2004) also studied the connection between religiosity and political orientation in the World Values Survey.

---

* *Arab Times*, Saturday, Novermber 1, 2008.

A strong theory of extremism should be able to explain not only why there has been an increase in extremism on religion-related issues over the last three decades, but why extremism seems to be more prevalent on these issues than on matters of economic policy such as taxation.

Extremism leads to vandalism, and not just violent vandalism, but undermining the economy through making radical decisions that result in a decline in production, low productivity of workers and a shortage of commodities and services.

During October 2008, *Al Ittihad Annual Forum* discussed many important issues related to the connection between social development and the positions of various blocs including religious movements. The forum, titled "Religion and Society in the Arab World", focused on stability, which is a key factor in economic growth and social development. Thus, any extremist act that jeopardise this stability must have negative impacts on development and investment rates, which would lead to unemployment and a decline in living standards.

It is enough to recall the tragedies of the countries that suffered the negative impacts of instability, such as Lebanon, Somalia, Iraq, Pakistan and Afghanistan including India and within the country, state of Assam in particular and the north eastern region in general.

Economic and serious political problems are the causes for terrorism and the focus should be emphasised on these problems as causes rather than the attacks, which are results. Extremism and terrorism can also sometimes be a reaction to extremism from the other side. Extremism and terrorism are not interchangeable terms and should be defined accurately. Furthermore, a distinction should be made between the different types of extremism and terrorism. It is true that all terrorists are extremists but not all extremists are terrorists. There are terrorists who use violence and another type who are national liberation groups.

World population has risen from 2.5 billion in 1950 to 6.0 billion in 1999 which further increased to 6.7 billion in 2008 and during the same period India's population increased to 1.15 billion (estimate for July 2008) comprised approximately one-sixth of the world's population. The imbalance in population growth seen over the last century will only intensify in the years to come. There are 216 languages with more than 10,000 native speakers in India. The largest of these is Hindi with some 337 million (the second largest being

Bangla with some 207 million). 22 languages are recognized as official languages. In India, there are 1,652 languages and dialects in total.[1] Almost 80 per cent of the Indians are Hindus, with 14 per cent of the population Muslim, making India home to the third-largest Muslim population in the world after Indonesia and Pakistan.

The North East of India (NER), with its plethora of ethnic groups, each asserting its identity obsessively has been a source of worry over the last sixty years. The region generally brings to mind two diametrically opposite images the first, a picturesque region abundant in forest and rivers, and the second, a terrain bludgeoned by bullets, bombs and bloodshed. When all other States of the country are making rapid strides towards progress and development in all spheres of life, the NER is still what it was a few decades ago. The Indian Government is not doing honestly enough for the actual development of the region to bring it on par with the other states of the Indian mainland.

The eight states of the North East have international boundaries with four foreign countries, China, Myanmar, Bangladesh, Nepal and Bhutan have all had a history of prolonged troubles. These states are a troubled legacy for India. Although their varied and rich natural resource endowments could provide the basis for rapid economic growth, but this has not happened due to various reasons.

Though insurgency movements are seen in Nagaland, Assam, Manipur and Tripura, there has been deepening of democratic process in the entire region. There is a positive signal towards peace and dialogue from this area, as can be evidenced from the state of affairs in Mizoram which is one of the most peaceful states in the country today.

It can be realised the intensity with which the 'aggressive linguistic nationalism' worked in the state of Assam when one will compare between the real and the manipulated population figures from 1951 census onwards. In Brahmaputra Valley, the percentage of Assamese speaking people increased from 42 per cent in 1931 to 73.1 per cent in 1951 and it further increased to 73.3 per cent only in 1961 while at the same time in the same valley, the percentage of Bengalee-speaking people decreased to 13.0 per cent in 1951 from 23.0 per cent in 1931 which further decreased to 9.8 per cent in 1961 (Dutta and Pradhan, 2003).

Political vested interests obviously play a decisive role in the development of ethnic conflicts, which if allowed to go on unabated will worsen the situation and endanger India's unity and integrity. Even when national funds are allocated, they never reach the targeted groups, because of the corruption of the bureaucrats, politicians and other mediators. In the absence of any serious attempts to correct these economic distortions, it may not be realistic to expect resolution of these ragging ethnic conflicts. Further, marginalisation of a section of the ethnic groups easily go for militancy for their survival. The issues involved are invariably mixed with questions of sharing economic resources and decision making power. The growing recourse to caste and ethnic mobilization in India's democratic politics has been the erosion of ideology and viable socio-economic programmes around which electoral and political mobilisation ought to take place. These followed a rise, both in number and political clout, of ethnic and region based parties (Dutta, 2005).

The process of modernization has also intensified the search for an identity on the part of the tribal communities. They are becoming conscious of the need to be a viable human resource. As a consequence, small and distinct local groups combine to form a bigger group and adopt a common appellation, through the creation of some socio-political organization. No doubt in identity movement for wider social base, there are ethnic and political overtones (Datta Ray, 1989).

The problem of identity became acute in recent years. In the process of the 'passing' of ethnic identities and politicalisation of ethnic groups, a number of 'secular' or 'non-ethnic' factors play a critical role. This includes the state, pace and pattern of economic development, political elites and forces, and outside subversion. Social and economic crisis is deepening faster than anytime in North East India. This crisis is the crisis of underdevelopment in capitalist framework. The capitalist model of development has failed to manage the crisis of economic backwardness. The NER as a whole is placed amongst the poorest regions in the country.

Dutta (1996) pointed out that the poorest section of the society in Assam has been badly affected. He observed that the richest group of population has been gaining much at the expense of the poorest section of the society. The extent of degree of inequality in the level of living in the state of Assam in NER is much more than what is taken to guide some of the decision making elements in connection with resource transfer from centre to the states of NER.

Again, Economic development is a prerequisite to peace. Government today is in no position to provide jobs to all educated youth. When an educated youth fails to get employment, he turns to insurgency. Unless we bring back peace and security to the region, we are bound not only to lose valuable years right now but also stay far behind the rest of the country in the match towards development and prosperity.

According to Paul Wilkinson (1986), the causes of revolution and political violence in general are also the causes of terrorism. These include ethnic conflicts, religious and ideological conflicts, poverty, modernization stresses, political inequities, lack of peaceful communications channels, traditions of violence, the existence of a revolutionary group, governmental weakness and ineptness, erosions of confidence in a regime, and deep divisions within governing elites and leadership groups.

One must realize that North East is a mini-India. There are more than 75 major population groups and sub-groups, speaking approximately 400 languages and dialects, of which there are about 168 in Arunachal Pradesh, 95 in Nagaland, 87 in Manipur, 100 in Tripura and 200 in Assam, Meghalaya and Mizoram (Madhab, J., 1999). Thus, the whole north-eastern India is a place with people of diverse races, cultures, languages and various dialects with different traditions. Because of prolonged insurgency in the region, despite abundance of natural resources (oil, gas, coal, granite, limestone, water and forest wealth) no outside investment has taken place.

Dutta (2002) showed that poverty is an important factor in the development of frustration of the young generation. Again frustration develops in the society due to unemployment and poverty which is also the consequence of food shortage. All these creates social chaos in the society and ultimately the frustrated people raise their ugly faces to create social disturbances through different nasty activities. Thus, extremism is a multicausal phenomenon and usually results from multiple causal factors such as economic, political, religious, and sociological among others.

Both these persisting syndromes of poverty and skewed distribution of income have played a very critical role in shaping the future of youths in these states. This has a far reaching consequence in the increasing number of unemployed people in these states and a generation of frustrated youth. In fact, a study done by the Ministry of Welfare in 1989 found that 88 per cent of the sampled drug addicts in Guwahati cited "frustration" as the reason for them to go for drugs.[2]

Assam Chief Minister Mr. Tarun Gogoi, while welcoming the ban on SIMI, called upon the Union Government to ban all such fundamentalist groups, including the Bajrang Dal (*The Times of India,* New Delhi, 2nd October, 2001). Several SIMI Offices in the state have been identified and action against their members would be taken soon. Some of the Islamic fundamentalist or militant organizations active in the state are Muslim United Liberation Front of Assam, Muslim Liberation Tigers of Assam, Islamic Liberation Army of Assam, United Reformation Protest of Assam, People's United Liberation Front and others. The presence of a large population of Bangladeshi immigrants, especially in border areas, makes it convenient for these organizations to operate (*The Statesman*, Tuesday, 2 October, 2001).

Dutta (1985) mentioned that much of anxiety of the smaller ethnic groups, particularly of the tribals of NER has been associated with the identity crisis which they have been facing due to various economic, social, cultural and political factors. In search for their roots sometimes they have been forced to take the agitational path. The frustration-aggression hypothesis of violence is prominent in the literature.

This hypothesis is based mostly on the relative-deprivation hypothesis as proposed by Ted Robert Gurr (1970), an expert on violent behaviours and movements, and reformulated by J.C. Davies (1973) to include a gap between rising expectations and need satisfaction.

The present study, keeping in view the above into account, has been designed under different heads. The study will examine some of the factors which are responsible for the extremism in the region in general and Assam in particular. The chapter attempts to present a modest account of how the issues of extremism, the nature of the state's response to the same and tries to formulate the problems in the process of development. The study will be made on the basis of published and unpublished secondary data. Due to extremism, it becomes impossible to make developmental works of the region. Thus, some suggestions will be put forward for the policy makers and planners of the region so that the developmental works of the region may be done properly.

Analysis and Discussion

The North Eastern Region of India is known for its vast natural resources and a cauldron of different people and cultures. But the tragedies of the region in general and Assam in particular that have been suffering the negative impacts of instability which hampers the overall economic development of the region.

Observing that the North East Region in particular has been a victim of "misdirected policies and planning" of the federal government, the Tripura Chief Minister Manik Sarkar said that "this region is now particularly backward in both physical and social infrastructure". He attributed this "growing feeling of discontent and frustration and a sense of injustice" to this imbalance. "We must make all efforts to dispel such negative and disruptive feelings, which can also drive the people, particularly a section of young and unemployed, to the path of extremism and other anti-national activities," the CM pointed out.

According to India's Health Ministry, India's population which was 238 million in 1947 touched 1.012 billion in March 2001 (Table 20.1) and is expected to be 1.263 billion by 2016. The share of population of NER, in comparison to all-India, increased from 2.89 per cent in 1951 to 3.78 per cent in 2001.

It is to be noted that from the pre-independence period, the percentage of Muslim population in the state of Assam has been increasing steadily from 16.23 per cent in 1911 to 30.92 per cent in 2001. During the period 1951-1991, the percentage of Hindu population in NER decreased from 65.61 per cent in 1951 to 60.92 per cent in 1991 while at the same time the percentage of Muslim population increased from 20.88 per cent to 21.56 per cent. The percentage of Christian population has also been increased from 6.34 per cent to 12.25 per cent. The proportion of Hindu population has been declining mainly due to increased proportion of population professing Muslim, Christian religions. As the Christian dominated states, viz. Nagaland, Mizoram and Meghalaya recorded a comparatively higher growth rate of population during the last two or three consecutive decades that definitely resulted in an increase proportion of population of Christian religion in North East of India. The decadal growth rate in NER recorded a very slow in case of population professing Hinduism during the study period. During 1971-1991, proportion of Hindu population increased at the rate of 47.91 per cent against the growth rates of 140.89 per cent for Christian, 79.04 per cent for Muslims. According to 2001 Census figures, the percentage of Hindu population in the state of Assam decreased to 64.89 per cent while the per cent of population in case of Muslims increased to 30.92 per cent and Christians to 3.70 per cent. The abnormal growth of population in the region has multiple causes. However, one of the reasons is heavy influx from the neighbouring countries before and after independence.

Table 20.1: Population Distribution and Illiteracy Rates in NER

States	*Full-fledged Statehood*	*Population (in million) in 1951*	*Population (in million) in 2001*	*Per capita Income (US$) in 1991*	*Illiteracy (in Per-cent) in 1991*	*Illiteracy (in Per-cent) in 2001*	*Female Illiteracy (in Per-cent) in 2001*
Arunachal Pradesh	1987	—	1.091	250	58	45.26	55.76
Assam	1947	8.029	26.638	171	47	36.72	43.97
Manipur	1972	0.578	2.389	153	40	29	40.30
Meghalaya	1972	0.606	2.306	175	.50	36.69	39.59
Mizoram	1987	0.196	0.891	215	17	11	13.87
Nagaland	1963	0.213	1.989	190	38	33	38.08
Sikkim	1975	0.138	0.540	164	43	31	40.00
Tripura	1972	0.639	3.191	121	39	27	34.59

Education can affect lives of people in several ways. It enables women to assume more autonomy or power in traditional gender stratified family settings and also in more egalitarian ones, giving them greater control over their own lives and a stronger voice in matters affecting themselves and their families. Access to educational institutions promoting skill development is a prerequisite for providing trained manpower. As per 1991 Census, literacy rate of NER was 58.09 per cent (all-India 52.2%), while in 2001 it was 68.5 per cent (all-India 64.8%). Mizoram has the second highest literacy rate in India.[3] Except Arunachal Pradesh (58%) and Meghalaya (50%), the illiteracy level of the region's population is below the national level (48%) according to 1991 Census while in 2001, percentage of illiteracy rate in the states of Arunachal Pradesh (45.26%), Meghalaya (36.69%) and Assam (36.72%) are above the national figure of 34.62 per cent. Female illiteracy is highest in the state of Arunachal Pradesh followed by Assam

(43.97%) and Manipur (40.30%) while it is lowest in Mizoram (13.87%). In the recent years, female education has come to the forefront of development planning for tackling various problems in the society.

It is clear that the resources allocated for both plan and non-plan expenditures have not been utilised for the purposes they were allocated for. Even if they were targeted to objectives such as poverty alleviation, public distribution system, health, education, drinking water and rural electrification, these resources either did not reach the target groups or had a huge leakage in the delivery mechanism.[4] In the absence of any monitoring and evaluation of these projects and related use of resources, the leakage and diversion of funds became a regular feature and gradually became institutionalised. Meanwhile, the resources kept coming in from Delhi regardless of how they were utilised. This continuous flow of resources in fact did consolidate the emerging institutionalised corruption.

Despite so much pumping of resources to the area, most of the states in the NER continue to remain in a state of poverty. Though the percentage of population below the poverty line has gone down steadily during the 20 years from 1973-74 to 1993-94, the numbers in absolute terms have in fact increased. For example, in small states like Arunachal Pradesh and Meghalaya, the percentage of people living below the poverty line has come down steadily from 51.93 to 39.35 per cent and from 50.2 to 37.92 per cent respectively during the period from 1973-74 to 1993-94, but the actual number of people below the poverty line has increased from 2.66 lakhs to 3.73 lakhs and from 5.52 lakhs to 7.73 lakhs respectively during the same period. Indeed, the total number of persons below the poverty line in the entire North East Region (including Sikkim) has increased from 10.9 million in 1973-74 to 13.49 million in 1993-94. This means 4.2 per cent (3.39% in 1973-74) of the people below the poverty line in India is concentrated in a land area of 7.97 per cent of the country. Moreover, the concentration of the people below the poverty line in the rural areas goes to show that the rural development programmes, particularly the poverty alleviation measures, have not really benefited the rural poor (Lama, 2001).

Wealth distribution in India is fairly uneven. With the top 10 per cent of income groups earning 33 per cent of the income. Despite significant economic progress, a quarter of the nation's population earns less than the government—specified poverty threshold of $0.40 per day. In 2004-05, 27.5 per cent of the population was living below the poverty line. Per capita income is found to be highest in the state of Arunachal Pradesh (us $ 250) followed by Mizoram (us $ 215) while it is lowest in Tripura followed by Manipur.

For providing employment opportunities in rural areas and thereby strengthening the rural economy, Khadi & Village Industries (KVI) plays an important role. It is observed that total number of employment in this industry was 2.85 lakhs in 2001-02 which increased to 3.09 lakhs in 2003-04 thereby an average increase of 2.83 per cent per year.

According to Census 1991, 55.54 per cent of the rural population had access to an improved water source. As on 1.4.2007, Department's figures show that out of a total of 15,07,349 rural habitations in the country, 74.39 per cent (11,21,366 habitations) are fully covered, and 14.64 per cent (2,20,165 habitations) are partially covered. Average access to drinking water is highest in class I towns (73%), followed by class II towns (63%), class III towns (61%) and other towns (58%).

The issue is how and where to use the money amassed through corruption. It is a common feature in NER that the earning of money is quickly reflected in the apparent consumption patterns of the people, and also in buildings, and cars and modern gadgets at home. More dangerously, it is reflected in the behaviour of the youth who have very limited entertainment options in the region. Since most of them would hesitate to go out of the state, they would like this easy money to be spent in the cities and towns of their own state. And one very fashionable way is to resort to expensive narcotics. Once they are in the chain of drug abusers it is then very difficult for them to get disentangled and so the process continues from a resort to anti-social activities and, often on to insurgency.

At the time of country's independence in 1947, Assam attracted attention of the entire nation for foreign national issue. During the years of Muslim League Ministry under Sir Mohammed Sadullah and before there was a heavy flow of people from East Bengal. It is possible that the Muslim League Ministry encouraged the land-hungry peasants from East Bengal to settle in the fertile plains of Assam in the name of agricultural development of the

State. Before independence, there had always been a latent fear in the Assamese mind of being swamped by the Bengali-speaking people and such suspicious were strengthened when Assam was included in the group "C" category by the Cabinet Mission. Taking language as an issue, the then leaders of Assam headed by Mr. Gopinath Bordoloi committed a serious blunder in Assam's history as a result of which there was every possibility of Muslim dominance in Assam. The separation of Bengali-speaking district of Sylhet from Assam in 1947 through a referendum known as "Sylhet referendum" greatly helped to calm Assamese fears of being outnumbered by Bengali speaking population but the path for future ethnic conflicts were cleared from that day onwards in Assam.

In 1951 Census, the rise in the population of Assamese-speaking people was substantial as the migrated Muslim population adopted Assamese as their language leaving their mother tongue Bengali. Meanwhile, the refugees from East Pakistan poured into the State in thousands leading to an abnormally high rate of population growth in the State.

It is observed, in this context, that every successive government in Assam since independence adopted an attitude that can set one community against another, one race against other etc., i.e. an attitude that can sharpen the divide among people in respect to either religion, race, or language. And by doing so, they might wrest political power but the sharp cleavage, once created, has struck its root deep and even after more than six decades of independence the level of backwardness in economy, communication, industrial investment etc. is writ large in the face of the region in general and the state of Assam in particular. Unless homogeneity is achieved in heterogeneity, progress lies distant. The political leaders, cutting across party lines, are, it seems, bent on letting loose and inferno for the people of the state and building a Tajmahal for them out of the public exchequer. Again party in power at the centre at present cannot be escaped from the accusations as NER is deliberately ignored by the Central Government so far as the problem of security is concerned though it sanctioned thousand crores of money during the period 1997-2003 (Tables 20.2 and 20.3) in connection with insurgency problems in the region.

Table 20.2: Expenditure in Security Arrangement of Police Force in NER

(Rs. in Crores)

Year / *State*	*1997-98*	*1998-99*	*1999-2000*	*2000-01*	*2001-02*	*2002-03*	*Total*
Arunachal Pradesh	—	—	—	1.00	1.90	0.95	3.85
Assam	131.91	78.86	52.17	63.97	92.86	68.01	487.78
Manipur	—	19.43	3.44	14.18	4.00	7.64	48.69
Meghalaya	—	—	—	3.21	0.60	8.35	12.16
Mizoram	—	—	—	—	—	—	—
Nagaland	—	35.61	17.88	7.50	12.71	22.42	96.12
Tripura	—	28.55	17.53	15.00	27.70	29.85	118.63

Source: *The Ananda Bazar Patrika*, 28th November, 2003.

The expenditure to control insurgency in NER has been increasing day by day. But ironically along with the expenditure to control insurgency, insurgency has been increasing by leaps and bounds. During the period of seven years, the states of NER have sanctioned crores of rupees in their budget. Side by side an amount of rupees 767 crore they have spent for police security out of the enhanced amount of Rs. 1,000 crore sanctioned by the Central Government. Among these seven states, Assam having an expenditure amounting to Rs. 487.8 crore, Tripura having Rs. 118 crore and Nagaland having Rs. 96 crore are at the top of the list. For the modernization of police force another Rs. 278 crore has been spent. In this sphere also Assam is on the top of the list along with the states of Tripura and Nagaland. The amounts spent for these states are Rs. 103 crore, Rs. 46 crore and Rs. 39 crore respectively. But the problems cannot be solved unless the governments both Central and the States try to appropriate the money in a proper way. The governmental information made it clear that despite the huge expenditure; normalcy cannot be brought in the region. Here both the Central and the State governments are a great failure (Dutta and Deb, 2007).

Only Assam, Manipur and Tripura are currently eligible for 100 per cent Central assistance under the police modernisation scheme in the North East. Meghalaya, Nagaland and Arunachal Pradesh, on the other hand, receive 75 per cent Central assistance; the state governments contribute the remainder. Mizoram and Sikim, which are peaceful states, are being kept out of the ambit of the upgraded police modernisation scheme. According to an

Table 20.3: Expenditure in Modernisation of Police Force in NER

(Rs. in Lakhs)

State / Year	1997-98	1998-99	1999-2000	2000-01	2001-02	2002-03	Total
Arunachal Pradesh	—	56	386	538	76	541	1597
Assam	1710	664	2272	2245	1821	1561	10273
Manipur	626	98	554	651	362	1149	3440
Meghalaya	—	122	474	635	325	488	2044
Mizoram	—	67	346	436	365	814	2028
Nagaland	616	108	452	651	593	1588	3908
Tripura	611	133	606	1381	832	1036	4599

official, it was primarily owing to the reason that the North-eastern states, which enjoy a plan size of Rs. 180 crore under this scheme, are actually allocated only Rs. 96 crore.

Preventing violent extremism is a fast-moving and complex challenge. It requires an awareness of the global, national and local context. These include sustainability and cohesion, crime reduction, wealth and employment, educational attainment, promoting equality of opportunity in housing and access to local services, regeneration, reducing inequalities and promoting equality of opportunity in housing and access to local services.

A review of different ethnic issues in NER proved that the ethnic conflicts in the region, in general, and in Assam in particular, were due to the religious, linguistic crisis of ethnic identity of different groups of people living in the region and the repressive attitude of the people in the mainstream of the region. Through different ethnic movements, the state of Assam is bifurcated into different states and the process of separation is still going on jeopardizing the unity and integrity of the region and threatening the security of the country. The ethnic movements in the region initially reflect the ethno-cultural aspirations of the people and finally deviate from the real path by turning the movements into violence of the insurgence for material gains (Dutta and Pradhan, 2006).

With 439 insurgency-related fatalities in 500 incidents of violence, Assam remained the most violent theatre of conflict in the states of NER in 2007 (Table 20.4). A close look at the table shows an increase of 81.4 per cent of total fatalities in 2007 in comparison to 2006. Fatalities among civilians and the insurgents have significantly increased in the State in 2007. An increase of 74.4 per cent was recorded in civilian fatalities between 2006 and 2007, while insurgent fatalities rose by 180 per cent, indicating a series of successes for the SFs.

Table 20.4: Insurgency-related fatalities in Assam: 2005-07

	Incidents	*Civilians*	*SFs*	*Insurgents*	*Total*
2005	398	173	7	74	254
2006	413	164	32	46	242
2007	500	286	24	129	439

Source: 2005 and 2006: Union Ministry of Home Affairs, 2007: Assam Police.

As indicated by Institute for Conflict Management database, insurgent violence was reported from 26 of Assam's 27 Districts in 2007, the north-eastern District of Lakhimpur being the only peaceful geographical entity. Assam Police sources indicated that the dramatic rise in civilian fatalities was solely due to the spate of ULFA sponsored violence against the Hindi speaking population in the eastern-most (Upper Assam) Districts of the State in January and another similar campaign against the trading community in the hilly Karbi Anglong District in August. However, given the fact that the bulk of the killings was the handiwork of four principal insurgent groups in the State, of which the influence of three was confined to four contiguous Districts, the claims of insurgent marginalisation do not hold conviction.

The neutralisation (killings, arrests and surrender) of 1,956 insurgents in 2007 notwithstanding, the state of insurgency in extended parts of Assam continues to evoke a sense of fear among common citizens. Assam Police sources further indicate that insurgents from various groups in the State were arrested in 2007 and a further 200 surrendered, considerably weakening the outfits. Nevertheless, extremist depredations continued, and the large number of civilian killings was compounded by the abduction of at least 75 civilians, of whom 55 were rescued, and an enveloping campaign of extortion.

There are a number of common features among the different extremist groups of NER, beginning with their varied political demands starting from statehood within the Constitution of India

Table 20.5A: Scheme for modernization of state police forces (MPF scheme) Funds released/utilization position as on 30-06-2005

Annual Plan Size: Rs. 77.40 crore	*Central funds released (Rs. in crore)*	*Per cent utilization*
2000-01	36.58	50.06
2001-02	38.59	48.19
2002-03	16.50	62.43
2003-04	36.52	93.67
2004-05	41.17	17.78

to re-demarcation of interstate borders to the expulsion of "foreigners" and outsiders. Many of these groups are said to have been working in close co-ordination with each other within and outside the region. The leadership of many of these outfits is known but untraceable as they are stationed outside India, in Bangladesh, Bhutan and Thailand. Since most of them are well equipped with sophisticated weaponry, they seldom hesitate to resort to violence particularly against the state armed forces.

It is to be noted from the figures of Table 20.5A that whatever be the amount of fund released by the government under different schemes, a big amount of money remain unutilized due to various factors. From Table 20.5B, it is striking to note that except for the year 2004-05, total allocated funds were released and the total expenditures also being made during the period 2001-06 under consideration.

Table 20.5B: Border Area Development Programme (Allocation and Release of Fund, Expenditure and Unspent Balance)

(Rs. in Lakh)

Year	*Allocation*	*Release*	*Expenditure*	*Unspent Balance*
2001-02	748.00	748.00	748.00	—
2002-03	748.00	748.00	748.00	—
2003-04	748.00	748.00	748.00	—
2004-05	748.00	998.00	399.00	599.00
2005-06	1081.00	1081.00	1081.00	—

Location has a significant impact on crime in India. In 2006, the highest crime rate was reported in Pondicherry with 447.7 per cent for crimes under Indian Penal Code which is 2.7 times the national crime rate of 167.7 per cent. Kerala reported the highest crime rate at 312.5 per cent among the states. Uttar Pradesh reported the highest incidence of violent crimes accounting for 12.1 per cent of total violent crimes in India (24,851 out of 2,05,656) followed by Bihar with 11.8 per cent (24,271 out of 2,05,656). Among 35 mega cities, Delhi reported 31.2 per cent (533 out of 1,706) of total rape cases. Madhya Pradesh has reported the highest number of rape cases (2,900) accounting for 15.0 per cent of total such cases reported in the country. Uttar Pradesh reported 16.9 per cent (5,480 out of 32,481) of total murder cases in the country and 18.4 per cent (4,997 out of 27,230) total attempt to murder cases. Jammu & Kashmir (33.7%), Manipur (33.0%), Assam (30.4%) and Daman and Diu and Pondicherry (29.4%) reported higher violent crime rate compared to 18.4 per cent at national level.[5]

A report published by the National Crime Records Bureau (Table 20.6) compared crime rate from 1953 to 2006. The report noted that burglary declined over a period of 53 years by 38 per cent (from 1,47,379 in 1953 to 91,666 in 2006), whereas murder has increased by 231 per cent (from 9,803 in 1953 to 32,481 in 2006). Kidnapping has increased by 356 per cent (from 5,261 in 1953 to 23,991 in 2006), robbery by 120 per cent (from 8,407 in 1953 to 18,456 in 2006) and riots by 176 per cent (from 20,529 in 1953 to 56,641 in 2006).

Table 2.6: Number of Crimes (Murder/Kidnapping/Robbery/Burglary/Riots)

Year	Total Cog. Crimes Under IPC	Murder	Kidnap-ping	Robbery	Burglary	Riots
1953	6,01,964	9,802	5,261	8,407	1,47,379	20,529
2006	18,78,293	32,481	23,991	18,456	91,666	56,641
Per cent Changes in 2006 over 1953	212.03	231.37	356.02	119.53	-37.80	175.91

Source: National Crime Records Bureau, Snapshots 1953-2006.

In 2006, 51,02,460 cognizable crimes were committed including 18,78,293 Indian Penal Code (IPC) crimes and 32,24,167 Special & Local Laws (SLL) crimes, with an increase of 1.5 per cent over 2005 (50,26,337). IPC crime rate in 2006 was 167.7 compared to 165.3 in 2005 showing an increase of 1.5 per cent in 2006 over 2005. SLL crime rate in 2006 was 287.9 compared to 290.5 in 2005 showing an decline of 0.9 per cent in 2006 over 2005).

Assam's Police-population ratio, at 178, is the lowest among the India's North-eastern States. According to media reports in December 2007, Assam had 7,776 vacancies including those of 6,695 constables, 17 Additional Superintendents of Police (ASP), 135 Deputy Superintendents of Police (DSPs), besides inspectors, head constables, and vacancies in other ranks. Bureau of Police Research and Development (BPR&D) data indicates that no recruitment took place in the State Police department for three consecutive years between 2002 and 2005, before 1,350 constables were inducted in 2005. It is remarkable to note that only 0.97 (less than 1) per cent of the total Police expenditure in 2005-06 was spent on training.

Table 20.7 shows the different insurgent groups who are more or less active in different states of NER of India. The first three groups of Manipur now operate from a unified platform, the Manipur People's Liberation Front (MPLF). The most prominent among the terrorist outfits of Tripura is the NLFT (National Liberation Front of Tripura). It employs terror tactics to effect mass conversion to Christianity (*The Statesman*, 1999, 2000; Ghosh, 1999) and is a predominantly Baptist (Protestant) organisation. Despite the efforts to resolve 35 year, long left wing extremism in the Indian subcontinent, the violence has been continuing and we are witnessing a gradual increase in the left wing extremists' activities in the region.

Over the years, both the state and the Central Government have used tactics from negotiations to military operations to bring stability and to rooting out militants in the region. Nevertheless, the region remains a potential tinderbox. The ULFA has been fighting for an independent Assamese homeland since 1979 and more than 15,000 people have lost their lives to insurgency in Assam during the past three decades.

Arunachal Pradesh, Assam, Manipur, Mizoram and Nagaland have a long international border with unguarded and rugged border points. When the state fails to protect the general population particularly those with economic power, the latter tends to organise their own security system sometimes by succumbing easily to the financial and other demands of the insurgents. Across the international border vigilance is poor and there are symptoms of "loose national controls" because of weak administration. So extraterritorial forces including some from Myanmar and Pakistan's ISI play a major role.

Table 20.7: List of Insurgent Groups in NER

State	*Extremist Group*	*Name*
Arunachal Pradesh	1. United Peoples' Volunteers of Arunachal Pradesh	UPVA
	2. United Liberation Volunteers of Arunachal Pradesh	ULVA
	3. United Liberation Movement of Arunachal Pradesh	ULMA
	4. Arunachal Dragon Force	ADF
Assam	1. United Liberation Front of Assam	ULFA
	2. Bodo Security Force	BSF
	3. Karbi National Volunteers	KNV
	4. Muslim Security Force	MSF
	5. Muslim United Liberation Tigers of Assam	MULTA
	6. Muslim Volunteers Force	MVF
	7. National Democratic Front of Bodoland	NDFB
	8. Bodo Liberation Tiger Force	BLTF
	9. United People's Democratic Solidarity	UPDS
	10. Dima Halim Daogah	DHD
	11. Rabha National Security Force	RNSF
	12. Hmar People's Convention-Democracy	HPC-D
	13. Bengali Tiger Force	BTF
	14. Islamic Liberation Army of Assam	ILAA
	15. Muslim Tiger Force	MTF
	16. United Liberation Militia of Assam	ULMA
	17. Muslim Liberation Army	MLA
	18. Barak Valley Youth Liberation Front	BVYLF
	19. Muslim Volunteer Force	MVF
	20. People's United Liberation Front	PULF
	21. Muslim United Liberation Front of Assam	MULFA
	22. Muslim Security Council of Assam	MSCA
	23. Kamtapur Liberation Organisation	KLO
	24. United Liberation Front of Barak Valley	ULFBV
	25. Karbi People's Front	KPF
	26. Revolutionary Muslim Commandos	RMC
	27. Adivasi Security Force	ASF
	28. Adam Sena	AS
	29. Islamic United Reformation Protest of India	IURPI
	30. Islamic Sevak Sangh	ISS
	31. All Assam Adivasi Suraksha Samiti	AAASS
	32. Student Islamic Movement of India	SIMI
	33. All Adivasi National Liberation Army	AANLA
	34. Islamic Tigers	
	35. Sadam Bahini	
	36. Harkat-ul-Jihad-al-Islami	
Manipur	1. United Nationalist Liberation Front	UNLF
	2. Peoples' Liberation Army	PLA
	3. Peoples Revolutionary Party of Kangleipak	PREPAK
	4. Kanglei Yawol Kanna Lup	KYKL
	5. Kuki National Front	KNF

(*Contd.*)

(Contd.)

State	Extremist Group	Name
	6. Kangleipak Communist Party	KCP
	7. Islamic Liberation Front	ILF
	8. Kuki National Party	KNP
	9. Hmar People's Convention	HPC
	10. Manipur Liberation Tiger Army	MLTA
	11. People's United Liberation Front	PULF
	12. United Islamic Liberation Army	UILA
	13. United Kuki Liberation Front	UKLF
	14. United Committee of Manipur	UCM
Meghalaya	1. Achik National Volunteer Council	ANVC
	2. Hynniewtrep Volunteers Council	HVC
	3. Achik Liberation Matgrik Army	ALMA
	4. Hajong United Liberation Army	HULA
	5. People's Liberation Front of Meghalaya	PLF-M
	6. Hynniewtrep National Liberation Council	HNLC
Mizoram	1. Bru National Liberation Front	BNLF
	2. Hmar People's Convention-Democracy	HPC-D
Nagaland	1. National Socialist Council of Nagaland (Isaac-Muivah)	NSCN-IM
	2. National Socialist Council of Nagaland (Khaplang)	NSCN-KM
	3. Naga National Council (Adino)	NNC (Adino)
Tripura	1. Tripura National Force	TNF
	2. National Liberation Front of Tripura	NLFT
	3. National Militia of Tripura	NMT
	4. Tripura and Tribal Commando Force	TTCF
	5. All Tripura Volunteer Force	ATVF
	6. All Tripura Tiger Force	ATTF
	7. Tripura Tribal Volunteer Force	TTVF
	8. Tripura Tribal Youth Force	TTYF
	9. Tripura Armed Tribal Commando Force	TATCF
	10. Tripura Tribal Democratic Force	TTDF
	11. Tripura Liberation Organisation Front	TLOF
	12. United Bengali Liberation Front	UBLF
	13. Tripura Liberation Force	TLF
	14. Tripura Tribal Action Committee Force	TTACF
	15. Tripura National Democratic Tribal Force	TNDTF
	16. All Tripura Bengali Regiment	ATBR
	17. Borok National Council of Tripura	BNCT
	18. All Tripura Liberation Organisation	ATLO
	19. Tripura State Volunteers	TSV
	20. Tripura Tribal Sengkrak Force	TTSF
	21. Socialist Democratic Front of Tripura	SDFT
	22. Tiger Commando Force	TCF
	23. All Tripura National Force	ATNF
	24. Tripura National Army	TNA
	25. Tripura Mukti Police	TMP

The role and grip of the state over certain administrative areas like law and order maintenance gets vastly eroded. This is what has been happening in the North East. The most vital examples are the business community and industrialists including those in tea, jute and timber, indirectly and tacitly supporting the insurgent activities by providing them with money under pressure on friendly terms or otherwise. A very crucial example is that of the Tata Tea Company's case of 1997. Tata Tea is one of the Indian giants and has a huge stake in the tea industry of Assam. The Tata Tea and five other unnamed companies were found to be providing funds to the militants, particularly the ULFA.

In a statement made in September 1997, Prafulla Kumar Mahanta, the then Chief Minister of Assam, stated that: "It is not that we are singling out the tea industry. Investigations are also on to ascertain which other companies, both in public and private sectors have paid the extremist groups and action will be taken against those found guilty....an inquiry has been initiated against government employees who were allegedly funding the National Democratic Front of Bodoland (NDFB), formerly the Boro Security Force. The audited financial accounts of the NDFB for 1994-95 and 1995-96 revealed that the outfits received money from sales tax, forest and motor vehicle inspectors."[7]

The Bangladesh connection of some of the militants is very well known. Clinching evidence of this was the arrest of ULFA leader Anup Chetia in Dhaka. In fact, a booklet published by the Ministry of Home Affairs pointed out that: "ULFA has reportedly started several income generating projects in Dhaka, Mymensingh, Narsingdi, Sylhet etc. which are run by money partly received as subscription from tea gardens in Assam and partly by donor agencies. In Dhaka, ULFA owns three hotels, a private clinic, two motor driving schools in Sylhet, it has a number of grocery shops and drug stores. In Mymensingh, it owns some poultry farms while in Narsingdi, it runs two schools."[8]

This Myanmar connection in the arms supplies to the North East became so serious that in 1995, the Indian and Myanmarese armies conducted a joint operation known as "Operation Golden Bird" on the Manipur-Myanmar border where at least 40 insurgents were killed. The commander of a counter-insurgency army corps stated later that the "militants in the North East and Myanmar actively aided by the Pakistani ISI are getting their arms supply from the flourishing arms market in the Far East."[9]

Government officials are increasingly falling prey to the attractions of links with insurgent groups. The document entitled *Bleeding Assam* published by the Union Ministry of Home Affairs accuses Assam government employees of being in association with the banned ULFA. The government to divert government funds or force them to do so under threat. At places resources allocated for development have not reached the beneficiaries, but have instead been used to finance ULFA's gun running, hence infrastructure development in Assam continues to be hampered with poorer communication links.[10]

Almost every state in the North East is affected by insurgent activities. Many parts of the North East have been declared as "disturbed areas" under the Armed Forces (Special Powers) Act, 1958.[11] There is an array of insurgent outfits, many of whom have emerged very recently.

It was for the first time that a huge congregation was witnessed in the North East, shouting slogans like "We want peace", people took to streets of Guwahati to express their resentment and condemn widespread militancy. Protestors were demanding eviction of illegal Bangladeshi migrants, fundamentalist forces and militants from the state. The agitated protestors requested the government to shed the soft posture against terrorism and fundamentalism in the state.

Kashmir and North-eastern states face the same problem, extremism and lack of economic development. But the Central Government play a double role in case of these two states. Kashmir gets more attention and a separate article (Article 370) of the Constitution governs the state. Why are the North-eastern states provided with the same exemptions and economic subsidies? It may be due to the fact that Kashmir is more important internationally.

Action Taken by the Government

"At the outset, let me say that I have always condemned violence and extremism in Assam and elsewhere and never hesitated to say that we can negotiate only with those who want peace, not with those who kill innocent people." But at the same time, the government would never compromise with the unity and integrity of the country or allow those who killed innocent people to go unpunished, Prime Minister Manmohan Singh said replying to the Motion of Thanks on the President's address in Lok Sabha.[12]

The Prime Minister also said referring to Assam and ULFA that "We will never hesitate to sit down and talk to a fellow Indian—howsoever misguided, he or she may be—if such conversation can bring peace to our people."

Winding up his visit to the trouble-torn Manipur, Prime Minister Manmohan Singh extended an open invitation to all groups including ULFA, who abjure violence, for talks to resolve all outstanding issues in the North East and expressed hope that a "humane" law would replace the controversial Armed Forces Special Powers Act.

Ministry of Development of North East has been consistently pursuing its efforts towards development of North East through various development measures and projects under the schemes formulated by the Government of India for development of socio-economic infrastructure in the NER. The Central Government has taken a number of measures to curb insurgency in the states of NER. The Government sanctioned a total of Rs. 144.30 crore by the Tenth Finance Commission to the North-Eastern States for Police Housing, Police Training, Police Telecommunications, construction of Police Stations/Outposts, repair and renovation of jails etc., upgradation of arms and ammunition, vehicles, communication and other equipments.

A package of initiatives, amounting to Rs. 6133 crore has been taken for the development of the North East which now stands at Rs. 7865 crore following inclusion of certain additional schemes in the package (the package includes schemes for development of the North East in priority sectors like Health, Education, Transport, Flood controls etc.

Delhi recently sanctioned the creation of a new counter-insurgency and anti-terrorist training facility at Dayapur in Silchar on the lines of the Army's Counter Insurgency and Jungle Warfare School at Vairangte in Mizoram.

"So far, 297.9 km of the international boundary has been fenced and work is on progress on the 148.7 km stretch. Altogether, 491.1 km border will be fenced", according to BSF Director-General, Mr. Ranjit Shekar Mushahary.

New security steps announced by the State Government in the last week of December 2007 include the plan to open 19 Police

Stations in the char (riverine) areas, 26 Police Stations in the Adivasi-dominated remote areas, and the filling up of 298 vacant posts in the Special (Intelligence) Branch of the Police Department.

Implications

All the issues have wide political, economic, military, health, environmental and psychological consequences that pose threats to Indian sovereignty, and to the political stability, economic and social equilibrium of the states of NER.

In these hilly states, local journalists are stuck between the devil and the deep blue sea in the form of the army and the militants. There have been instances where editors have been threatened for refusing media coverage to the militant organisations. Those who bow down to their demands are harassed by the army and police on charges of assisting the militants.

Apart from destroying some of the main pillars of the society, especially the youth, the corridor status has given the North East an artificially high cost economy.

Assam is one of the states in NER that are connected to the Indian mainland by a very thin strip of land. Since the independence of India in 1947, this region has witnessed the rise and fall of a number of insurgent and ethno-nationalist movements against the Indian state. The region has also been neglected in terms of socio-economic development and hence provides a fertile ground for recruitment of disaffected youth in Assam who want to vent out their anger against the Indian state.

The June 1999 bomb blast in New Jalpaiguri railway station in north Bengal, killing many Kargil bound soldiers, has serious implications. The subsequent claim by the ULFA that it did this bombing with the help of the ISI should in fact be an eye opener to security personnel, policy makers and civil society at large in the region particularly when it took place in an area which is the meeting point for four countries: India, Bangladesh, Bhutan and Nepal.

The ULFA has, no doubt, suffered a series of setbacks since the December 2003 military operations in Bhutan. The '28th battalion' of ULFA remains the outfit's premier strike force, responsible for all its attacks in the Upper Assam Districts. The 'battalion' has traditionally used the virgin territory of Arunachal

Pradesh and Nagaland to travel between Assam and Myanmar, a movement that remained largely undisrupted till November 2007. The warming up of ULFA's ties with the NSCN-K has apparently created an acrimonious war between the NSCN-IM and the ULFA, erstwhile partners in terror, resulting in the NSCN-IM refusing any right of movement to ULFA cadres through Naga territory. Augmented SF deployment in Arunachal Pradesh had already created serious problems of transit for the ULFA. IJLFA's routes to Bangladesh, mostly through the Garo Hills of Meghalaya, however, remain undisrupted.

On November, 27 Suspected Black Widow militants shot dead 10 unidentified saw mill workers and injured eight others in two separate attacks at Bithorgaon under Umrangsho police station in the NC Hills District of Assam. On December 13 of the same year, All Adivasi National Liberation Army (AANLA) militants successfully carried out an explosion in the New Delhi Rajdhani Express in the Golaghat District, killing five persons.

On January 1, 2008, Chief Minister Gogoi unveiled the routine and now tried 'three-pronged strategy'—on the political, law and order and developmental fronts—to deal with the insurgency in the State. This, however, appeared to be little more than the usual political rhetoric, long used by successive regimes in the State to disguise their ineptitude over the previous years. Except for the temporary dip in violence in the preceding years, a trend that appears to have been decisively reversed in 2007, Assam has very little to show in terms of its improved capacities to rein in the insurgents. Even after three decades of insurgency, the initiative continues to remain in the hands of the insurgents, a reality that is unlikely to change in near future and it confirms the fact when the blasts continue to occur in different corners of the state even in 2009.

Conclusion and Suggestions

It is recognised that while a security response is vital it will not, on its own, be enough. Winning hearts and minds and preventing individuals being attracted to violent extremism in the first place is also crucial. Peaceful co-existence of all different religions and harmonious relationship between all religions is something which is most essential for promoting enlightenment and peace in the society. In fact, it will be worthwhile to conduct a nation-wide campaign vigorously. The responsibility of promoting such a campaign naturally falls on the shoulders of those who belong to moderate sections of opinion in every religion as well as on the shoulders of all the civil society organizations.

The non-governmental voluntary service organizations or civil society organizations need to address themselves to this frightening situation associated with religious extremism. A climate, an opinion against extremism ought to be generated. State power alone cannot achieve such a goal. There will be no terrorism in a country when the civil society of the country will not encourage it at all. Terrorism in India is uncontrollable because the civil society does not have guts to protest really. Never our Government have been able to motivate people to stand together firmly against human rights and human values. The citizens of the country, irrespective of economic division, want to live a contented life. Economic inequality between different classes of people should be narrowed as far as practicable. The Day Indians would think as one nation and start honouring its own self there would be no terror in our country.

As a society we must defend and promote our shared and non-negotiable values: respect for the rule of law, freedom of speech, equality of opportunity, respect for others and responsibility towards others.

In developing this action plan, we have drawn on the recommendations from the Preventing Extremism Together working groups; debates with local communities; roundtable meetings with theologians, academics, practitioners and community groups; and the views of key partners including the intelligence agencies, the police, local government and other government departments.

Almost all the news channels have beamed the episode with vivid description of serial bomb blasts in Assam. But no channel have devoted enough time to condemn it and to encourage civil society to stand up against it. Reporting the matter repeatedly is one thing but discouraging the terrorism is another responsibility. The vivid show of terrorism is not enough. Thus, it is necessary for the media to devote enough time to discourage the event too.

Disaster Management System of the region should have take active part seriously and honestly as soon as it is needed. Thus, thc governments of the region should take proper care for the upgradation of the Management. The governments also should build defence mechanism, against terrorism.

Identifying the factors that make someone vulnerable to become involved in violent extremism is the first step towards anticipating and addressing the issue. There is a common view that there is insufficient information about what causes a person to become a violent extremist. There are many instances where information held by Intelligence and informers is not being shared with the police because of concern about how that would be interpreted by the local police authority. Thus, it needs to be an understanding among the intelligence branch, informers and police front line staff of the sort of information that is required. It needs to develop more coordination and consistent systems for collecting and making sense of the information available locally.

It should be made clear that it is not acceptable for leadership organisations merely to pay lip service to tackling violent extremism. Governments should give priority in its support and funding decisions to those leadership organisations who actively work to tackle violent extremism, supporting community cohesion and speaking out for the vast majority who reject violence.

Women can play a vital role in building strong communities and tackling violent extremism. It is important to enable their voices to be heard and empower them to engage with disillusioned youths. The important task is to take direct responsibility for those areas where Government action is required and to provide sustained support and encouragement to those organisations displaying true leadership.

It is not the military operation but the dialogue for peace with the militant outfits that has brought some order to the NER. Dialogue with the M.N.F. remains the only example of the culmination of a successful peace process that ended militancy in Mizoram in 1986. Experiences such as the Mizo Peace Accord, however, have not been replicated. Other peace deals such as the Shillong Accord in 1975 with the N.N.C. in Nagaland, the 1988 agreement with the Tripura National Volunteers in Tripura, the Bodoland Autonomous Council agreement of 1993 with the Bodo militants in Assam have all fallen through as new factions, dissatisfied with the terms of the agreement, have resumed hostilities under new leaderships.

It may be suggested that more government intervention for all-round development, better service from the North Eastern Council (NEC), prevention of infiltration and sealing of international borders are urgently needed. It should not be voted in favour of further reorganization of the state as it may be harmful for national integration and economic development. It should be done more for all low-income groups whatever their faith or ethnicity. While tackling violent extremism is a national priority, the nature of the challenge can vary greatly from place to place. Working with local communities to deliver local solutions is the key. This is not just about local authorities, it is about wider cultural activities and inter-faith work in the communities. It is this type of activity that brings people together and emphasises that there is more that unites all than divides all.

NOTES

1. Rupert Goodwins. Smashing India's Language Barriers. ZDNet UK. And Mother Tongues of India According to 1961 Census.
2. M.N. Karna, *Assessment of Drug Abuse, Drug Users and Drug Prevention Services in Guwahati*, Shillong, Department of Sociology, North Eastern Hill University, and Ministry of Welfare, Delhi, Government of India, 1989.
3. *Source*: Draft Report of the Task force on Development Initiatives for the NER, September 2005.
4. Indicators: non-plan expenditures have gone up many fold. The share of the central government in the revenue has gone up to over 80 per cent in many of the states.
5. Snapshots (1953 - 2006), National Crime Records Bureau and Snapshots - 2006, National Crime Records Bureau.
6. Statement given by the Chief Minister of Assam, Prafulla Mahanta, *Telegraph*, Calcutta, 22 September, 1997.
7. *Hindustan Times*, Delhi, 25 October, 1998.
8. *Outlook*, Delhi, 1 February, 1999.
9. *Bleeding Assam*, Ministry of Home Affairs, Delhi, Government of India, 1998 as quoted by *Hindustan Times*, Delhi, 24 October, 1998.
10. Ministry of Home Affairs, *Annual Report 1995-96*, Delhi, Government of India, 1996.
11. Press Trust of India (PTI)—Posted online: Thursday, March 8, 2007 at 17:39 hours 1ST.

REFERENCES

Davies, T.R. (1973): "Aggression, Violence, Revolution and War". in *Handbook of Political Psychology,* San Francisco: (ed.) Jossey-Bass, Jeanne N. Knutson, pp. 234-60.

Dutta, B. (1985): "The Reemergence of Folklore in North East India", *Man and Life,* in Vol. II, No. I & IL Calcutta.

Dutta, P.C. (1996): "Quality Variation of some food items of consumption in the North Eastern Region (NER)", *IJRS,* Vol. 28, No. 1.

Dutta, P.C. (2002): "Population Growth and Environmental Crisis in North East India: Problems and Remedies" in *Development Priorities in North East India* (ed), B. J. Deb, Concept Publishing Company (P) Ltd., New Delhi.

Dutta, P.C. (2005): "Problems of Ethnicity in North East India" in *Perspective of Security & Development in North East India* (ed) S.K. Agnihotri (IAS) and B. Datta Ray, Concept Publishing Company (P) Ltd., New Delhi.

Dutta, P.C. (2006): "Issues and Problems of Ethnicity in Assam" in *Ethnic Issues, Secularism and Conflict Resolution in North East India* (ed.) Bimal J. Deb, Concept Publishing Company (P) Ltd., New Delhi.

Dutta, P.C. and B.C. Pradhan (2003): "Demographic Changes, Racial and Linguistic Conflicts in Assam of North Eastern Region ", proceedings of the National Seminar on Social Transition in the North East (UGC Sponsored), Hailakandi, 8th December, 2003.

Dutta, P.C. and Y. Deb (2007): "Problems and Prospects of the Peace Process in Assam" in *Terrorism and Human Rights in North East India* (ed.) Asok Kumar Ray and Bimal J. Deb, Om Publications, New Delhi.

Datta, Ray, B. (1989): *Tribal Identity and Tension in North East India,* Omsons Publications, New Delhi.

Gurr, Ted Robert. (1970): *Why Men Rebel.* Princeton, New Jersey: Princeton University Press.

Lama, Mahendra P. (2001): "India's North East States: Narcotics, Small Arms and Misgovernance" in *Ethnic Studies Report,* Vol. XIX, No. 2, July 2001.

Madhab, Jayanta (1999): "North East: Crisis of Identity, Security and Underdevelopment," *Economic and Political Weekly,* Bombay, 6 February, 1999.

Norris, Pippa, and Ronald Inglehart (2004): "Sacred and Secular: Religion and Politics Worldwide," *in Cambridge Studies in Social Theory, Religion, and Politics,* Cambridge University Press, Cambridge, UK.

Wilkinson, Paul (1986): "Terrorism: International Dimensions." in *Contemporary Terrorism,* pp. 29-56: Facts on File, New York.

21

Extremist Organisations in Manipur and their Ideologies

Oinam Sareeta Devi

Manipur is a land of the Indo-Mongoloids, on the extreme North East of India and is a natural fortification surrounded by the hills. The state had remained isolated for a long time from the mainland socially, politically and culturally. So the people of the state, at large, still have a sense of racial alienation from the rest of India. The population, roughly 25 lakhs, comprises two sections of peoples, namely (i) the valley, predominantly the Meiteis and (ii) the hill tribes comprising the Nagas and the Kukis, en-block of 33 scheduled tribes and more. Politically Manipur was an independent kingdom till the last Anglo-Manipuri war of 1891, which saw the fall of Manipur's Independence in the hands of the British. The Union-Jack was hoisted on the soil of Manipur on the 27th April, 1891 at Kangla, the ancient seat of power followed by hanging of the national heroes like Prince Tikendrajt, Thangal General, and so many others to be mentioned. The Manipuris could not easily forget the holocaust of the said war and humiliation they suffered and its repercussions are still looming large in everyone's mind with a remorseful sense of vengeance. After the war, Manipur was administered by a king of Manipuri origin installed by the occupying forces under the British Suzerainty. Manipur, however, retained the status of a princely state. The British paramountcy in India ended in 1947. But it was shortlived as Manipur was formally merged to Indian dominion by virtue of the Merger Agreement of 1949 which is still to be admitted by a large section of the people particularly the youth who have a strong zeal of Manipuri nationalism.

The history of Manipur was filled with constant fighting and warfare amongst the clan principalities and tribal village chiefs to show one's supremacy over the another. Even the tradition of the notorious head-hunting was widely prevalent for a long time in the past. However, the martial tradition got melted down, to a great extent, after the advent of the Hindu Vaishnavism among the valley of Manipuris, which is based on *Prem-Bhakti* and simultaneous baptism of the hill tribes into Christianity. These historical facts apart, the Manipuris are generally peace loving and hospitable and well known for their polished culture and beautiful dances. But situation now is like a bitter pill for Manipur which was once acclaimed as the Jewel of India by a person none other than Pandit Jawaharlal Nehru, the former Prime Minister of India as the state has been completely seized under the grip of series of armed conflicts as fall out of the ongoing violent revolutionary movements by numerous plain and hill based extremist groups for the last half a century leaving her social, political and economic condition mercilessly in shambles. The citizens, en-block, are entirely trapped in a state of conflict situation in between the warring groups. Sound of gunshots and shrill cries of the innocents has become the fashion of the day. Life is becoming uncertain, anybody may become a victim at any time depending upon one's fortune.

The resurgence of the extremist groups anywhere in the world is prominently the by-product of the socio-political and economic situation of the land and her people. Likewise, the first salvo of the armed struggle was echoed at a time when the national pride of the Manipuris, particularly of the youths who had learnt much about the defeat of 1891 war and subsequent Merger Agreement of 1949 was shattered due to torturous design of the Colonial rulers. Their hopes and aspirations had been lost, and they were unable to surrender to the situation of the time as they had always been a strong zeal to fight. Here we may cite from a work—"Everything on this earth can be made into something better. Every defeat may be cause of later resurgence. Every visitation of distress can give a new impetus to human energy. And out of oppression those forces can develop which bring about a new re-birth of the national soul." It may, therefore, be rightly presumed that the first extremist organization came into being on the soil of Manipur as planted by some diehard young men who followed the legacy left by the independent rulers of the land and later by Hijan Irawat who went underground and mobilized the people for armed struggle, way back in 1949. He was the only serious social reformer of the 20th Century Manipur who himself resigned from the all-powerful State Durbar to fight against the repressive measures of the then feudal lord Maharaja Churachand Singh (1891-1930). Irawat went underground after the warrant to arrest him was issued by the Government of Manipur on 21st September, 1948. He had later established the Manipur Red Guard Army declaring a resolute armed struggle for an independent Socialist Republic of Manipur in 1950 at Burma. He died as a unsung hero, quietly at Tangbo in Burma on the 26th September, 1951. The tragic end of Irawat and the legacy left by him was considered as one of the multi-dimensional causes of the revolutionary movements in Manipur. It may be pertinent here to point out the other causes, which could be apparently the origin of the ongoing armed struggles. Some of the prominent factors are: (i) The long and unique tradition and culture of the state based on the belief of imagined good olden days of Manipur which got buried in the course of history with the sacrifice of the national heroes who martyred for the motherland, (ii) The Agreement on the Merger of Manipur with Indian dominion signed on October 15, 1949 at Shillong, which is still unacceptable to a large section of the populace, (iii) The rampant corruption in the administration having a severe impact on the youth losing their self-confidence leading to all sort of social conflicts, (iv) Worsening socio-economic condition and high rate of unemployment, a direct blow to educated youth who lost vision of the future and lastly, (v) Indifferent attitude of the Union Government towards the North East.

As soon as the Irawat era ended in 1951, a revolutionary group in the name and style of Manipur Revolutionary Nationalist Party (MRNP) was founded during 1953 with an avowed objective towards 'restoration of the independence of Manipur'. The party died down very soon after the mass arrest of its members and no important tell-tale imprints were left. Then came the powerful Meitei State Committee in the scenario. It was also the product of the post-Irawat days, founded in 1964 by his followers, mostly the peasants who believed in Irawat's armed struggle and interestingly some of them were ex-Red Guards. A group of the said committee even went to Nagaland and participated in the Tartar Ho (Parliament) of the then Federal Government of Nagaland as part of their plan to set up an organisation with its Head Quarters at Keibi Taretkhul on the North Eastern part of Imphal which happened to be a hot bed during the early part of Irawat's movement. Evidently, the objective of the Meitei State Committee was to establish a non-exploitative Socialist Independent State in Manipur and the committee also had the strong conviction to preserve the racial identity of the Meiteis and to protect it from the bondage of the Hindu colonisation and influence of Vaishnavism which had been enforced by the Pro-Hindu Kings upon his subjects from the time of Garibnawaj (1714-1754) onwards. The Committee did not last for long.

On the other hand, the Naga extremist organisations had spread widely in the hill districts of Manipur well before the revolutionary movements in the valley started simmering. Those movements were greatly influenced by the Naga Nationalist Council (NNC) which was formed in Nagaland way back in 1946, as a show of Naga solidarity, under three principles of: (i) Sovereignty, (ii) Non-Violent approach, and (iii) Non-cooperation with the Government of India. The rebel Nagas declared Independence on 14th August, 1947 and thereafter the Naga Voluntary Plebiscite was held in Nagaland on 16th May, 1951, which showed that 99.9 per cent of Nagas voted for independence. It was the beginning of a fierce armed conflict and hectic exercises to find out a solution. The first cease-fire between the Government of India and Federal Government of Nagaland was declared on 25th May, 1964 covering whole of Nagaland and a good part of Naga inhabited area of Manipur, which lasted only up to 1967. The NNC split after signing the Shillong Accord 1975 which was apparently executed without consulting its leader A.Z. Phizo, as some influential members of the council left the parent body to form the National Socialist Council of Nagaland (NSCN) under the leadership of Isac Swu, S.S. Khaplang and Th. Muivah of whom the last one hailed from Ukhrul district of Manipur. The same group split again into two groups, viz. NSCN (IM) and NSCN (Khaplang) and resumed their armed conflicts between the Naga National Army and the Government of India unabated till the signing of the second Cease Fire Agreement between the Government of India and National Socialist Council of Nagalim

(NSCN) on 1st August, 1997 with a vision to end the Naga Conflict by means of peaceful political solution. The peace process is still continuing but a political solution acceptable to both parties is yet to be seen. The NNC and the break-way NSCN (K) faction are determined not to accept any solution other than sovereignty. But, the NSCN (IM), retracting a bit from its earlier stand for an absolute Sovereignty, is now asking for the unification of Naga-dominated areas of Manipur, Assam and Arunachal Predesh under one umbrella of Nagalim as an agenda of the new peace proposal which is not acceptable to the people of Manipur in particular.

Again, coming down to the valley, 1960s and 1970s saw the birth of many more extremist organisations in the name of the United National Liberation Front (UNLF), People's Liberation Army (PLA), the People's Revolutionary Party of Kangleipak (PREPAK) and the Kangleipak Communist Party (KCP) etc. The UNLF was founded under the leadership of late Arambam Somorendro Singh, a well-known playwright and social activist on 24th November, 1964. Many people have considered the front as an offshoot of the Pan Manipuri Youth League (1955-56), which was formed to bring about the solidarity of the ethnic Mongoloids of the North East India. The UNLF had an early setback, split between senior leaders and young blood due to ideological differences. Late Sudhir, a member of the break way group led the formation of the Revolutionary Government of Manipur (RGM) in 1969 at Sylhet and later the rival faction assassinated him. The founder of the UNLF, himself left the organisation and cameover ground. After braving the early setbacks, the party is now well on track under the charismatic leader R.K. Meghen *alias* Sanayaima as the General Secretary of the party, which is one of the most powerful extremist organisations operating in the state. The PLA is another powerful revolutionary group established by late Nameirakpam Biseshwar reorganizing the faction ridden RGM on 25th September, 1978. It had shot in the national limelight as the most powerful extremist group during 1980s and the Revolutionary People's Front (RPF), the political wing of PLA, was set up on 25th September, 1979 to give a stronger impetus to their revolutionary movement which had spread under Irengbam Bhorot *alias* Chaoren as the president of RPF and its supreme commander. This is also the only major extremist organisation, which had no factional feuds within the party, which is becoming a draconian problem in the modern armed revolutionary movement of the state.

The political ideology of the above organisations is more or less similar as both of them are destined to continue the armed struggle to restore the lost status of Manipur as "Independent" entity. Apart from the issue of sovereignty, they are pursuing to bring a change in the socio-economic and cultural front of the state through drastic reformations. Strictures to ban the sale of liquors, use of narcotic drugs and screening of Hindi films are a few examples to cite. Besides these reformative operations both the armed revolutionary groups are determined to regain the territory of the state lost in different courses of history.

The People's Revolutionary Party of Kangleipak (PREPAK) is another powerful extremist group founded on 9th October, 1977 at Koubru hill, roughly 10 kms on the north of Imphal by late R.K. Tulachandra, a well learned young man at his mid-thirties, with the objective to establish an independent sovereign state of Manipur. The party, which was once running as one of the most powerful revolutionary groups is evidently faction ridden and is now in the process of re-organising the cadres to regain strength. The Kangleipak Communist Party (KCP), another valley based extremist group facing the problem of fragmentation, was established on 15th May, 1980 by Maipak Sharma at Heirok village of Thoubal District of Manipur after break from the erstwhile PREPAK and lead from late Y. Ibohanbi *alias* Baji who was Assistant Commander at the time of formation. He took the reign of the party as the commander in-chief and formed his own group in the same year. As the name itself suggests, the objective of the KCP, which stands for the poor peasants and workers, is to take up arm for freedom and to bring an egalitarian society. After the death of its popular leader Ibohanbi, the party's image has been slackened due to factionalism and frequent rivalries among the top leaders of this militant group, once very strong in some parts of the state.

The Kangleipak Yawon Kanna Lup (KYKL) is another powerful militant group formed at Bangladesh Head Quarters of PREPAK on 25th May, 1994 with a vision to bring unification of the revolutionary groups operating in Manipur and to continue armed struggle unitedly for restoration of Manipur's lost independence. One significant move of the KYKL is the massive operations to end the virus of corruption in the administration particularly in the education department and also to protect the ethnic identity of the Manipuris by introduction of the Meitei Archaic Script (Meitei Mayek) as compulsory subject in the schools in which the Operation Kangleipak is viewed as the effective measure to streamline the present education system of the state. The tradition of factionalism, in itself has become a threat often to almost all the organisations in the state. KYKL also had to face the same predicament during late 1990s.

Apart from these major groups, a number of armed militant organisations were founded on ethnic line to fight either for a separate homeland or to defend the interest of the minorities within state. Among them mention may be made of some notable armed groups as: Kuki National Front (KNF-1988) later splitted into KNF (P) and KNF (MC); Kuki Liberation Army (KLA-1992); Kuki National Organisation (KNO-1998); and United Kuki Liberation Front (UKLF-2000) etc. There are more militant groups like the People's United Liberation Front (PULF), the North East Minority Front (NEMF) and Islamic National Front (INF) etc. There are many other minor militant groups founded only to protect the interest of their own tribes. It is an enormous task to pinpoint the actual number of the extremist organisations due to frequent factional feuds and multiplicity in numbers. It is also found difficult to confirm the who's who of the leadership of these organisations due to the same reason. Reportedly, there are about 25 extremist groups operating in different parts of the state.

But interestingly, a total of 18 militant groups, 7 from the United People's Front (UPF) and 11 from the Kuki National Organisation (KNO) entered into a tripartite Agreement signing the Suspension of Operation (SoO) on 22nd August, 2008 with the Centre and the Government of Manipur. Pu Thanglianpau, the chairman of the UPF who considered the unity of the 18 armed militant groups in sharing the negotiation table as a political milestone, "The SoO Agreement was signed to give peace a chance and for that matter, to arrive at a lasting honourable political solution." The agreement is hopefully moving forward and time will tell what would be the outcome in the end.

Conclusion

As a result of the prolonged exposure to frequent arm conflicts between militant outfits and state sponsored security forces, the people of Manipur, at large, have learnt enough about the art of living dangerously. The number of widows who lost their spouse in the so-called encounters whether genuine or fake, has been on the rise and, therefore, the corresponding crime associated with terrorism has also steadily increased from 281 in 2006 to 542 as per record up to November 2010. Both the national highways connecting the State with the mainland are apparently under control of the militant outfits causing hardship to innocent public due to extortions and killings perpetuated by the unknown extremists or the anti-social elements in the name of insurgency. Virtually, Manipur is turning into a killing field. Claims and counterclaims centring fake encounters, are becoming the fashion of the day. The number of death toll of the youth is alarming. These are only a few instances of numerous merciless massacres faced by the people. But the victims are often daily wage earners and poor peasants including innocent women and youth of the state. The gloomy stories of these glaring events are not a secret document as the news is often flashed in the state or the national dailies. But, it is everybody's misfortune that nobody came to the rescue of the poor and innocents who had no option except crying helplessly.

Every wise man would say that brute force cannot suppress people's revolution. The ongoing militancy is a political one and it is, therefore, to be solved by peaceful means through dialogue and understanding. But nothing came out practically and the people are suffering due to sagging economy and price hike of the essential commodities in the local market due to ongoing disturbances, high level corruption and weak governance in the wake of militant outfits waging war for the sovereignty of Manipur. Both the centre and the state are demanding peace for development and on the other hand a large section of the people are also demanding development for peace. Let their arguments go on. But, no time should be wasted to bring an end to the ongoing armed conflicts to avoid further bloodshed and aimless massacres in the state. The people who are caught in the battle of the guns are longing to see initiation of the peace process. It was more than once that the Chief Minister of Manipur appealed on the floor of the Assembly to the extremist organisations to come to the negotiating table. But nobody knows whether it was a sincere proposal or a publicity stunt. There was no concrete formulation determining the basis for the peace negotiation. This apart, the deliberate acts of killings are going on and the number of dead lying in the morgue is swelling. It is apparent at the time of writing this chapter that the Manipur Government has no immediate plan for the Peace accord as Pradeep Phanjoubam rightly viewed that the talk initiative by the State government would be a mere show than of substance.

If the government is serious enough and committed to bring normalcy in the state the foremost agenda must be to bring a congenial atmosphere free from tension and mistrust amongst the general people and to stop the terror unleashed by the state sponsored forces and militant outfits as well. The latest data of the Home Ministry of Government of India has clearly detailed the abuses by paramilitary forces that is unlikely to prove helpful in tackling extremism in the North East. The youth should be given a chance to regain their self-confidence, which stands shaken due to alarming scale of unemployment (roughly 23% of the total population), political corruption and massive repressive operations in the name of curbing the militant activities etc. According to the Draft Report of the 'Peace Progress and Prosperity in the North East Region: Vision 2020' produced by the Ministry for Development of North East Region (DONOR), the problem in the North East is squarely due to weak governance. So, the government should do everything possible for immediate redressal of the wrongs perpetuated so that the human psyche of the collective milieu is regenerated for a new hope and vision. Along with this, the apprehensions of racial discriminations and the clamour of sovereignty simmering in the mind of youth, as fall out of the tortuous and massive operations and deprivation of the democratic liberty need to be dispelled first as the foremost agenda to end the gruesome war on militancy in the state.

It is true that there is no one who would like to make Manipur into a chaotic zone and instead everyone will surely have a longing for peace free from virus of corruption and racial discriminations. In this regard, the Union Government needs to initiate corrective measures and instil confidence in the youth who constitute the most important resource of the state.

REFERENCES

Karam Manimohan Singh, *Nupi Lan (Women's War of Manipur)*, Karam Premlata Devi, 2006.

N. Joykumar Singh, *Revolutionary Movement in Manipur*, Akansha Publishing House, 2005.

North East India Council for Social Science Research, Shillong, *Terrorism and Human Right in North East India*, Om Publication, New Delhi, 2007.

North East Sun, October 16-31, 2008, Vol. XIV, No. 6, pp. 10-12.

Sangai Express (Manipuri Local Daily Newspaper), dated 19-10-2007.

Sangai Express (Manipuri Local Daily Newspaper), dated 4-11-2008.

Soyam Chattradhari, *Manipur Itihasta Irawat*, Soyam Publication, Manipur, 1972.

Tarapot Phanjoubam, *Bleeding Manipur*, Har-Anand Publication, New Delhi, 2003.

Tarapot Phanjoubam, Eikhoigi Ereipak, *Priyobarta Mangang*, Imphal-East, Manipur, 2007.

The Telegraph (North East), 12-1-2009.

22

Extremism and Urbanisation Among the Tribals of Tripura

Malabika Das Gupta

Introduction

Since it is an empirically established phenomenon that urbanisation accompanies economic development[1], and 'extremism and development' is identified as a sub-theme of the national seminar on Extremism in North East India, the present chapter deals with extremism and urbanisation among the tribals of Tripura.

Relationship between Extremism and Urbanisation among Tribals: The Theoretical Issues

The level of urbanisation in a state can increase over time if one, some, or all of the following things occurs/occur: (a) new areas are included within the boundaries of the existing towns of the state, (b) a net addition to the number of towns takes place in the state, (c) a net natural growth occurs in the urban population of the state, and/or (d) net migration occurs in the urban areas of the state.

Similarly, the level of urbanisation among the tribals in a state can also increase over time if a large number of tribals live in areas that get included within the boundaries of the existing towns when they grow in size or if new towns develop in areas where there is a large concentration of tribal population.[2] The level of urbanisation among the tribals in a state can also increase over time if, when the total tribal population of the state increases, there is a net addition to the tribal population of the urban centres as a result of the natural increase of the tribal population of these towns and also if there is a net migration of tribals to the urban areas of the state from other countries, other states and the rural areas of the state.

Though a wide variety of reasons can lead to the migration of tribals to the urban areas of the state from other countries, from other states and from the rural areas thus increasing the level of urbanisation among the tribals of the state concerned, a part of the tribal migration to urban areas of the state under consideration may be induced by the incidence of extremism in the country or area of origin of the tribal immigrants.[3] However, the incidence of extremism can sometimes also lead to an outflow of urban tribals of the state concerned to other countries, other states or the rural areas of the state and lead to a fall in the level of urbanisation among the tribals there. So, theoretically, it is possible for extremism to lead to either an increase or a decrease in the level of urbanisation among the tribals of a state and whether or not extremism will raise the level of urbanisation among them will depend on the relative strength of these two opposite forces in a state at a particular point in time.

Objectives and Scope of the Study

The chapter will attempt to examine whether extremism in Tripura has had an impact on the level of urbanisation among the tribals of the state where the level of urbanisation among tribals in Tripura will be measured by the percentage of tribals residing in the cities and towns of the state or by *u* where

$$u = \frac{\text{Number of tribals living in the urban areas of Tripura in a particular year}}{\text{Total tribal population of Tripura in that particular year}} \times 100$$

The focus of the study will be on:

(a) examining the part played by extremism in the urbanisation of tribals in different phases of extremist activities in Tripura, and

(b) dealing with the future of extremism-related urbanisation in the state now that the incidence of extremist-related violence has come down in the state.

It may be noted that the study is an attempt to examine if extremism has had a part to play in the urbanisation of the tribals of Tripura. It does not attempt to measure the exact contribution of extremism in the urbanisation of the tribals of Tripura *vis-à-vis* the contribution of the other factors leading to urbanisation among them.

Rationale for the Choice of the State for the Study

Tripura has been singled out for examining if extremism has had any impact on the level of urbanisation among the tribals of the state because the state has been a hotbed of extremist activities from the 1980s onwards though extremist activities are supposed to have abated somewhat in the state in recent years.[4] Another reason for concentrating on Tripura for examining whether extremism has had any influence on urbanisation among the tribals of the state is that a continuous dataset on the relevant variables for the study is available for the state from 1961 onwards. This is not true of Mizoram, Manipur, and Assam, three other states of the region that have been plagued by extremism at different points of time.[5] Another reason for dealing with Tripura is that researchers have not explored the relationship between extremism and urbanisation among the tribals of this state before.[6] Last but not the least, the familiarity of the author of this chapter with the ground realities prevailing in the state and the opportunity she got to do some fieldwork in the state on the topic, thanks to her ICSSR Senior Fellowship research project, 'Urbanisation and the Tribals of Tripura' determined to a great extent her choice of the state on which the seminar paper concentrates.

The Background of the Study

(1) A brief note on urbanisation among the tribals of Tripura from 1961 to 2001

(a) Urbanisation among the Tribals of Tripura before 1961

Tripura has a comparatively recent urban history. Agartala, the only town of the state before 1961, was founded about in the year 1844 (Hunter, 1973:497) and was the capital of the princely state. The population of the town was reported in 1864 to number about 875 (*ibid*: 495). The break up of the population of the town on the basis of its ethnic composition cannot be found from the secondary data sources but since the population of the town is said to have comprised almost entirely of the Raja's relatives and retainers (*ibid*: 496) and given the fact that the Tripura Rajas were tribals, it may be conjectured that the urban population of Tripura was mainly of tribal origin. However, the level of urbanisation among tribals must have been very low in late nineteenth century Tripura because the majority of the tribals of the state lived in the hills and were shifting cultivators.

Table 22.1 shows the total population, urban population and level of urbanisation in the state from 1901 to 1951. Like the earlier period, during this period also, data are not available separately for the tribal and non-tribal residents of urban Tripura because the Scheduled Tribes had not been notified at the time of the 1951 Census. It is evident from the table that the level of urbanisation in the state showed an upward trend from 1941 onwards. This trend was mainly due to the arrival of refugees from the neighbouring areas of British India before independence and from East Pakistan after the partition due to communal tension in the region. These refugees were mostly Bengalis who settled in Agartala and even if the town had been predominantly tribal earlier, with the arrival of the refugees, its demographic balance shifted in favour of the Bengalis (Census of India 1951). Consequent on the influx of the Bengali refugees in Agartala, the only town of the state till 1961, the tribals of the town became not only a small proportion of the tribal population but also of the urban population of the state.[7] The percentage of tribals in the urban population of Tripura went down during this period not because the tribals left the town in large numbers following the refugee influx but because they were swamped by the massive inflow of Bengali refugees into the town.[8] According to Jagadish Debbarma, one of the tribal respondents for the study from Agartala whose family has lived in the town for four generations, there was no out-migration of tribals from Agartala in large numbers in the wake of the influx of the refugees. Though many tribals living in Agartala sold their land to the newly arrived refugees, most of them did not become landless as a result and did not have to leave the town because of their landlessness. On the contrary, some tribals who owned property in the outskirts of the town sold these lands to the refugees and moved into the town proper raising the level of urbanisation among the tribals of the state. According to Jagadish Debbarma, only a few tribal families of Agartala left the town and settled down in nearby villages as a result of the refugee influx because after selling a part of their lands to the refugees, they were left with very small parcels of land in the town or because they found the town crowded and not very pleasant to live in after the refugees poured into the town in large numbers.

Table 22.1: Total population, urban population and the level of urbanisation in Tripura (1901-1951)

Year	*Total population*	*Urban population*	*Level of urbanisation*
1901	173325	6415	3.70
1911	229613	6831	2.98
1921	304437	7743	2.54
1931	382450	9580	2.50
1941	513010	17693	3.45
1951	639029	42595	6.67

Source: Census of India 1951, Vol. XII, Assam, Manipur and Tripura, Part IIA.

(b) Urbanisation Among the Tribals of Tripura from 1961 Onwards[9]

This period is dealt with separately because from the 1961 census onwards, the census data allow us to calculate urbanisation among the Scheduled Tribes of the state.[10]

Table 22.2 shows the total population, urban population, and ST urban population of Tripura from 1961 to 2001 as well as the level of urbanisation in the state as a whole and among its STs during the period under consideration. It shows that both the level of urbanisation in the state and the level of urbanisation among its STs have increased over time but the table also shows that throughout the period, during every census year, the level of urbanisation among the STs has been much less than the level of urbanisation in the state.

Table 22.2: Place of STs in population, urban population and level of urbanisation in Tripura, 1961-2001

Year	*Population*		*Urban population*		*ST population as % of total population of state*	*ST urban population as % of total urban population of state*	*Level of urbanisation among*	
	Total	*ST*	*Total*	*ST*			*Population*	*ST population*
1961	1142005	360070	102997	3698	31.53	3.59	9.02	1.03
1971	1556342	453161	162360	5485	29.12	3.38	10.43	1.21
1981	2053058	583920	225568	7668	28.44	3.40	10.99	1.31
1991	2757205	853345	421721	14081	30.95	3.34	15.30	1.65
2001	3199203	993426	545750	25429	31.05	4.66	17.06	2.56

Source: Census of India, different years.

(2) A Brief Note on Extremist Activities in Tripura[11]

There were two major episodes of extremist activities in the state during the period in question.[12] An ethnic riot took place in Tripura in 1980. It started in Mandai and spread to other areas of Tripura. Atrocities were committed against the Bengalis in tribal-dominated areas and against tribals in the Bengali-dominated ones. Both tribals and non-tribals were affected by the killings, arson and looting that took place in the state and many had to abandon their homes for their own safety. Lives were lost in both communities and people became homeless but the situation was brought under control within a short time.

The 1990s saw the rise of tribal extremism in the state and a Bengali backlash followed. The extremist uprising in the state that started in the 1990s had a much wider and a more long-lasting impact. Tribal extremism and its Bengali backlash brought developmental activities practically to a standstill in the interior areas of the state where most of the tribals of the state live. Educational institutions became virtually non-functional particularly in the tribal areas due to extremist depredations. The incidence of extremism is believed to have declined in the state in the very recent past though it has not died out totally.[13]

Extremism and Urbanisation among the Tribals of Tripura

(a) Need to Examine Town Level Data for the Study

Though it has to be admitted that extremism may be just one of the factors that can influence the level of urbanisation among the tribals of Tripura, we shall try to examine if the level of urbanisation among the tribals of Tripura over time bears any relationship with the incidence of extremism in the state. The overall figures on urbanisation among the tribals of Tripura as a whole that are given in Table 22.2 are not particularly revealing facts in this respect as neither the incidence of extremism nor its impact on urbanisation has been uniform in all areas of the state and aggregate figures for the level of urbanisation among tribals in the state as a whole hide more than they reveal. This question can, therefore, be best answered with respect to data on the tribal urban population of the towns of Tripura over time.

Table 22.3 gives the census data on the population and ST population residing in the urban centres of Tripura from 1961 to 2001. The Table also calculates the percentage of STs in the population of each town of the state during the period from 1961 to 2001. Table 22.4 calculates the rate of growth of the ST population of the urban centres of Tripura during the period under consideration.

Though at the level of the state as a whole, the urban ST population has increased from one decade to the next, as shown in Table 22.3, this is not true for all the towns of Tripura during the entire period of time under review. Like their total population, the ST population of Agartala, Khowai, Kailashahar, Sabroom, Amarpur, Jogendranagar, Gandhigram, Pratapgarh and Badharghat increased from one decade to the next between 1961 and 2001. In Udaipur, Belonia, Sonamura, Kamalpur, Kumarghat, Teliamura and Dharmanagar, the ST population had decreased in absolute terms in certain census years between 1961 and 2001. In Udaipur and Belonia, the tribal population went down in absolute terms in 1981 though the population of these two towns increased in 1981 compared to 1971. The same thing happened in Sonamura and Kamalpur in 1991 while the total population of both these towns increased between 1981 and 1991. In Kumarghat and Teliamura, both the total population of the towns as well as their ST population went down markedly in 2001. In Dharmanagar, the ST population went down in 2001 compared to 1991 while the population of the town increased from one decade to the next throughout the period from 1961 to 2001. Table 22.4 shows that even among the towns that registered a steady increase in their total and ST population between 1961 and 2001, the rate of growth of the ST population of Agartala and Khowai declined between 1971 and 1981, of Kailashahar between 1981 and 1991 and of Sabroom between 1991 and 2001.

(b) Methodology Adopted for Dealing with the Research Questions

Did extremism have a part to play in bringing about the changes in the number of ST urban residents or the rate of growth of the number of ST residents of the different towns of Tripura between 1961 and 2001 that have been noted in Tables 22.3 and 22.4? Instead of dealing with all the urban centres of Tripura for which the

Table 22.3: Population, ST population and ST population as per cent of population of urban areas of Tripura, 1961-2001

State/Town/ City	*Population*					*ST population*					*ST population as % of population of city/town*				
	1961	*1971*	*1981*	*1991*	*2001*	*1961*	*1971*	*1981*	*1991*	*2001*	*1961*	*1971*	*1981*	*1991*	*2001*
Agartala	54878	100264	132186	157358	189998	3346	4822	6100	8601	15616	6.10	4.81	4.61	5.47	8.22
Khowai	8782	9338	10722	12552	17689	102	221	306	532	1443	1.16	2.37	2.85	4.24	8.16
Dharmanagar	13240	16858	20806	25897	30790	47	77	182	358	232	0.35	0.46	0.87	1.38	0.75
Kailashahar	8575	10602	12938	16166	20286	53	86	290	481	845	0.62	0.81	2.24	2.98	4.17
Udaipur	8778	13924	16304	18223	21758	88	173	102	308	528	1.00	1.24	0.63	1.69	2.43
Belonia	8744	11374	12054	13274	15760	62	106	72	75	202	0.71	0.93	0.60	0.57	1.28
Sonamura			6380	8136	10074			178	77	154			2.79	0.95	1.53
Kamalpur			3688	4300	5143			158	133	429			4.28	3.09	8.34
Sabroom			3340	4766	5768			118	248	471			3.53	5.20	8.17
Amarpur			7150	8550	10861			162	253	503			2.27	2.96	4.63
Kumarghat				14641	11593				1120	578				7.65	4.99
Teliamura				27668	19605				776	118				2.80	0.60
Jogendranagar				26990	34850				34	57				0.13	0.16
Gandhigram				7538	10669				55	93				0.73	0.87
Singarbil				9160					136					1.48	
Barjala				16954					72					0.42	
Pratapgarh				13972	26837				147	275				1.05	1.02
Badharghat				35576	47713				675	1136				1.90	2.38
Ranirbazar					11003					6					0.05
Narsingarh					6820					117					1.72
Kujaban (part)					7343					236					3.21
Indranagar (part)					17807					65					0.37
Gokulnagar					9659					598					6.19
Kanchanpur					7679					965					12.57
Ambassa					6045					762					12.61
Total Tripura	102997	162360	225568	421721	545750	3698	5485	7668	14081	25429	3.59	3.38	3.40	3.34	4.66

Source: Census of India, different years.

decadal rate of growth of the tribal population can be calculated, Agartala, Udaipur and Kamalpur were chosen for attempting to answer this question. Knowledgeable people familiar with the course of extremist activities in the state and its impact on urbanisation among the tribals of Tripura, officials of the Department of Urban Affairs and of the Agartala Municipal Council, Udaipur Nagar Panchayat and Kamalpur Nagar Panchayat were interviewed to examine if extremism has affected urbanisation among the tribals of these urban areas and if so, how.

Agartala was selected for this exercise because as can be observed from Table 22.3, the city has contributed the most to urbanisation among the tribals of Tripura. Udaipur and Kamalpur were purposively selected for study because it is a well-known fact that the rural areas surrounding the former were badly affected by the ethnic riot of 1980 and of the latter by extremist activities in 1990. The reason for restricting our choice to only these two towns was that on the basis of discussions with knowledgeable people and government officers and peoples' representatives, it became obvious that while the decline in the number of ST residents of Udaipur in 1981 as compared to 1971 and Kamalpur in 1991 as compared to 1981 could be ascribed to extremist activities, this explanation was not valid for the decline in the number of STs living in other towns in some census years. Therefore, among this group of towns, the study was confined to Udaipur and Kamalpur.[14]

Some tribal families that had migrated to Agartala during the period 1961 to 2001 were also interviewed in Agartala to examine if their presence in these urban centres was due in some ways to the incidence of extremist activities in the state. The tribal families interviewed were residents of wards with a big ST population. They were purposively selected by knowledgeable people in Agartala, including a Member of the Agartala Municipal Council so as to include a cross-section of migrants from rural areas. Though the number of families interviewed was not large, the families selected represented the whole spectrum of rural-urban migrants in the urban centre and increasing the size of the sample would not have added more to our knowledge. In addition to these families, some ST families that had come to the city from rural areas and had then left Agartala again to take up residence in the rural areas of Tripura during the period in question were also interviewed to examine if their migration from the rural to the urban area and back again to the rural area had anything to do with the incidence of extremism in the state.

(c) Findings from Interviewing Knowledgeable People and Officials

As shown in Tables 22.3 and 22.4, Agartala, the capital city of the state contained most of the urban tribal population of Tripura. The tribal population of the city increased in every census year from 1961 onwards although the rate of growth of the urban ST population of Tripura slowed down in the decade 1971-81 before gathering momentum again in 1981-91 and 1991-2001. According to the knowledgeable people and the officials interviewed the slowing down of the rate of growth of the ST urban population of Tripura in the decade 1971-81 had some connection with the ethnic riot that erupted in the state in 1980. Though there were a few instances of tribal families of Agartala moving out of the city and taking shelter in tribal villages near Teliamura temporarily, there was no mass scale out-migration of tribals from the city as a result of the ethnic riot even though a fear psychosis was created and the tribals of the city tended to move into the tribal-dominated areas of the city like Banamalipur and Krishnanagar as they felt safer there. However, the ethnic riot slowed down the stream of migration of tribals into Agartala from the villages to take advantage of the facilities and amenities available there for some years and both these tendencies led to a slowing down of the rate of growth of the tribal population of Agartala in 1971-81.[15] The wave of extremism that swept through Tripura from the 1990s onwards had a much more marked and lasting impact on the urban presence of tribals in Agartala. Extremist activities perpetrated by both tribal and Bengali extremists caused many tribals to move to the city to escape extortions, arson, looting and threat to life in villages. In some cases, excesses by the CRPF and the police personnel during their combing operations to flush out tribal extremists from the areas where they held sway also caused some tribal migration to the city. As it was no longer safe for tribals to commute to and from Agartala for work from nearby villages because Bengali extremists could attack them when they passed through Bengali settlements, some tribals who were commuters to Agartala from their villages found it safer to settle down in the city. Educational institutions in tribal areas had become practically non-functional from the 1990s as school teachers who were mostly Bengalis were afraid to travel to their place of work in tribal villages for fear of being abducted or killed by the extremists. As schools in many tribal areas practically closed down as a consequence of extremist activities, tribal students had to move to Agartala to ensure that they could attend classes regularly without any disruption. Some tribal students also migrated to Agartala because young villagers were extremely vulnerable in their villages. Even if they did not subscribe to the extremist ideology, they were in constant danger of being forcibly recruited by extremists and were also in danger of being picked up by the police or by the para-military forces fighting extremism and tortured on the suspicion that they were extremists or were aiding or abetting them. Parents of many tribal children also moved to Agartala to ensure that the education of their wards would not be disrupted by extremism. Political activists belonging to the ruling party were hounded out of their villages by extremists and were forced to seek shelter in Agartala and the government rehabilitated the leaders among the surrendered extremists in the capital city. All this gave a fillip to the growth of tribal population in Agartala from 1990 onwards.

As Table 22.3 shows that the ST population of Udaipur went down from 173 in 1971 to 102 in 1981, registering a 41.04 per cent decrease between 1971 and 1981 as shown in Table 22.4 although the population of the town increased between 1971 and 1981 and also throughout the period from 1961 to 2001. According to informed sources, the decline in the ST population of the town, which, in any case, always constituted a small proportion of the total population of the town as shown in Table 22.3, was due to the extremist activities let loose by the ethnic riots that swept the state in 1980. The villages surrounding Udaipur like Maharani and Hadra were badly affected by the riot and this made the tribals of Udaipur very nervous as they were in a minority in the town. Rajnagar village, situated across the Gumti river from Udaipur, had a big tribal population. Bengali extremists attacked the tribals of Rajnagar and tribal homes were torched in the village. This created a fear psychosis in the minds of the tribal residents of the town who fled to the interior villages. Many of the tribal government employees sought transfers in safer areas and left the town in the wake of the ethnic riots in 1980, lowering the number

Table 22.4: Rate of growth of ST population of towns/city, Tripura (1941-71 to 1991-2001)

State/Town/City	*Rate of growth of ST population of town/city*			
	1961-1971	*1971-1981*	*1981-1991*	*1991-2001*
Agartala	44.11	26.5	41	81.56
Khowai	116.67	38.46	73.86	171.24
Dharmanagar	63.83	136.36	96.7	–35.2
Kailashahar	62.26	237.21	65.86	75.68
Udaipur	96.59	–41.04	201.96	71.43
Belonia	70.97	–32.08	4.17	169.33
Sonamura			–56.74	100
Kamalpur			–15.82	222.56
Sabroom			110.17	89.92
Amarpur			56.17	98.81
Kumarghat				-48.39
Teliamura				-84.79
Jogendranagar				67.65
Gandhigram				69.09
Singarbil				
Barjala				
Pratapgarh				87.07
Badharghat				68.3
Ranirbazar				
Narsingarh				
Kujaban (part)				
Indranagar (part)				
Gokulnagar				
Kanchanpur				
Ambassa				

Source: Table 22.3.

of tribals in the town in 1981 that is observed in the census figures. According to the informants, after the situation returned to normal in the state and also around Udaipur, many of the tribals who had left the town in a panic returned to the town. Since the 1990s, some tribals living in nearby villages also migrated to the town in order to avail of better educational opportunities available there as the educational system of the tribal areas had broken down due to extremist activities in the state in general and around Udaipur in particular. In addition to this, with the development of the town, its administrative and other functions increased and this led to the growth of the ST population of the town as tribals formed a considerable portion of the government employees posted in Udaipur. The combined effect of all these factors was to increase the tribal population of Udaipur from 1990 onwards.

Though the population of Kamalpur recorded an increase during every census year from 1981 onwards when Kamalpur became a town for the first time according to the census definition, the ST population of the town went down from 158 in 1981 to 133 in 1991. STs formed 4.28 per cent of the population of the town in 1981 but this percentage dropped to 3.09 in 1991 (Table 22.3). Most of the tribal residents of Kamalpur were government servants who came from the surrounding villages and lived in rented accommodation in the town. In the early 1990s when extremist activities in Tripura had reached a peak, some of these government servants left the town and moved back to their native villages near the town where they felt relatively safe since tribals constituted a majority in these villages. The STs residing in Kamalpur expected a communal backlash against them in the town as a result of the atrocities that were perpetrated against the Bengalis of Srirampur village situated near the town by tribal extremists since they formed a minuscule percentage of the town population and felt vulnerable there. When extremist activities became less frequent in Tripura and a semblance of normalcy was restored in the state, many of the tribals of the town who had moved out of Kamalpur returned to the town though a handful of them also migrated to Agartala and Khowai. The tribal population of Kamalpur increased quite sharply in 2001 because some tribal government servants were transferred to the town and also because better educational facilities available in the town acted as a magnet, drawing more tribals into the town from the surrounding villages.

(d) Findings from the Field Study in Agartala

According to the knowledgeable people who were interviewed, among the new rural to urban ST migrants to Agartala from the rural areas of the state are five types of people—students, rickshaw pullers, employees, political activists and surrendered extremists. Altogether, 13 sample individuals or households were purposively selected for the study to capture the situation of typical tribal migrants to Agartala from the rural areas of the state. The sample consisted of 3 students, 6 employees, 1 rickshaw puller, 2 political activists and 1 surrendered extremist who had migrated to Agartala after 1990. Table 22.6A summarises the data obtained on the place of origin and the socio-economic conditions of these migrants, the

Table 22.5: Contribution of towns/city to urbanisation among ST population in Tripura (1961-2001)

Town/City	*Contribution of the town/city to urbanisation among STs*				
	1961	*1971*	*1981*	*1991*	*2001*
Agartala	0.93	1.06	1.04	1.01	1.57
Khowai	0.03	0.05	0.05	0.06	0.15
Dharmanagar	0.01	0.02	0.03	0.04	0.02
Kailashahar	0.01	0.02	0.05	0.06	0.09
Udaipur	0.02	0.04	0.02	0.04	0.05
Belonia	0.02	0.02	0.01	0.01	0.02
Sonamura			0.03	0.01	0.02
Kamalpur			0.03	0.02	0.04
Sabroom			0.02	0.03	0.05
Amarpur			0.03	0.03	0.05
Kumarghat				0.13	0.06
Teliamura				0.09	0.01
Jogendranagar					0.01
Gandhigram				0.01	0.01
Singarbil				0.02	
Barjala				0.01	
Pratapgarh				0.02	0.03
Badharghat				0.08	0.11
Ranirbazar					
Narsinggarh					0.01
Kunjaban (part)					0.02
Indranagar (part)					0.01
Gokulnagar					0.06
Kanchanpur					0.1
Ambassa					0.08
Tripura	1.03	1.21	1.31	1.65	2.56

Source: Tables 22.2 and 22.3.

reasons for their migration, and their future plans regarding their place of stay. Out of them, 3 students, 5 employees, 2 political activists and the surrendered extremist or 11 out of the 13 respondents, constituting 84.62 per cent of the total sample, had migrated to Agartala because of extremism-related reasons. The students had become residents of Agartala because the educational system of the villages they came from had become virtually non-existent due to extremism and they considered the educational institutions in Agartala to be better. They were also of the opinion that studying in Agartala was a better option because private tutors were available in the city whereas none of the school teachers stayed in the village and returned to Agartala as soon as their classes were over because of the extremist terror. Five of the employees had decided to settle in the city for the education of their children even at the cost of commuting to their places of work everyday because the school system in the tribal villages of the state existed only in name due to extremism. The political activists of the CPI(M) were forced to move out of their village by the extremists and settled down in Agartala under duress. The surrendered extremist who was interviewed was an important leader of an extremist outfit. The Government of Tripura rehabilitated him in the capital city and provided him with security coverage, probably because relatively speaking it was easy to keep him under surveillance in the city and also to ensure that he was not a victim of revenge killing.[16] Table 22.6B summarises the details about 2 respondents who had fled from their village to escape from the extremists and had lived in Agartala from 1990 to 2006. They had returned to their village subsequently after the situation has improved somewhat with the decline of extremism in the state and were interviewed in the Hezamara Block headquarters.

(e) Some Observations and Questions Regarding Extremism-related Urbanisation among the Tribals of Tripura Emerging from the Study

- It is apparent from the field study that the relatively better off sections of people who lived near the urban centres could migrate to Agartala when they were adversely affected by extremism.[17] This seems to be due to the fact that they had better chances of bearing the costs of relocating themselves in new surroundings, had a kin group in the urban areas on whom they could depend and could take the risk of settling down in a new area because of the political and economic clout they wielded.
- STs reacted differently to extremism at different points of time. As an aftermath of the 1980 ethnic riot, some tribals living in the urban centres that were studied moved out of the towns temporarily, though not in large numbers, while extremism in the 1990s led to the growth of urbanisation among the tribals. The difference may be ascribed to the fact that the ethnic riot was a sporadic incident confined only to certain rural areas of the state and was quickly snuffed out. It did not lead to a long-

lasting disruption of normal life in the state and its rural areas. Though it led to a fear psychosis among the ST urban dwellers, it did not lead to a mass-scale and permanent movement of STs from urban to rural areas or a massive and permanent influx of tribals from villages to the towns. The extremist problem that began in the state in the 1990s was a long-drawn out affair that is not fully over as yet. It has had a wide-ranging effect practically throughout the state. Villages including tribal villages have been vulnerable and the tribals of the state have been the victims of tribal and Bengali extremism. Tribals have also had to suffer on account of excesses committed by the police and the paramilitary forces in their drive against tribal extremists as at times they have treated all tribal people as potential extremists or at least, as their collaborators. Since the urban areas have not suffered from extremist attacks and the educational and health care institutions have not come to a standstill in them as a result of extremist activities, the tribals who are in a relatively advantageous position have left the villages and have settled down in the comparative safety of the towns in the wake of extremist activities that have racked the state since the 1990s.

Future of Extremism-related Urbanisation among the Tribals of Tripura

It is widely believed that extremism is on the wane in Tripura and the heyday of extremism is over in the state. How is this development likely to impact extremism-related urbanisation among the tribals of the state? One possible outcome is that urbanisation among the tribals of the state will decline as there may be an exodus of the urban tribals who had left their village homes under the threat of extremist depredations to the rural areas they came from once the incidence of extremism declines. Secondly, a decline in urbanisation among the tribals of Tripura may be noticed as the incidence of extremism-induced migration of tribals to the urban areas of the state in search of safety and security may gradually fall when there is a gradual return to normalcy in the state.[18] However, it is equally possible that though a part of the tribal migration to urban areas was induced by extremism, once the tribal migrants who were driven to urban areas by extremist depredations have stayed in urban areas for a certain length of time and have become used to living in the city and enjoying the facilities and the advantages it offers, they will not think of returning to the villages they came from even when conditions become normal in the state. Even if the first generation extremism-induced tribals decide to go back to the villages of their origin, it is quite likely that the children of these migrants who have very few links with and often no memories of their parental villages and are often city born and bred will not take part in the exodus. Besides, with the restoration of normalcy in the state, the prospects of development of some interior areas with a large tribal population into urban centres may rise. For example, towns like Kanchanpur and Ambassa, the new census towns of 2001 in Dhalai district, which is tribal dominated (54.03% of its population was tribal in 2001), where the percentage of tribals in the population was large compared to the rest of the towns of the state in 2001, may develop into full-fledged statutory towns in the 2011 Census with a burgeoning tribal population. Again, Khumulung, the headquarters of the Tripura Tribal Areas Autonomous District Council, can also develop into a town in the 2011 census. The growth of towns that have a relatively large tribal population that are located in tribal majority areas may lead to further urbanisation among the tribals of Tripura in future. *In situ* urbanisation of tribals can also take place in other tribal-dominated areas of the state and along with it, tribals from the surrounding tribal villages can flock to these new towns to take advantage of the facilities and amenities offered by them and thereby increase the level of urbanisation in the state.[19] Statutory towns like Sabroom, Khowai, Kamalpur, Kumarghat, Amarpur, Kailashahar and the capital city of Agartala that had a relatively large percentage of Scheduled Tribe population as per the 2001 Census as shown in Table 22.3 may experience more growth with the demise of extremism and less diversion of state funds for the maintenance of law and order in the state. Urban development in these towns may induce a further dose of tribal migration into these urban centres so that urbanisation among the tribals of Tripura may increase in future.[20]

Whether increased or decreased presence of tribals will prevail in future in the urban centres of Tripura as a result of the decline in extremism in the state is a matter of conjecture because since the easing of extremist activities in the state, there have been instances of both types. For example, as can be seen from Tables 22.6A and 22.6B, out of the 4 tribal party members of the CPI(M) in the sample who had to flee their homes in villages and seek safety in Agartala, 2 have stayed back in Agartala. One respondent continues to live in Agartala because her son goes to school there and commutes to the Block Headquarters everyday. The other has built a house in Agartala and will continue to live in the city because he prefers to live there now. On the other side of the scale are instances of extremism-affected respondents who want to return to their villages or have already returned to their native villages. Two of the political activists interviewed who had been hounded out of their village by extremists and had taken shelter in Agartala have returned to their village and plan to stay there to continue with their political work but interestingly enough, the sons of one of the respondents have stayed back in the city and do not intend to return to their native village. While all the students in the sample who came to study in Agartala because the educational system in the tribal villages had broken down completely as a result of extremist activities want to stay on in Agartala after they finish their education, all the parents who migrated to Agartala to ensure that their wards could get good schooling facilities in a terror-free atmosphere in the city and endured quite a lot of hardship in the process want to return to their villages after retirement even though they feel that their children may not emulate them and become villagers.[21] The surrendered extremist expressed his preference for staying on in revenge killing by his former accomplices if he returned to his Agartala permanently probably because he was afraid of village. The probability of getting the best possible rehabilitation package and of being successful if he launches a fresh political career if he is based close to the seat of power in the capital city has been a factor in his decision-making.

In any case, extremism-induced migration is just one of the causes of urbanisation among the tribals of the state. Migration to urban areas takes place among tribals for education and employment opportunities offered in towns and with rising aspirations, filling up the tribal quota in jobs and more affirmative action being taken to improve the social and economic conditions of the tribals of the state, more rather than less urbanisation among the tribals of Tripura is likely to occur in future.[22]

Table 22.6A: ST migrants who have come to Agartala after 1990

Respondent	*Migrated to Agartala from*	*Socio-economic particulars about respondent or his/her family*	*Reasons for migrating from village*	*Preferred place of stay in future*
1	Jolaibari village	Respondent and his wife work in the Education Department, Government of Tripura. Respondent is posted in Lembucherra and his wife is posted in Esrai. Both have to commute to work from Agartala. Respondent lives in own house in Agartala and has agricultural land and rubber garden in native village. Father is a prosperous farmer in native village.	For the education of the children partly because extremists have played havoc with the educational system in the villages of Tripura.	Both the husband and the wife would like to go back to their native village when they retire but they are not sure that their children would like to go back to the village.
2	Madhabbari village	Respondent works in the Education Department and is posted in Urmai High School. His wife works in the PWD and is posted in Agartala. Respondent has to spend a lot of time in commuting to and from work everyday. He lives in his own house in Agartala.	For the education of the children partly because extremists have played havoc with the educational system in the villages of Tripura.	The couple would like to return to their village when both of them retire but the children may want to stay on in Agartala.
3	Village near Teliamura	Respondent employed in a private school in Agartala. Has agricultural land in the village which he gets cultivated by bargadars.	For the education of the children partly because extremists have played havoc with the educational system in the villages of Tripura.	Wants to return to the village after retirement.
4	Village near Teliamura	Respondent works in a government school in Golaghati. Has to spend two hours everyday in travelling to the school where he works. Lives in rented accommodation in Agartala.	For the education of the children partly because extremists have played havoc with the educational system in the villages of Tripura.	Would like to return to native village after retirement.

5	Village in North Tripura District	Respondent is Executive Engineer in PWD is posted in Agartala at present. Studied in North East India Institute of Science and Technology. Has built own house in new tribal neighbourhood in Agartala. Wife nursing tutor in G.B. Hospital in Agartala. Father prosperous farmer in native village.	Has been posted in Agartala.	Plans to go back to village after retirement but feels that his young children who were born in Agartala may not want to stay in the village.
6	Village near Champaknagar in West Tripura District	Respondent is Senior Assistant to Minister of Fisheries, Government of Tripura Lives in a Government Quarters Complex in Agartala. His children study in Agartala. He has agricultural land in his native village which he has given out to sharecroppers.	Respondent used to commute to work in Agartala from his native village everyday by bus In 1990, the bus he missed while coming to work was attacked by Bengali extremists near Teliamura. All the tribals who were in the bus were forced to get off and were beaten up. In the evening the respondent returned to his village along with other tribal government employees living in or near his village in a hired taxi with a police escort and he decided to shift his residence to Agartala to avoid taking the risk of travelling through areas where Bengali terrorists held sway. This incident shocked the respondent who decided to move to Agartala to avoid the risky journey to and from the village everyday.	Respondent wants to settle down in his village after retirement but he is not sure whether his children would like to go back to the village with him.

(Contd.)

Respondent	Migrated to Agartala from	Socio-economic particulars about respondent or his/her family	Reasons for migrating from village	Preferred place of stay in future
7	Hezamara Block Headquarters	Respondent is the Vice Chairperson of Hezamara Block Panchayat and is a local leader of the CPI(M) has a house in Hezamara and has built a house in Agartala. Commutes from Agartala daily for her official and political work. One of her sons went to college in Bangalore and is now preparing to go abroad for a degree in Management. Her other son is in school in Agartala.	Respondent was forced to leave her home in Hezamara by extrermists in the 1990s.	Respondent has decided to stay on in Agartala for her son's education.
8	Hezamara Block Headquarters	Respondent is Extension Officer of Hezamara Block Panchayat. Has built his own house in Agartala and commutes to work everyday. Parents live in Hezamara.	Respondent was forced to leave his home by the extremists in the 1990s.	Respondent wants to stay on in the city as he has grown used to living in Agartala.
9	Lembucherra village	Respondent was a landless agricultural labourer in the village. He works as a rickshaw-puller in Agartala. He lives in rented accommodation in the city with his whole family.	Respondent could not make both ends meet in village. He also migrated to give better educational opportunities to his children in the city.	Respondent wants to return to his village when he becomes old.

10	Village near Teliamura	Respondent is a surrendered extremist leader. He lines in a government officers' residential complex in Agartala and the government provides him with security guards 24 hours a day. His wife has got training in sewing and tailoring as a part of the rehabilitation package and his children are studying in a missionary school in the city.	Did not divulge but according to knowledgeable people, surrendered extremists of high rank are given rehabilitation in Agartala for reasons of their safety and for the relative ease with which their activities can be kept track of in the city. The surrendered extremist leaders also prefer to live in the city because it is the focii of power and bargaining with the powers that be.	Wants to stay on in Agartala.
11	Village near Agartala	Respondent is a college student. Studied in school in Agartala also. Father prosperous farmer in village. Stays in shared rented accommodation with other tribal students. Spends long holidays in village.	Educational facilities better in Agartala.	Wants to stay on in Agartala.
12	Village near Jirania	Respondent is a school student. Stays in shared rented accommodation with other tribal students. Father retired government pensioner and has agricultural land. Spends long holidays in village.	School in Agartala is of a better quality. Private tuition available in city whereas in the village, teachers commute from the city and do not stay in village after school hours and cannot give tuitions.	Would like to stay on in Agartala provided he can get a job.
13	Village near Mandai	Respondent studies in an open school. Stays in Agartala with brother and shares rented accommodation with other tribal students. Spends long holidays in village. Father prosperous farmer in village.	Educational facilities better in Agartala. Private tutors available.	Wants to stay on in Agartala even when his education is over.

Source: Field Survey.

Table 22.6B: ST respondents who have moved from Agartala to rural areas

Respon-dent	*Migrated to Agartala from*	*Socio-economic particulars about respondent or his/her family*	*Reasons for migrating to and from Agartala*	*Preferred place of stay in future*
1	Hezamara Block headquarters	Respondent is Chairperson of Hezamara Block Panchayat. Is a local leader of the CPI(M) party in Hezamara. Has his own house in Hezamara and lived in Agartala as a tenant.	Respondent had to leave Hezamara due to extremist threat in the 1990s. He was forced to live in rented accommodation in Agartala till 2007 and commuted to Agartala for work and organizational work of the party in Hezamara during this time and never spent the night at Hezamara for fear of being kidnapped by the extremists. Now that conditions have become normal in the Block, he has returned to his native village.	Wants to stay in Hezamara in future but his sons are still living in Agartala.
2	Hezamara Block headquarters	Respondent is an elected member of the Hezamara Block Panchayat. He is a member of the CPI(M) party.	He was abducted by the extremists from Hezamara in 1990, but he escaped from their clutches and went back to Hezamara. He was abducted by extremists again and was taken to Bangladesh by them. He was freed by them on payment of ransom by his family. After he was released by the extremists, he decided to move to Agartala. Now that conditions have returned to normal in the Block, he has returned to Hezamara.	He wants to stay in Hezamara.

Source: Field Survey.

REFERENCES

Government of India, Census Reports of Tripura of different years.

G. Bhattacharyya, *Refugee Rehabilitation and its Impact on Tripura's Economy*, Guwahati: Omson's Publication, 1988.

M. Das Gupta, 'Shifting cultivators and extremism in Tripura', *Social Scientist*, No. 398-399, Vol. 34, No. 7-8, July-August 2006.

________, *Economic Impact of Raids on the Shifting Cultivators of Tripura*, Kolkata: The Asiatic Society, 2008.

W.W. Hunter, *A Statistical Account of Bengal*, Vol. VI, Delhi: D.K. Publishing House, 1973 (Reprint edition).

NOTES

1. Edwin S. Mills and Charles M. Becker, *Studies in Indian Urban Development*, Published for the World Bank, New York, Oxford and London: Oxford University Press, 1986, Chapter 2.
2. The level of urbanisation among tribals will rise with the inclusion of new areas with a tribal population within the boundaries of existing towns or the growth of new towns in areas that have a tribal population provided that tribals do not leave these areas when they become urban.
3. Under normal circumstances, tribals may migrate to urban areas of the state concerned from other countries, other states or the rural areas of the state for education and jobs and to avail of the other facilities that are available there. City lights may also attract tribal migrants to urban areas.
4. The genesis, causes and the history of extremism in the state are not dealt with in this paper.
5. Mizoram did not become a separate entity till the 1971 census, there was no census in Assam in 1981, census data for Manipur excluded three districts in 2001.
6. In Mizoram on the other hand, researchers have dealt with the role of regrouped villages to end insurgency and extremist activities in the state in the growth of urbanisation in the state.
7. The refugees who came to Tripura in 1941 as a result of the Ampura riots near Dhaka went back to British India after normalcy was restored or relocated themselves in Calcutta if they were affluent but the refugees who came to Tripura in the wake of the communal riots immediately preceding and following the partition of the country did not return to their homes in East Pakistan and many of them chose to stay in Agartala. The town alone harboured 19,286 or nearly 20 per cent of the 1,01,200 displaced persons recorded in

Tripura in the 1951 Census. The refugees preferred to stay in Agartala because many of them belonged to non-agricultural classes and bought property in the town with the cash they could bring with them. Agartala was a preferred place of residence for many refugees because it offered them possibilities of earning a living. It was possible for them to secure a livelihood in the town by taking up petty trades or becoming casual labourers. It was also possible for them to start petty businesses in the town or to get jobs in different government departments. The displaced persons also preferred to live in Agartala because living in the town made it easier for them to get rehabilitation assistance provided by the government, as Agartala was the state capital (Bhattacharyya, 1988:23).

8. Unlike the Bengalis, very few tribals left East Pakistan and entered Tripura during this period and the few tribals who did leave East Pakistan and migrate to Tripura settled down in the villages and not in Agartala, thus tilting the demographic balance of the town in favour of the non-tribals.
9. From the year 1961 onwards, the words 'STs' and 'tribals' are used synonymously in this paper.
10. The Scheduled Tribes of Tripura were notified before the 1961 Census.
11. To repeat, the genesis and causes of extremism in the state are not discussed in this paper.
12. Apart from these two major episodes of extremism in the state, Tripura has been affected by extremist activities in the Chittagong Hill Tracts of Bangladesh that made Chakma refugees take shelter in the state. Extremist activities directed against the Riangs in Mizoram led to Riangs taking refuge in Tripura but these out-of-Tripura acts of extremism did not lead to the growth of tribal urban population in the state as the tribals taking shelter in Tripura settled in the rural areas of the state or were accommodated in refugee camps located in the rural areas of the state. Had their numbers been sufficiently high, the tribal population of Tripura would have increased substantially and brought down the level of urbanisation among the tribals in the state but this was not the case.
13. Since the early 1990s as a safety measure against possible extremist attacks, all north bound civilian vehicles in Tripura on the National Highway linking Tripura with the rest of India had to travel in a convoy with armed CRPF personnel travelling in jeeps and trucks escorting them up to Kumarghat. Only daytime movement of civilian vehicles was allowed on the Assam-Agartala road. As a result of the easing of the situation, there is a talk of withdrawing armed escorts for civilian vehicles travelling on the National Highway.
14. The number of tribal people living in Belonia declined in 1981 because many ST government servants living in the town were transferred to other places. The decline in the number of tribals living

in Sonamura in 1991 was due to the transfer of ST government servants from the town. In Kumarghat and Teliamura both the population and the ST population declined in 2001 because the area of these towns decreased in 2001. There was a decline in the number of STs living in Dharmanagar in 2001 compared to 1991 because a significant proportion of the tribal government servants bought land outside the town, built their own houses there and left Dharmanagar.

15. Temporary refugee camps for riot-affected tribals were set up in Agartala but they were disbanded within a short time and the tribals who had been given shelter in the camps returned to their villages. So, the presence of tribal refugees in Agartala did not succeed in reversing the decline in the rate of growth of the tribal population in Agartala that is observed in Table 22.3 for the period 1971-1981.
16. Although the respondent granted an interview, he did not provide any information about what had prompted him to move to Agartala from his native village. The information about him was gathered from his neighbours and other tribals in the government housing complex where he lived.
17. For example, the Jhumia tribals of Tripura, one of the most economically and socially backward groups of people in Tripura, who were exposed to grave extremist threats and had to flee their hamlets in the interior hills of the state camped in the open on the Assam Agartala highway for safety. The government rehabilitated these families in a number of regrouping villages located in forest areas near roads and police stations (Das Gupta, 2006). The rank and file elements among the surrendered tribal extremists who were mostly recruited from poor families and had no training or skills, were housed in heavily guarded camps in rural areas in interior of the state and were given vocational education and training for their rehabilitation (Das Gupta, 2008).
18. Not only that, with the return of normalcy in the state, there will gradually be fewer and fewer surrendered extremist leaders who were rehabilitated in urban centres of the state and mainly in Agartala city in the past. However, their numbers are so limited that it may not have a significant impact on urbanisation among the tribals of Tripura.
19. However, there is always a possibility that when an area where tribals form a sizeable portion of the population develops into a town, a large section of its native tribal population will leave the area and retreat into interior areas away from the town.
20. However, though the abatement of extremism can increase the number of urban tribals, if extremism led to mass-scale murder of tribals, the total tribal population also increases when extremism is on the wane by reducing the death rate among the tribals and the

impact of the combined effect of a rise in the number of urban tribals and an increase in the number of tribals cannot be predicted. But the decrease in the death rate among tribals as a result of the impact of extremism among them could not have been very high and by and large, it will have a negligible effect on the level of urbanisation among the tribals of Tripura.

21. Tribal migrants to the city as a result of extremist depredation belonged to an older age group than the student migrants. They also maintained a close relationship with their families in the village and had fixed assets there. As older people and first generation migrants, they felt less at home in the city than the students who do not wish to return to the village. Probably because of their age also, they were less enamoured of the city lights than the tribal students and could think of returning to their villages after retirement.
22. A factor that may stem the tide of urbanisation among the tribals of Tripura is the development of growth centres in the rural areas of the state. Rural growth centres are being set up in developed willages of the state as nodal centres for facilitating the development of their surrounding areas. It is hoped that these centres will become focal points of development in the future. The growth centres have good infrasturcural facilities and provide services and marketing facilities for local products for the surrounding rural areas. The rural growth centres have planned markets, community halls, motor stands, good roads and communication facilities including telecommunication facilities, banks, post offices, agricultural service centres, health and educational facilities. In 2004-05, funds were sanctioned for developing 17 growth centres in different parts of the state. 13 of them are already functioning. More rural growth centres have been sanctioned in 2005-06 and 2006-07. An electrician from Hezamara Block who had to travel to Agartala city to get work was interviewed in the Hezamara Rural Growth Centre where he has a shop in the shopping complex now. He said with the coming up of the growth centre, he did not need to go to the city as he could get enough work there itself. The growth centres that have come up near Khowai at Asharambari and Ampura have also reduced the flow of ST migrants from nearby villages to the town. Government's scheme of giving ownership rights over rubber gardens to STs has also had the same effect according to knowledgeable people interviewed in Khowai.

23

Extremism: Ideology and North East India Phenomenon

Kshireswar Borah

(I)

Today, one can form or organise a terrorist group over night. The term 'terrorist' and 'extremist' are not same or synonymous. Without weapon 'terrorists' have no meaning, but an 'extremist' may also be without arms like Gandhian non-violent extremist. Of course, armed struggle is also one of the means to attain an end out of thousand and one means and methods of movement subject to some exceptions or exemptions. International Humanitarian laws have upheld such armed conflict between and among countries. The separatist movement from autonomy to sovereignty, insurgency to belligerency, rebellion to freedom fighting has adopted such violent tool for their destiny. Someone is freedom fighter while someone else is a terrorist. Scholars have categorically opined that national liberation movement is some- what different from the terrorist led one. Now-a-days, the secessionist or liberation movements have adopted violent method to fight against colonial legacy and foreign subjugation.

(II)

If we search for a universally accepted definition of the term 'terrorism' one has to observe only one-sided, subjective and prejudicial reflection. Academicians and scholars of different fields of the world have opined terrorism as follows:

Victoria Schofield viewed as many as 109 variations in the terrorism definition and his own definition is "unlawful acts of violence committed in an attempt to overthrow a government and a system of government which rules by intimidation."[1]

J.N. Sexena, the Indian expert is cited recurrently, "Legally speaking terrorism focused upon the effect, while self-determination deals with casual relationship. While terrorism is a human wrong, self-determination is arguably a human right."[2]

Major General Asfor Karim states, "Guerillas unlike terrorists, do not attack the common people, as popular support is important to them."[3] He makes a classification of six kinds of insurgencies—secessionist, revolutionary, restorational, reactionary, conservative and reformist. According to Karim, the South Asian insurgencies are mostly secessionist type from regional autonomy to total independence.

The post-World War Western definition of terrorism is put forward by Paul Wilkinson covering not less than a hundred terrorism publicists. The leading authority of contemporary terrorism classified the political terrorism as follows: (1) war terror, (2) suppressive terror, (3) revolutionary terror, and (4) Sub-revolutionary terror.[4]

(III)

The maxim could have been slightly altered in the context of the emerging Narco-terrorism, Bio-chemical terrorism, Nuclear terrorism and so forth. Terrorism by now encompasses the Catholic terrorism in nothern Ireland, Islamic terrorism of Taliban's in Afghanistan, Sleepers Falung Gong of China, Hindu and Islamic terrorism in India, Buddhist terrorism in Sri Lanka and above all state terrorism, proxy war, assassinations, massacres committed by the underworld gangs such as CIA[5], ISI and DGFI of Bangladesh as the state level agencies.

The UN legal regime on terror free world has began since 1929. Out of these the major conventions on offences committed are Board Aircraft (Tokyo, 1963), unlawful seizure of Aircraft (Hague, 1970), Unlawful Acts against the safety of the Civil Aviation (Montreal, 1971) crimes against internally protected persons includiag diplomatic Agents (1973), taking of Hostage (UN, 1973),

Maritime Navigation (1988), Safety of fixed platforms (1988), Plastic Explosive (1991), Tourist Bombing (1997), Financing of Terrorism (1999) and Kathmandu Regional Convention on terrorism (1987).[6]

These 12 treaties have been adopted by the community and two more major initiatives under active consideration of UN lying are Global convention against Terrorism and Nuclear Terrorism. Proposals about bringing terrorism and drug trafficking within the scope of International Criminal Court (ICC) set-up in 2002 are on the record.

The International Convention for Suppression of Terrorist Bombing (15 December, 1997) and Suppression of the Financing of Terrorism (9 December, 1999) adopted by UN on the basis of 12 discussed treaties are significant developments. The United Nations Security Council (UNSC) resolution 1267 (1999) had given teeth to demand hand over Osama-bin-Laden to US for 11/9 WTC terror, 20LeT terrorists for 26/11 Mumbai Carnage to India.

Similarly, the Resolution 1373 (2001) of UNSC also paved the way to publicise state obligation against financing, planning, preparation or support for terrorist acts. The asylum-seekers would not have participated in such activities as per the said resolution. In order to support national liberation movement, resolution 2548 (11 December, 1969) adopted by UN General Assembly against terrorist crimes on mercenaries. The onus of resolutions by General Assembly 2625 (24 October, 1970), 2734 (16 December, 1970), 3103 (12 December, 1973), and 579 (1985) get teeth of *modus operandi* from the principles of the aforesaid treaties and conventions.

(IV)

As thrust area of this chapter is North East India, the most vulnerable and restive region of India and the world, let us now assess extremism in the above line. North East India occupies 8 per cent of India's total geographical area and 4 per cent of total population. Until North East Areas (Reorganisation) Act, 1971 seven States such as Assam, Meghalaya, Manipur, Tripura, Mizoram, Nagaland and Arunachal Pradesh stood under the same umbrella. Sikkim, the Himalayan kingdom integrated to India in 1975 also now incorporated under North Eastern Council (NEC).

Meghalaya became a tribal state in 1969 (42nd Constitutional Amendment) and elevated to separate full-fledged state by the 1971 Act. Nagaland became a Union territory in 1956 and declared statehood in 1963 after boycott of the 1952 General Election by Naga National Council (NNC). The NNC believes that they have been deceived by the 'Hyderi Agreement' which deprived them to pursue the Naga customary laws in civil and criminal justice. As a protest they declared complete independence on 14 August, 1947[7] just before a day of free India.

The 'Shillong Accord' was signed in 1975 without the presence of Phizo, Khaplang and Issac Muiva and resulted in formation of National Socialist Council of Nagaland (NSCN) in 1980 which adopted the violent path for their independence. In 1988, NSCN was split into two separate groups NSCN(K) and NSCN(IM) for their internal differentiation between the duo. The NSCN(IM) declared ceasefire in 1997.

After much fratricidal bloodshed both these factions reconciled in 2007 and attended the 'peace summit' (4th) with the Government of India (GoI) for sovereign Nagaland or greater Nagalim.

Next to Nagaland, Manipur gave birth the people's Liberation Army (PLA) in 1978 adopting the violent way for complete independence. Prior to annexation on 15 October, 1949 with India Manipur was an independent Princely state ruled by Maharaja. Their boundary had extended up to Kabaw Valley of Myanmar. The 1950 aborted movement popularly known as 'Pan-Mongoloid Movement' is an attempt to unite the Mongoloid ethnic race of NE India for a sovereign nation of the Mongoloid people.[8] After PLA almost a dozen of insurgent outfits emerged with the demand of regional autonomy to secession or total independence and have been operating in the state. The noted among them are Revolutionary People's Front (RPF), United Liberation Front (UNLF) in 1986, People's Revolution Party of Kangleipak (PREPAK) a valley based Meitei insurgent group who claimed an independent state embracing geographically all NE states except western part of Assam and a part of Tripura. Kangleipak Communist Party (KCP), Hmar People's Convention (HPC), Kuki National Organization (KNO), Kuki National Army (KNA) are other outfits of Manipur. The KNA demanded autonomous state near Myanmar for Kukis while other claimed 'Kuki-homeland' covering Ukhrul, Senapati, Imphal and Kuki dominated areas of

Nagaland, Assam and Manipur with 22.32 sq.km geographical area having nine districts and thirty three recognized Scheduled Tribes. The five hill districts Chandel, Churachandpur, Tamenglong, Senapati and Ukhrul dominated by tribal and the state land laws prohibited Meitei (the largest community) and non-tribal to buy land and settle in the hills. The four valley districts (2.23 sq.km.)—Imphal East, Imphal West, Bishnupur and Thoubal are a mixture of more or less all tribe representatives.[9]

As a result of British fallacious policy the hill area was administered by British political agent and valley was allowed to rule by Meitei king. British also rehabilitated Kuki before the Naga with an intention to fight against Burmese, Lushai and Naga tribes. Manipur had first experience of Hmar-Kuki conflict (1959-60) for regrouping the hill tribes as 'Kuki' or 'Naga'. Since then the last decade erupted with Naga-Kuki, Kuki-Paite, Kuki-Meitei and Kuki-Tamil intra-community conflict.[10]

Assam the doorway for the NE region witnessed emergence of militant group since 7 April, 1979 at the twilight of foreigners movement which was concluded on 15 August, 1985 with an Accord with the Government. Since then United Liberation Front of Asom (ULFA) has been fighting against the Governments of India and Assam. The ideology which ULFA adhered is that Assam is a colony of Indian alien rulers after the treaty of *Yandabo* in 1826. Prior to this treaty between British and Burma Assam had independent ruler. Till now several thousand ULFA militants were killed, 5 thousand surrendered and 3 thousand are in jail custody. On 24 June, 2008 one battalion out of total 4 has unilaterally declared truce and sheltered in designated camp. But one company 'B' among them is still on the war path along with the remaining three battalions, namely 109, 709 and 27. Torture, rape, molestation, fake counter, secret killings, abduction, kidnapping, ransom, involuntary disappearance, illegal detention were mounted during this period. Nobody is spared including businessmen, politicians, teachers, students and cultivators. Political assassination, massacre and use of third degree methods became the order of the day. Both the civilians and security personnel suffered a gross violation of human rights. Since 27 November, 1990, three major Army operations have been concluded up to 1994. These are operation Bajrang, Rhino (I & II) and Sher-e-Dil etc.[11] The ULFA has constituted a 10 member Peace Consultative Group (PCG) in 2005 and after 3 rounds of discussion with GoI it remained virtually a defunct body.

Like ULFA another Scheduled Tribe (Plain) terrorist outfit Bodoland Security Force (BSF) was formed on 3 October, 1986 for a sovereign Bodoland. This secessionist terrorist outfit has changed its name to National Democratic Front of Bodoland (NDFB) on 25 November, 1994. The NDFB declared truce on 8 October, 2004 and reshaped new ledership by throwing Ranjan Daimari *alias* D.R. Nabla on 8 December, 2008. Bodoland Liberation Tigers (BLT) another Bodo militant outfit emerged in 2000 with autonomy demand became overground on 10 February, 2003 and are at present ruling Bodoland Territorial Area Council (BTAC) with four districts of lower Assam of Brahamaputra Valley, namely Chirang, Baksa, Udalguri and Kokrajhar forming Bodoland People's Front, a regional political party. Two years ago one more Bodo insurgent outfit Bodoland Royal Tigers Force (BRTF) also evolved. The aim and object of this outfit is not still properly highlighted.[12]

Another tribal terrorist outfit Rabha Viper Army (RVA) although born for autonomy issue in Goalpara and Kamrup District seems to be inactive at present. The two hill districts of Assam—North Cachar and Karbi-Anglong under Sixth Schedule status are now demanding separate tribal state demand under Article 244-A of the Constitution since 1992. Dimasa National Security Force (DNSF), a terrorist outfit manifested in 1992 with a separate 'Dimasaland' demand organised by few Dimasa youth with the financial aid of the then Minister of Assam G.C. Langthasa. In 1994, 26 militants of DNSF surrendered. The dissident DNSF militants formed a new outfit breaking away from the original group and came to be known as 'Black widow' *alias* Dima Halam Dauga (DHD-J) under Jewel Garlosa. The remaining faction is known as DHD-N under Dilip Nunisa which had declared truce in 1 January, 2003.[13]

In Karbi-Anglong United People's Democratic Solidarity (UPDS), a terrorist outfit also evolved for separate statehood and declared ceasefire on 1 October, 2002. Now, they are waiting for dialogue and negotiation. Other insurgent outfits of Karbi-Anglong with same agenda and footings are—United Karbi National Liberation Front (UKNLF) born on 24 September, 2008, United Tribal Democratic Movement (UTDM), United Karbi-Anglong and NC Hills Liberation Front (UKANCHLF) and Karbi-Anglong and

NC Hills People's Front (KANCHPF). Moreover, the hill settler Bodos in the region operated in the name of NDFB and BLT. All these hills outfits take assistance of arms, technology and outside links mainly from NSCN and ULFA.[14]

Some other terrorist outfits working in Assam from the last part of this decade are from Adivasi and Koch-Rajbanshi. Adivasi community belonging to tea and ex-tea garden workers who originally migrated from Bihar, Orissa, Madhya Pradesh, West Bengal during British regime are now claiming for Scheduled Tribe status in Assam like their counterparts in India. The noted among them are Adivasi National Liberation Army (ANLA), Birosa Commando Force, Cobra Militant, Adivasi Tiger Force and Chah Janajati Mukti Force. Out of these outfits Adviasi Cobra Militant of Assam and Birosa Commando Force have declared ceasefire on 15 September, 2001 and 15 October, 2004 respectively. Initially, Koch-Rajbanshi terrorist outfit was born for ST status demand which subsequently claimed separate 'Kamatapur State' to be carved from some parts of Bihar, West Bengal and Assam. This outfit now evolved as Kamatapuri Liberation Organization is spreading nexus with ULFA and Huji of Bangladesh.[15]

Similarly, more than 17 Muslim fundamentalist terrorist outfits have been working in Assam in different regions. The visible groups are—Muslim United Liberation Tigers of Assam (MULTA), Harkat-Ul-Mujahidin (HuM), Muslim United Liberation Front of Assam (MULFA), Muslim Liberation Army (MLA), Muslim Volunteers Force (MVF), Independent Liberation Army of Assam (ILAA), Islamic Security Force of India (ISFI), Jamat-e-Islami (JeI), Muslim Liberation Tigers of Assam (MLTA), United Social Reform Army (USRA), Islamic Sevak Sangha (ISS), United Reformation Protest of Assam (URPA), Student Islamic Movement of India (SIMI), People's United Liberation Front (PULF), Students Islamic Organization (SIO) and Islamic Liberation Army (ILA). The root and network of all these outfits are in Pakistan and Bangladesh.[16] United Liberation Front of Barak Valley (ULFBV), a terrorist outfit came into existence in 2001 for autonomy in the valley to the Riang tribes against the exploitation of the Muslim and Mizos in the valley. All the cadres of the outfit have surrendered at Pragjyoti Cultural Complex of Guwahati on 30 September, 2008.[17]

It is crystal clear from the above study that in Assam, a maximum number of terrorist organizations are active across the world. Approximately, 27 outfits have been working in this region for sovereignty, separate state, autonomy and ST status demand. Although some of them already surrendered, declared truce or ceasefire, weapons are still in their hand to enable them to commit any crime.

Tripura Upajati Juba Sangha (TUJS) a democratic organization was born in 1967 from which extremist group Tripura National Volunteer Force (TNV) evolved. Next to TNV, National Liberation Front of Tripura (NLFT) had emerged in 1989.

TNV the extremist group emerged under the leadership of Bijoy Hrangkhawl in July 1979 with the aim to establish an independent Tribal state of Tripura by ousting legally constituted government through armed struggle. After eight years of insurgency in Tripura a tripartite agreement was signed in 1988 by Indian Government, Tripura Government and TNV. But no solution could be achieved as new outfit NLFT emerged newly. [18]

Twelve militant outfits in Tripura had been evolved since 1947 onwards. The visible groups are — National Liberation Front of Tripura (NLFT) 1989, All Tripura Tiger Force (ATTF) 16 September, 1993, Tripura Resurrection Army (TRA) May 1994, Tripura Tribal Youth Force (TTYF), 3 December, 1993, Sengkrak, October 1993, Tripura Liberation Organization (TLO) 16 January, 1994, Tripura Tribal Volunteer Force (TTVF) 21 November, 1993, All Tripura Volunteer Force (ATVF) September, 1994, Ahinksha Tripura Bharat Suraksha Force (ATBSF) 23 June, 1994, Social Democratic Force of Tripura (SDFT) 27 January, 1995, Tripura Security Army (TSA) 30 January, 1995 and Tripura Tribal Democratic Force (TTDF) 2 November, 1993.[19]

After Several rounds of talk an agreement between Tripura government and ATTF was signed on 23 August, 1993.

After the establishment of District Council in Meghalaya in 1951, agitation started to remove the nominated members. In 1960, Assam Government decided to introduce Assamese as officical language and All Party Hill Leaders Conference (APHLC) was formed demanding separate statehood and accordingly got full-fledged status in 1972. [20]

Militancy in Meghalaya started with the formation of Meghalaya United Movement (MUM) in 1989 by Khasi Youth. The separate Garo-land demand was raised by another militant outfit Achik Liberation Matgrik Army (ALMA) in 1991. In 1992 another insurgent group Hynniewtrep Voluntary Council (HVC) emerged to fight social evils specially among Khasi youths. After one year Hynniewtrep Achik Liberation Council (HALC) was formed in 1992 with an objective of separation.[21]

Currently, People's Liberation Front of Meghalaya (PLF-M) and Achik National Liberation Army (ANLA) have been active.

In 1990, Indo Barma Revolutionary Force (IBRF) was formed jointly by NSCN(K), UNLF and ULFA for co-ordination among the NES ultras. Prior to it, Biseswar Singh founder Chairman of PLA united Assam, Meghalaya, Manipur, Tripura, Mizoram and Arunachal groups in 1981 before negotiating with GoI.[22] Assam Association (1903), Asom Chatra Sanmilan (1919), Asom Sahitya Sabha (1917), Assam Samgrakshini Sabha (1926) etc. were based on the sentiment of 'Assamese Nationalism' rather then 'Indian Nationalism.'[23]

The contemporary situation is that all the NES extremist groups are taking shelter and aid for training or technology with the neighbouring border countries like Bangladesh, Pakistan, Myanmar, Bhutan, Nepal and China.

(V)

It is apparent from the foregoing analytical evidence that the statistical and empirical amount of extremist groups in NE India is approximately sixty. Nowhere in the world crossed this limit till this date. All these outfits are in the range from total secession or independent or sovereignty, separate state, regional autonomy and reclaiming identity like ST status and so on. These features have highlighted by the leading authorities of the world about the South Asian terrorism.

NOTES

1. International Terrorism: A humanitarian Challenge. N. Sanajaoba, *Human Rights—Current Issues*, Omson, New Delhi, 2004.
2. *Id.* at 4.
3. *Ibid.*
4. *Ibid.*
5. *Id.* at 2.
6. *Id.* at 6.

7. Insurgency in North East; with special Reference to Manipur and Nagaland, Sukhendu Mazumdar, *Insurgency in North East India*, B. Pakem (ed), 1997.
8. *Ibid.*
9. *Ethnic Conflict and National Integration in North East India: Problem and Solution*. Aheibam Korieng Singh Maibam Ratankumar Singh Manipur, 2008.
10. *Ibid.*
11. Human Rights violation in Assam (1990-92), LLM dissertation GU, by Kshireswar Borah.
12. *Manab Adhikar—Neeti Aru Prayog*, Kshireswar Borah, 2008, Guwahati.
13. ASDC written statement before the Justice Rajkumar Manisana Singh Inquiry Commission, 2008.
14. *Amar Asom*, at 4, 25 December, 2008.
15. Supra n. 12.
16. *Assam Tribune*, at 1, 10 October, 2008.
17. *Assam Tribune*, at 1, 31 September, 2008.
18. Supra n. 7, *Tribal Insurgency in Tripura; Prospective and Issues*, Chandrika Basu (Mazumder).
19. *Id*. at 359-362.
20. Supra n. 7.
    Background Note on militancy in Meghalaya, S.K. Agnihotri, 1997.
21. *Ibid.*
22. Supra n. 7. *Insurgency in Manipur*, C. Jashua Thomas, 1997.
23. Supra n. 7. *Politics of seccessionism in North East India: A case of Assamese* by Girin Phukan, 1997.

24

Terrorism, Insurgency and International Humanitarian Law in the North East Region

R.C. Borpatra Gohain

Concept of Terrorism

Since time immemorial, the innocent civilians have been made the soft targets and victims of terrorist activities. It has assumed, by now, the magnitude of global hydra-headedness. Terrorism is a multi-dimensional social phenomenon with its relative sequential variations. It confuses the experts in international laws or the government representatives to arrive at an agreed point pertaining to a comprehensive and universally accepted definition.

However, the Convention for the Prevention and Punishment of Terrorism of 1937 defined acts of terrorism in a very comprehensive term referring only to criminal acts but not specifying which acts are illegal in the context of terrorism. The draft UN Comprehensive Convention on International Terrorism formulated by Ad-Hoc Committee defined terrorist acts to be an offence within the meaning of the Convention, whereby if any person, by any means, unlawfully and intentionally causes *inter alia* death or serious bodily injury to any person or serious damage to public or private property, including a place of public use, a state or government facility, a public transportation system, and infrastructure facility or the environment.

Terrorist attack on human lives and property not only brings suffering and distress to the individual victims but also have far reaching consequences for the life of a nation. The killing in Sarajevo of the Austrian Crown Prince in 1914 triggered the outbreak of the First World War. Along with that the revolution of 1917 disrupting the Russian Empire, brought an end of a long period of stability in 19th century Europe. The 20th century witnessed a spate of terrorist activities all-over the world. Such activities perpetuated to the 21st century and is characterized by appalling acts or cruelty against civilian, perpetrating with the sole aim of terrorizing the civilian population of a country at war.

The Algerian war of independence, the crushing of independence movement by the Soviet Union, the involvement of Americans and allied forces in Vietnam, the mass killing of Cambodian people, the wars in the Middle-East to mention a few, indicates that acts of terrorism are parts of an armed conflict.

Right of Self-Determination and Anti-Colonialism

The roots of the principle of Right to Self-determination with the decolonization can be traced back to 12th century. Many scholars trace the idea of self-determination in Greek polis. During the Middle Ages, and in the wake of the propagation of Judaism, Christianity and Islam, the freedom of choice of individuals were collectively exercised.

The term self-determination first gained recognition in Western Europe. The rise of nationalism stressing the self-identification of the people with the state, paved the way of evolution of the doctrine. In the 19th century, subsequent to the French Revolution and the Napoleonic imperialism, the Right to self-determination emerged as the doctrine of political revolution.

In the 20th century, the two world wars and its consequentiality made the global community to unite and the Charter of the United Nations emerged and is followed by many international declarations and instruments giving recognition to right to self-determination.

The National Liberation Movements having recognition of international law since the 2nd half of 20th century strengthened and expedited the worldwide de-colonisation process. The UN Committee of 24 monitors the de-colonisation process. The political developments after the 2nd World War witnessed dramatic territorial re-alignments and liberation of an additional 140 colonised nations.

In the North Eastern Region, the insurgent groups, regional political parties and other organizations have been claiming their rights to self-determination in varying degrees.

International Humanitarian Law in North East Region

The four Geneva Conventions of 1949 and the two Additional Protocols of 1977 formed the basis of International Humanitarian Laws. The Rome Treaty of 1998 formulates the policy of fixing Individual Criminal Responsibility on the wrong doers for committing genocide, crime against humanity, war crimes and aggression (not yet finally defined). The entire set of humanitarian law and treaties relating thereto, govern both international armed conflict situation and non-armed conflict situations, based on the principle of non-derogability.

The universal human right, i.e. the Right to Self-Determination is recognized by the United Nations Charter (Articles 1-55) and the two covenants on 1966, it constitutes the corner-stone of UN General Assembly Declarations, Security Council's Resolution, Judgments of the International Court of Justice and several other significant principles of contemporary international law.

Article 1, common to both International Covenants of 1966 guarantees the people's right to exercise self-determination. India, like few other countries, retains certain reservations on the universal right of dependent people, despite UN Human Rights Commission's strictures; the Government of India has been treating the National Liberation Movements in the North East, Punjab and Kashmir as ordinary law and order problem.

The problem of insurgency in Assam arose, when claim of the Right to Self-Determination has proven that Assam had never been a part of India till the signing of the Treaty of *Yandabo* in 1826. Even Congress leader like Gopinath Bordoloi asked for a separate political constitution for Assam.

Insurgency, National Liberation Movement and other resistant movements are within the fold of international armed conflict and therefore, the International Humanitarian Laws, Geneva Conventions and other relevant legal provisions are applicable in such conflict.

In the North East region, there are many draconian laws making them discriminatorily applicable only to the region, which are in operation since India obtained independence. These laws are —

1. Assam Disturbed Areas Act, 1955.
2. The Armed Forces Special Power Act, 1958.
3. Assam Maintenance of Public Order, 1953.
4. Nagaland Security Regulation, 1962.
5. National Security Act, 1980.

These Acts have conferred wide ranging powers to the Army, and Para-military forces like CRPF, BSF, Assam Rifles and the State police, the misuse of which results into violation of human rights. These laws have failed to contain the liberation movements and insurgency in the region but help increase the number of such groups day by day. Uptil now there are as many as 37 nos. of insurgent groups operating in Assam.

International committee is fully agreeable to confer right to self-determination on fulfilling certain criteria by the Liberation Movements. The Government of India is also agreeable to grant Right to Self-Determination to those liberation groups acting within the national boundaries on fulfilling any of the following criteria:

1. The people are under foreign domain.
2. If the people are under internal domination.
3. People under domination under different race or group.

Whether a liberation movement belongs to the category no. 1 or category 2, as mentioned above depends on certain criteria. The 1st category is an issue which is both national and international in nature. In the second category that is the liberation movements there are primarily international issues. However, if they are found to be taking resort to only terrorist activities, they will definitely fall under 1st category.

Before the exercise of the Right to self-determination, whether it is internal or external what is needed is either a referendum or a plebiscite on the issue.

In case of the offences falling in category 1, Article 3 common to all Geneva Convention, International Humanitarian Laws, other norms of International customary laws befitting to the required circumstances must be taken resort to, to contain such offences. The non-state actors like insurgents and Liberation Movement Organization are also equally bound by such mandate. They must also show due respect to the valued human rights.

It may be mentioned that on June 15, 1995, the then Prime Minister P.V. Narasimha Rao agreed to the pre-conditions imposed by NSCN (IM) to come to the negotiating table and the conditions were—

1. Discussion on sovereignty (Greater Nagaland),
2. Discussion must be at Prime Minister level, and
3. The discussion must be in some foreign countries.

All these pre-conditions have been accepted and for last 14 years, the discussion is in continuity. The same principle, based on the doctrine of equality, should be followed in case of other insurgent groups. It is a political issue and it must be solved on the basis of a political will of the government at centre.

25

The Tripura Crisis and Dilemma

[A General over-view of what might have gone wrong since 1947 in Tripura]

Surajit Sen

It is a well known fact that the British ruled over India for more than a century, ever since the Battle of Plassey and the Battle of Buxar. Starting as a trading company, the British began to expand their territorial conquest over India to harness India's immense wealth – natural and capital wealth. With time they even thought of carving an empire in India, and to a great extent, even succeeded in it. With the growth of Indian Nationalism, the Britishers found it difficult to contain this dream of theirs. The only way possible for them was to follow the policy of 'Divide and Rule'. It worked wonders for them. They were quick to realize the fact that if the Hindu-Muslim unity could be destroyed, then they would be able to rule over India for ever. Keeping this in mind, they portioned Bengal – the richest province in British India, citing inconvenience of governance. To further divide India on communal lines, they gave impetus for the emergence of Muslim League as a counter attack to mainly the Hindu dominated Indian National Congress. When they left India, they perhaps created the greatest divide by partitioning India into two parts – India and Pakistan. This led to a gory spectacle of communal riots, in which several thousands of people lost their lives in the name of religion, and several more thousands became homeless and had to live as refugees in their country, which was their own before partition. This had led to rise of several outfits all-over India, who have been trying to find a place for themselves in their country. With time, radicalism increased, and these outfits turned into extremist organisations – some feeling that their socio-ethnic organization has been badly affected, while others feeling that they have been given nothing in India, even when they have left everything in their ancestral home, while others felt that their political aspirations would never be possible in such a sea change. This effect can also be clearly seen in India's North East, especially in the state of Tripura. This chapter, thus, makes a humble attempt to find out what might have gone wrong since 1947 in the North East, and more so in Tripura.

Brief Background of Tripura

Tripura is a land-locked state in the Indian Union. A formerly princely state, Tripura joined the Indian Union on 15th October, 1949 and became a Union Territory in 1956. A full statehood was granted to Tripura in January 1972. Tripura is the smallest state, in terms of area, among all the seven North Eastern States of India. It shares a territorial boundary with Assam (53 kms) and Mizoram (109 kms) in the North East; and an international boundary with Bangladesh (856 kms). The state is predominantly hilly and often inaccessible, with as many as nineteen different tribes residing here.[1] 'Kok-Barak' is the main dialect for inter-tribe communication, though Bengali is the official state language. The 2001 Census Report shows that the population of the state stands at 31,91,168 people, out of which only 30.95 per cent are tribals.

Genesis of Extremism in Tripura

The crisis in Tripura is mainly because of the conflict that has arisen between the tribals and non-tribals of the state. For a long time, there seemed to be harmony between the tribals and non-tribals. But during the later half of 1970s, organized tribal militancy started spreading in the state.[2] A few causes for the emergence of extremism in Tripura can be listed as follows:

(a) Strong feelings of social and economic deprivation (as the non-tribals began to get the cream of social and economic benefits).
(b) Insecurity combined with communal/ethnic feelings (the

tribals felt as second-class citizens in their own land and thought that their own identity, culture and tradition are at risk of being lost for ever as they could not get the exposure).

(c) Ambition for political power (ever since Tripura received statehood, it has had only one Tribal Chief Minister from 1993-1997; leading to a fear that politically too they would be alienated from their own land).

(d) A long international boundary with Bangladesh, without proper fencing, facilitates arms smuggling, infiltration and provides safe hideouts to extremists from North East region, including Tripura. Needless to point here that the first of Pakistan and DFGI of Bangladesh work hand in hand to help these extremists in their survival.

However, the point to be noted here is that all these factors would have risen had the colonial rule not sowed the seeds of separatism and communalism. Needless to say here that the Government of India is also to be blamed for its unrealistic approach in dealing with several problems.

For this, one may have to delve deep into history since the time the Britishers left India. "The final partition of Bengal in 1947 was a disaster for Tripura", says Subir Bhaumik.[3] It is a known fact that partition has left indelible marks in the history of the two nations – India and Pakistan – but the scar of which is significantly felt by India in the extremist movements, especially in the North Eastern states of the country and Jammu and Kashmir. The partition of 1947, opened avenues for the majority Hindu Bengalee of erstwhile East Pakistan (Bangladesh) to migrate into India. Tripura having historical contacts with Bangladesh was left open for the settlement of these immigrants. This for ever changed the demography of the state of Tripura and led way for "A fierce ethnic conflict that has ravaged the tiny state" for the last three decades.[4] The Indian Government ignored the demographic complexity of the state while rehabilitating the Bengali refugees from Bangladesh. This changed the tribal dominated states to become a non-tribal dominated state where the tribals were reduced from 64 per cent in 1864 to 52 per cent in 1901, 37 per cent in 1951 and 29 per cent in 1971—when the final flow of immigrants came from Bangladesh[5] owing to the Hindu cleansing done by the Bangladeshi Muslim government.

Since times immemorial, Tripura had a long standing relation with Bengal. The Kings of Tripura controlled large tracts of eastern Bengal (Bangladesh) like Comilla, Chittagong, Noakhali and Dhaka divisions of Contemporary Bangladesh. In 1280 A.D.; with the submission of Ratna Fa to Mughisuddin Tughril, the Tripuri Kings invited many Bengalis of high castes to their courts. Many of the Bengalis were even related to the 'Boro Bhuiyans' of Tripura.[6] However, the migration started gaining momentum since the first half of the 20th century, with first the divide of Bengal (East Bengal and West Bengal in 1905), then the partition of India (East Bengal becoming a part of Pakistan, and its christening as East Pakistan), and final the independence of East Pakistan from Pakistan and its becoming a nation known as Bangladesh in 1971.

In the early 20th century, the kings of Tripura invited several non-tribal Hindu peasantry from East Bengal to the state to augment the revenue, offering settlement of cultivable land in the valley at a low rent. The king also employed several educated non-tribal Hindu Bengalis in the state administration, and over the years, these Bengalis accepted Tripura as their homeland. However, the native tribals always regarded them as aliens, though the relation between the two was relatively stable till the tribals had majority. But trouble started in the 1940s when the Hindu Bengalis migrated into Tripura following the anti-Hindu riots in East Bengal and the turmoil of partition.[7]

With change in demography – the majority tribals becoming a minority in their own land, failure of the government, both central and state to provide the tribals with tangible support in mainstream political, social and economic fields, and the feeling of alienation resulted in the rise of anti-Hindu Bengali sentiments among the tribals. These feelings mixed with adventurism and aids from foreign agencies got stronger in the later part of 1970s. This resulted in the untoward ethnic violence that took place in June 1980 where more than 1300 tribals and non-tribals were killed, with a heavy loss to property.[8]

Effects of the Colonial Legacy

The genesis of extremism in Tripura can be said to have begun with the influx of immigrants from East Bengal, following the partition of India. Had the then Indian Government realized that instead of filling up one state with all the immigrants, they should be settled in different states also, then such a disaster and dilemma would never had arisen.

The anger and frustration of the Tribal population of Tripura saw its first armed movement, known as "Senkrak" in the 1960s. But the movement was controlled and suppressed by the Government officials. However, this became the mother of all extremist groups in Tripura. On 12th December, 1980, the All Tripura People's Liberation Organization (ATPLO) was formed in Bangladesh. With time several extremist organizations began to grow and flourish in Tripura. At the present moment, extremism in Tripura is dominated mainly by two groups – National Liberation Front of Tripura (NLFT) and All Tripura Tiger Force (ATTF). Both the groups are armed with sophisticated weapons, well trained men, having links with other insurgent groups of the North East and also with the ISI of Pakistan and DGFI of Bangladesh.[9]

The main demands of these groups are:

(i) Liberation from 'neo-colonialism',
(ii) Removal of non-tribals, especially Bengalis,
(iii) Furtherance of indigenous culture, and
(iv) Instilling consciousness against exploitation.[10]

Thus, from these demands, it becomes amply clear that these extremist organizations feel that the root cause for their agitation has been a loss of culture and identity in their own land because of immigration.

Thus, the crisis and dilemma faced today by Tripura is a great error of judgment made at the time of independence by India and, thereafter, when the Indian Government unrealistically settled a major chunk of refugees from Bangladesh in Tripura. The mistakes of the Past as now come as a glory sore for Tripura Chief Minister, Shri Manik Sarkar; the only way for a proper solution to all unrest in the state is through proper negotiations and talks.

NOTES

1. www.tripurapolice.com

2. *Ibid.*
3. Subir Bhaumik, *Disaster in Tripura.*
4. *Ibid.*
5. H.M. Bareh, *Encyclopedia of North East India*, Vol. viii.
6. H.L. Chatterjee, 'Glimpses of Tripura's History', *Tripura Review*, 15th August, 1972.
7. Ramashray Upadhyay, *Tripura Bleeds—In the Crossfire of Mainstream Political Parties and Virulent Ethnic Conflict.*
8. www.tripurapolice.com
9. *Ibid.*
10. *Ibid.*

26

Wave of Ethnic Revival and Extremism among the Chin-Kuki-Mizo (Zo) People in Manipur

S. Thangboi Zou

Introduction

Despite its popular usage, "extremism" defies clear definition, let alone analysis. It appears to be a blanket term covering all sorts of violent, conflicts, fundamentalism, terrorism and radicalism. Extremism denotes any political organisation which takes up arms or other forms of extreme way in order to pursue its political goal. It is important to locate the social roots of violence and extremism in modern India which – in the apt words of V.S. Naipaul – is the site of "a million mutinies". Those described as "extremists" surely must have points of view and visions of future possibilities, howsoever absurd they may be. Indeed, both moderate and extremist groups may exist within the body of an association. Any armed movement, no doubt, is a form of extremism.

India's North East is home to multiple nationalities and ethnic minorities. In spite of all its limitations, the democratic experiment in the North East has come a long way. A return to the old order of tribal kinship and clan polity is inconceivable. What we witness at present is perhaps not the *revival* of primordial identities of the past; but it is the *construction* of modern ethnic identities *vis-à-vis* the newly created nation-state of India. After the British departure from the political theatre of independent India, various politically conscious tribal leaders in the North East became anxious about their future political status. They developed in them the ambition of seeking and enjoying different administrative status of their own which ultimately made them to resort to violence to achieve their political ambition. Many leaders of the present-day underground outfits of the region argued that the political integration of the region to India was done without the approval of the people themselves.

The capacity of India to contain armed insurgency and to maintain its territorial integrity against domestic challengers has never been seriously doubted. But on their respective home turf, militant outfits have proved resilient enough to continue their low-intensity war in defending their sectional interests. Therefore, extremism—in any form and from any source—is a scourge to society. In a democratic setup, a mechanism needs to be in place to filter routine dissent. It does not augur well, therefore, when violence increasingly becomes accepted as legitimate instrument of ethnic or identity assertion.

Ethnic Streams in Manipur

Manipur is situated in the extreme north-eastern part of India, bordering Burma for about 352 kilometres in the East and South of it. It covers an area of 22,327 sq.km with a population of around 23 lakh (2001 Census). The state is divided into 9 districts. Manipur has 29 recognized Scheduled Tribes and 3 non-tribal groups. They belong to various ethno-linguistic traits. The ethnic groups can be broadly classified into three categories: Meitei, Naga and Chin-Kuki-Mizo. All of them belong to Mongoloid stock of race and Tibeto-Burman language family but varied from one another. The Meiteis are concentrated in the Valley and are the dominant population group of the state. The Naga and Chin-Kuki-Mizo groups inhabit the hill areas surrounding the plain of Manipur.

Manipur in the post-India's independence saw a great deal of political consciousness in the face of ethnic revival among different tribes of the Naga and Chin-Kuki-Mizo group. Extremism in the state may be generally categorized into three streams: the valley (Meitei) stream who believed that the Manipur king was forced to access into the Indian Union, and who are fighting for sovereignty; the Naga stream, who has been fighting for integration of all Naga inhabited areas in Assam, Nagaland, Manipur and Arunachal Pradesh; and the third stream is the Chin-Kuki-Mizo or Zo group, who has risen up to claim for their ethnic autonomous 'homeland' within Manipur and across international border to Burma. This form of ethno-nationalist movement with certain degree of patronage, moral and material support from the people of each ethnic group has given rise to militancy in Manipur.

Manipur is facing problems on economic, political, social, ethnic and administrative fronts that it could not arrest the problems of such extremist mode of socio-political mobilization in the state. Presently, there are around 30 armed militants operating inside the state consisting of almost all ethnic groups. With many armed groups among the hill tribes on the one hand and valley based groups on the other hand, peace and tranquillity seems to be a distant dream in the area.

Identity of Chin-Kuki-Mizo or Zo People

Apart from Naga group of hill tribes, there are also the Chin-Kuki-Mizo tribes who inhabit a large extent of geographical areas in Manipur. They are also found in Mizoram and Burma. Generally, these Chin-Kuki-Mizo people are called by different names in different regions of their settlement. Those living in Burma were known by a common name 'Chin' (Khyan in Burmese) while those living in Manipur and Assam are known as Kuki and those in Mizoram as Mizo. The so-called Chin are an indigenous race of Myanmar known to outside as Chin but who identified themselves as *Zo* (pronounced Zou). Of late, many scholars collectively refer to the Chin-Kuki-Mizo group as 'Zo' people based on historical, anthropological and linguistic affinities of the ethnic group. According to tribal mythology, the Zo people believed that they came out from a cave called *Khul* or *Chhinlung*, which is believed to be located somewhere in southern China while some believed it to be in Tibet.

The travel account of an Italian Missionary called Father Sangermano mentioned the word "Jo", for the first time ever, in his record in 1783. He also further wrote that "this people lived to the west of Chin mountains between 20° 30′ and 21°30′ north latitude, and is a petty nation called Jo [Yaw]. They are supposed to have been Chin" (Sangermano, 1833: 43). Grierson (1905:1) also mentioned the name 'Zo' to denote the Kuki-Chin people in his writings. He wrote "The name (Kuki or Chin) is not used by the tribe themselves, who used title such as Zo or Yo or Sho". A local writer Sing Khaw Khai mentions in his book '*Zo People and Their Culture*' that the British administrative officials, while carrying out the history of their newly colonised hill regions in Burma, found the same ethnic groups of people in different areas speaking different dialects and bearing various names. They were the tribes known to India as 'Kuki' and in Burma as 'Chin' (Khai, 1995:1). However, this group of people do not seem to prefer being called by their awarded nomenclature—'Chin'. "No single 'Chin' word has explicit reference to all the people we customarily called Chin, but... the peoples have a special word for themselves....which appears as Zo, Yo, and the like" (Lehman, 1963).

This people who exhibited almost the same cultural traits are called by different names. Regarding the Kuki terminology, Grierson (1995:905, 906 reprint) also clearly mentioned that "Kuki is an Assamese or Bengali term, applied to various hill tribes, such as the Lusheis, Rangkhols, Thados, etc. It seems to have been known at a comparatively early period." He further admitted that this term being a conventional one "there being no proper name comprising all these tribes ....I have, however, to avoid confusion, retained the old terminology (Kuki)." Here, Grierson was referring particularly to this (Zo people) living in the present Manipur and Mizoram hill areas. The word Kuki is, more especially, used to denote various tribes which have successively been driven from the Lushai and Chin Hills into the surrounding country, i.e. the present Manipur, Assam and Tripura. However, he wanted to signify that those people who are in Burma region are called Chin. The term Chin is not used by the tribes themselves, who use the titles such as Zo or Yo and Sho.

The Zo people who have settled in the Lushai Hills later came to be known with a new term 'Mizo'. The term Mizo is taken from Zo. Here, the term *Mi* means man, and *Zo* is the name of a person, who is strongly believed to be the progenitor of the Kuki-Chin-Mizo people. The Mizo were originally known as Lushei, but they discarded because of the fact that the Lushai signifies only a particular clan or community who originally used Duhlian as their language or dialact. Lushai is synonymous with Duhlian. Grierson (1904) mentioned that Duhlian is believed to be the founder of the Lushai proper. However, the Lushai geneology is mainly drawn from the Sailo family who is the ruling as well as the most influential family of the Lushai speakers. Besides the Lushai or Duhlian linguistic group, other families were also found, such as "Ralte, Hmar, Paite", who speak Duhlian at later stage. There are more than ten clans among the Lushai families. The new name 'Mizo' came to be the unifying term for these families in the modern period.

Regarding the substantiation of their identity as Zo, Major J. Shakespear[2] wrote, "...all these tribes are called by us Lushai, and by themselves as *Zao* (Zo)." Gopalakrisnan has written the similarity of Mizo *vis-à-vis* the Kuki-Chin group of Manipur:

"The term Mizo got momentum in the 1940s. The Manipur Mizo Integration Council included a large number of tribal groups within its fold. Even the Thado, Vaiphei and Gangte were brought under this broad terminology" (Gopalakrisnan, 1996:148).

Whatever the case might be, we want to make a statement that the so-called Chin-Kuki-Mizo groups of tribes are linguistically and ethnographically homogeneous. While the people in Mizoram have no problem accepting 'Mizo' as a common nomenclature, the same people in Manipur have not arrived into a common agreement.

Ethnic Revival and Extremist Movements of the Zo People

Manipur had seen quite a lot of ethnic awakenings in the post-independence period. Several Kuki-Chin-Mizo or Zo tribes living in the State had claimed their respective identities based on linguistic attributes. There are more than 10 languages spoken by the Kuki-Chin-Mizo group in Manipur alone. Under the Constitution of India (Scheduled Caste/Tribe) Order, 1950 and the Modification Order of 1956, the Government of India officially gave recognition to the following tribes of the Kuki-Chin: Aimol, Anal, Chiru, Gangte, Hmar, Kom, Maring, Any Mizo/Lushai, Paite, Simte, Sukte, Thado (Kuki), Vaiphei and Zou.

Although historians and writers stated lengthily of cultural and linguistic affinities of these people, the wave and feeling of alienation based on ethnicity and identity had been persistent. Instead of adhering to one common appellation, every group preferred to obtain different identities based on languages or dialectical accent of their own which has proven to be the main cause of disintegration among the Zo people. Interestingly, one imperative point to note is that all the languages have similarity and are often overlapping one another. Brief study on the ethnic movements of the Kuki-Chin-Mizo or Zo people in Manipur is being stressed on the paper.

The wave of ethnic revival among the Zo people had already begun prior to India's independence. The implication of Khul (the Cave where they are believed to emerge from) identity and its ethno-political awakening had started since 1940s. After India's independence, plethora of political and socio-political organisations in Manipur hills made their presence felt. The Kuki National Assembly (KNA) and later Khul National Union were noticeably one of the earliest political bodies that emerged as blanket organisation covering all the kindred tribal groups. KNA was officially established in 1946 at Imphal. It was the earliest political unit of the Kuki-Chin comprising other kindred tribes such as Thadous, Paites, Vaipheis, Simtes, Anals, Koms, Gangtes, Hmars, Koirengs, Zous, etc. The demand for a Kuki autonomous state by KNA within the framework of Indian Constitution was made in 1960s whereas the demand for a separate district was made in the 1970s (Ray, Asok Kumar, 1992).

In fact, the Khulmi Union was the fallout of misunderstanding between the then Thadou leaders and that of other sister tribes within KNA. The KNA was seen to have been dominated mostly by the Thadou speaking group that other kindred tribes started to float a new organisation known as Khulmi Union in 1947. The Khulmi Union consisted of all Kuki-Chin tribes other than the Thadou tribe under its umbrella. It had been ideologically in conflict with the KNA for quite some time. The inception of the Khulmi Union is vividly described by Prim S. Vaiphei in the following lines:

> "During 1947-50, the Kuki ethnos with the exception of the Thadous organised themselves in one body and named it Khulmi (means people of the 'Khul' cave) Union...The Khulmi Union was the organisation encompassing the following tribes: Aimol, Mayaon, Monsang, Maring, Mate, Chiru, Chothe, Hmar, Anal, Paite, Gangte, Simte, Kom, Koireng, Lamkang, Vaiphei, Zou, etc. (Vaiphei S., 1995:128).

However, Khulmi Union did not exist long. When the Khulmi Union failed to fulfil its aspiration every group started to float their own organisations. The Paite, a Kuki-Chin tribe in Manipur, formed its political organisation called Paite National Council (PNC) in 1956. The Hmar National Union (HNU) came into existence in 1962 to integrate all the Hmars of Manipur and other states. Apart from the mentioned larger groups, other smaller tribal groups also started to establish their own political organisations. The Zou tribe in Manipur formed its apex political body (Goswami, 1979: 72, 74) as United Zomi Organisation (UZO) in 1958. The Gangtes established Gangte Tribe Union (GTU) in 1958, the Vaipheis as Vaiphei National Organisation (VNO) in 1960, the Simte formed Simte National Council (SNC), the Mizo/Lushais as Manipur Mizo Union (MMU) and so on. All these organisations in collusion with the larger groups such as the KNA, PNC, and HNU had once demanded the demarcation of the Tribal Areas and also for constituting an autonomous district in the Tribal areas of Manipur.

The Mizo unification movement went parallel to the Kuki movement. The movement of Mizo National Union and its offshoot the Mizo National Front for a separate spread its wing across the Kuki-Chin inhabited areas of Manipur that it earned support from the latter in Manipur too. The Kuki National Assembly also lent support to the Manipur Mizo Integration Council in their demand for a single administrative unit. The Kuki-Chin areas were also, in fact, included within the arrangement for the greater Mizoram which, however, could not materialise.

The one and only major point of perpetual disagreement among them has been the question of identity. Pan-tribal movement in the context of Chin-Kuki groups have taken dimension. Terminologies like Kuki, Khulmi, Mizo, Zomi, Eimi, Chingmi, etc. as common name to envelop all the kindred groups had evolved though any existing choice has not led them into a consensus till today. Deviation and tension had surfaced as a result of national identity movement. The tension was of two-fold: tension between the tribes and the State or Government, and, the tension within the tribes themselves.

There has also been a tendency among members of some clans to raise their clan status to full-fledged Scheduled Tribes as in the case of Mate clans and Thangkhal section of the Zou tribe and so on. One crucial enquiry Gopalakrisnan (1996) made is: "will such tribal territorial and linguistic recognition serve as positive step for uplifting the socially and politically backward areas?"

Hmar Movement

The Hmar people settle mostly in the northern part of Mizoram and the south-western part of Manipur. The Hmar movement initially originated in Mizoram and later spread to other parts of Hmar inhabited areas of Manipur and Assam. During the demarcation of the boundary of the Mizo district in 1948, the Mizo Union is said to have not pressed the case of the Hmars to get the Hmar inhabited areas of Manipur and Assam included in the Lushai Hills district (Goswami, 1979:58). They were also disappointed with the Mizo Peace Accord of 1986 which failed to meet their demand of a 'Greater Mizoram' integrating all areas inhabited by the Hmar in Mizoram, Cachar district of Assam, and Manipur under a single administrative unit. So, in order to stir for the movement of integration of the said territories of the Hmar and set up a separate administrative body, a political party known as Hmar People Convention (HPC) was formed in Mizoram in 1986. They also wanted to maintain a separate identity in Mizoram that they demanded for the official recognition of Hmar tribe in Mizoram too.

Since 1987, the HPC waged an armed struggle for autonomy, which further reached to extreme level and violence in the 1990s. In 1992, HPC representatives and the Government of Mizoram mutually agreed to hold ministerial level talks. A Memorandum of Settlement (MoS) was signed at the Mizoram capital, Aizawl on July 27, 1994, for establishing the Hmar Autonomous Council or 'Sinlung Development Council' in the northern parts of Aizawl district in Mizoram and subsequently, the HPC militants surrendered along with their arms. However, dissatisfied with the implementation process, a section of the cadres parted ways with the over ground HPC and formed the HPC-D in 1995. The purported objective of the outfit over the years has changed from an autonomous district covering the north and North East Mizoram to a full-fledged Hmar State (*Hmar-ram*) consisting of the Hmar inhabited areas of Mizoram, Manipur and Assam.

Kuki Armed Movements

Some writers are of the view that the Kuki movement against the British's aggression into their territory which began a long period of time culminated in the so-called Kuki Rising of 1917-1919. The Thadou and Zou of the Kuki-Chin tribes in Manipur engaged in war with the British soldiers. However, after resisting the advancing British troops for almost three consecutive years, they were defeated by the latter. This uprising against the hegemony of the British is called 'Kuki Rebellion' by the foreign writers and 'Kuki Rising' or *Zou-Gal* (Zou-War) by the local scholars and writers. Although scholars view it in varied perspective, a song composed by Mangzathang, a Zou warrior in the midst of the war denotes a clear picture of defending their forefather's land than the misconstrued idea of mere rebellion against the British authority. The song goes:

> "Tuizum Maangkang kiil bang hing khang
> Zouta kual zil bang liing e,
> Pianna ka gamlei hi e, phal sing e!
>
> (Free translation)—
>
> The seafaring White Imperialist (The British) coils like the 'kiil' plant
> Tremors of earthquake do quiver the Zou world,
> 'Tis the land of my birth, I shall not part with it!
>
> (Zou, David, 2005:89)

Moreover, geographically the Kukis are scattered, particularly so in the northern hills and mountains of Manipur. They also suffered heavy blows from the persistent confrontation with the Naga rebels. The indifference of the State administration to their political and economic plight seemed to compel them to regroup and reorient their perspectives in order to safeguard their security and protection against any possible aggression by other people. Most of the armed movements of the Kukis had their stimulation and compulsion from external forces, from which they had felt the need to safeguard their ethnic identity and geographical space as well. In the light of this, the cause and genesis of the Kuki armed movements can be attributed to the prolonged conflict between the Thadou-Kuki and Naga on one hand and consequent revival of ethno-nationalism among them on the other hand.

Formation of Kuki National Army (KNA)

P.S. Haokip's *Zalengam—The Kuki Nation* (2008 reprint), mentions detail about the formation of the first Kuki armed movement. It states that, the post-independent India and Burma saw the Kuki leaders in the zeal to continue their fight against the division of their "ancestral land by the international boundary drawn without their consent" or to have a larger autonomy in both the countries. To restore their perceived "lost lands" Kuki National Organisation (KNO) with its armed and extremist group Kuki National Army (KNA) was formed in 1988 somewhere in the Indo-Burma border in Manipur. The KNO proposed the reunification of their "lost" territory. It further stresses that, in India, the Kuki National Assembly formed in 1946 initially proposed "sovereignty for the Kukis". Continuation of the movement made by the early Kuki National Assembly was one of the main purposes of the KNO. It claims that in the 1950s and 1960s, the Kukis had appealed for the recognition of Kuki states; one each in Burma and India if the two countries want to integrate parts of Kuki territory within their respective nations.

Therefore, the main objective of the KNO/KNA based mainly on recognition and restoration of their "ancestral land" which they call *Zalengam* or the independent land. It wanted the concerned government, i.e. India and Burma, to recognize that "the Kukis were an independent people before the advent of the British colonialists". Further, it also supported restoration of statehoods for all ethnic nationalities in Burma for which KNO is also a member of Federation of Ethnic Nationalities of Burma. So, it seems to have larger interest on the issue of Burma in the initial stage of formation while no lesser in India too. The KNO/KNA's area of operation includes Sagaing Division in Burma, Chandel, Ukhrul, Sadar Hills, Churachandpur districts of Manipur and parts of Assam. The organisation takes the responsibility of co-ordinating different Kuki revolutionary groups. There are, presently, more than ten militant groups belonging to various Kuki-Chin tribes operating under the banner of KNO.

Haokip (pp. 378-79) also further stressed about the plight of the Kukis in Burma and the reason as to why the KNA resorted to violence:

> "In Burma, KNO have had to resort to violent means against the Military Junta from 1991 to 1999. The Burmese government has disregarded the fact that Kukis live on their ancestral lands. Kuki village boundaries have been removed. Traditional form of governance, i.e. Haosa (chieftainship) system has been abolished. Ethnic Burmese populations, extricated mainly from Rangoon and Mandalay, have been transplanted to Kuki areas with a view to rendering the indigenous people a minority. Developments in the Kuki areas are non-existent. The problems faced by the Kukis and their political demands have been brought to the notice of the Indian and Burmese governments, the United Nations and other international and regional forums."

Kuki National Front (KNF)

The formation of another Kuki armed group in Manipur called the Kuki National Front (KNF) came in parallel with the formation of the KNO/KNA. KNF was formed on May 18, 1988 in Sadar Hills subdivision of Senapati district of Manipur with the main objective of curving out a Kuki homeland or Kukiland encompassing all the Kuki inhabited areas of Manipur and other north-eastern states. Nehkholun, the founder president of KNF wrote about the reason and objective of KNF formation and its reason of resorting to extremism. While justifying the demand of Kukiland, he expressed thus:

> "Whereas the Constitution of India, Schedule (1 to 4) and Articles 244 and 244(A) provide that the tribals of the North Eastern India may or shall have the administrative units of their own; whereas the other tribals of Meghalaya, Mizoram, Arunachal Pradesh and Karbi Anglong, etc. can get administrative forums and whereas the Kukis are of the same class, status and children of India, there is no reason as to why separate statehood for them cannot be created".

It can be surmised from the above statement that the KNF was formed in order to assert the Kuki identity and carve out a separate autonomous state for the Kukis parallel to the status of other sister states in the North East India. However, ethnic clash between the Naga and Thado-Kuki gave KNF the responsibility to add its attention from their main objective to protecting the Kuki people from its rival group whosoever. So, the KNF along with the KNA was engaged in turf war with the NSCN (IM) between 1993 and 1995 where several numbers of Kuki and Naga lost their lives.

Zomi Nationalist Movements and Formation of Armed Groups

The Zomi nationalist movement was started as an attempt to unite all the Chin-Kuki-Mizo (Zo) people of the North East India as well as Burma. It had began contemporary to the inception of Mizo National Front purportedly formed to establish a separate state for all the so-called Mizo, and under the banner of 'Mizo' which actually was synonymous with the Zomi terminology. The term Zomi is also derived from 'Zo' (the generic name for the Chin-Kuki-Mizo people). Zomi is also the reverse term of Mizo. The Zomi proponents contended that 'Zomi' is a more appropriate term for the generic name for the Kuki-Chin-Mizo people than the terms 'Mizo', 'Chin' or 'Kuki' as such. In a move to launch the Zomi unification process and integrate all their inhabited areas of Burma and India, T. Gougin Zou founded the Zomi National Congress (ZNC) in January 21, 1972 at Daijang village, Churachandpur district in Manipur. The activities of ZNC, although shortlived, had stirred in the minds of the people a revived political consciousness to the far extent.

The ZNC is instrumental to the birth of Zo Re-unification Organisation (ZORO) which came into being as an offshoot of the ZNC under whose banner the First World Zomi Convention on Re-Unification was held at Champhai, Mizoram from May 19-21, 1988 (Keivom 2008: 198). ZORO, which was formed during this Convention, highlighted the cause of Zo or Zomi re-unification and political emancipation to the highest world body, the UNO, and the world leaders by submitting memorandum to Butrous Ghali, the then UN Secretary General, John Major, the Prime Minister of England and Bill Clinton, the President of USA and to the Prime Minister and the President of India (1990-1995). Zomi

Revolutionary Volunteer (ZRV) was formed in India as the armed wing of ZNC.

The ZNC in Burma got recognition as a political party and contested the Burma General election in 1990. Two of its candidates by the persons of Thanglianpau and Chinsianthang were elected under the constituencies of Tedim Block and Tonzang Block of the Chin Hills respectively (Neihsial, 2008:55). However, the ZNC in India saw its excitements for a short period of three years, after which no trace of its movements and activities has been found till date. Nevertheless, its offshoot organisation, ZORO, although in a dormant state, still upholds its existence.

Zomi Revolutionary Army (ZRA)

The formation of Zomi Re-Unification Organisation (ZRO), a political organisation and its armed wing Zomi Revolutionary Army (ZRA) is more like the reformation of the defunct ZNC and its armed wing ZRV. ZRO along with its armed wing ZRA was formed in 1993, under the initiative of the Paite tribe. In 1992, there occurred a clash between the Paite and Thadou in Lamka town over some minor issue. The Paite then felt necessary for them to keep an armed organization in order to defend themselve from the Thadou who had already had armed groups. Then, Paite Commando was formed, which however, was re-named Zomi Revolutionary Army (ZRA) with the intention of incorporating other Kuki-Chin tribes also. The political objective of the ZRO/ ZRA is "to protect the interests of the Zomi communities from the onslaught of any community or group" and bring all the Zomi people, divided by State boundaries in various countries, specifically in Myanmar (Chin State), India (Manipur and Mizoram) and Bangladesh (Chittagong Hills Tracts), together under one administrative unit, called 'Zogam', or 'Zoland'.

Unsurprisingly, the ZRA came into conflict with its kindred Kuki militants in 1997. The ZRO operates in tandem with its father-figure organization, the Zomi Council. The Zomi Council, at present, consists of, under its umbrella, several Kuki-Chin (Zomi) tribes such as Paite, Simte, Vaiphei, Zou, Tedim-Chin (Sukte), etc. The outfit, ZRA primarily operates in the Paite and Zou dominated areas of Churachandpur district of Manipur, especially in Thanlon and Singngat sub-divisions bordering Myanmar and Mizoram. Its activities have also been noticeable in the bordering areas of Mizoram with Manipur.

Ideological Clashes, Territorial Tussles, Inter-Tribal Conflicts and Repurcussions

Various Zo political organisations had seen a lot of conflicting ideologies in them, let alone the extremist groups. Ideological clash, territorial tussle between various extremist groups had been instrumental in sparkling ethnic conflict among them in Churachandpur district in the 1990s. Churachandpur is located in the southern part of Manipur bordering Myanmar. Though officially known as Churachandpur, the local residents call it *Lamka,* meaning the confluence of Tedim, Tipaimukh and Sugnu Roads. It is one of the fastest developing towns in the State and is inhabited by the Chin-Kuki-Mizo (Zo) tribes that it could be dramatically called the Zo town. The Zo people like the Paite, Thadou, Hmar, Vaiphei, Simte, Tedim-Chin, Gangte, Mizo, Zou, etc. who speak slight different but almost the same languages lived in the district since time immemorial.

The 'Kuki-Zomi' Conflict

As already mentioned, the Khul Union was the first outcome of ideological clash and crack between the leaderships of the Thadou tribes and other Kuki-Chin tribes. Since the inception of the Khul Union—though it lasted for short period of time – it played an important role in further weakening the socio-political integration of the Kuki-Chin people in Manipur. In the process, many old Kuki tribes such as the Moyon, Monsang, Lamkang, Maring, Koireng, Kom, Purum and others shifted their affiliation from Kuki to the "Naga sub-nation". However, the Hmar, Paite, Zou, Vaiphei, Simte, etc. did not associate with any of the larger umbrella body—Kuki or Naga. Then, in the 1990s, a new organization known as "the Seven Tribes", under the initiative of the Paite, was founded in Churachandpur in order to unite all the mentioned minor tribes. The Seven Tribes organisation was then changed to "Zomi Re-unification Organisation (ZRO) with its foundation day observed on 20th February as "Zomi Namni" (Haokip, Rebecca 2008:191). With the objective of uniting all the tribes under the Zomi nomenclature and ensuring the political security for them an armed wing Zomi Revolutionary Army (ZRA) was installed.

On the other side of development, the Kuki National Front (KNF), with its main political objective of unifying all the kindred tribes under the Kuki nomenclature, spread its wings and influence over the southern parts of Manipur in Chandel and Churachandpur districts. The KNF which collected social taxes only to the Thadou tribes then also started to collect from other tribes in Churachandpur. The non-Thadou tribes did not want to accept the fact that they had to pay taxes to the KNF. So, the ZRA appealed to the KNF not to tax persons affiliated to the Zomi group. In this way, tension started to gain ground between the two armed groups. The Paite-Zomi took this step of KNF as an attempt to impose the Kuki identity upon them whereas, the KNF suspected the ZRA of conniving with its rival Naga militants against the Kukis. Hence forth, there took place many incidents of kidnappings and murders between the two groups, whereby the innocent civilians were often the victims.

Nonetheless, an internal discord within the KNF also played a role as a driving force of the conflict. The KNF split into two—the original KNF or KNF (President) and the KNF (Military Council), due to leadership and internal dissension in 1996. Then, feuds over territorial control and dominance took place between the two factions. This tussle led the 'President' faction to move down to Churachandpur town and its surrounding areas thereby causing further scuffle with the ZRA who had already established their command over large chunk of areas in Churachandpur. In one way, the conflict can be indirectly related to territorial issues among the armed groups.

The actual violence started on June 24, 1997 when a group of KNF mowed down ten Paite tribes from a village near Churachandpur town believed to be cadres of ZRA which the latter refuted vehemently. In retaliation, hordes of the Paite youth started to burn houses belonging to the Thadou inside the town and attacked the localities of the Thadous around it. Thereafter, the carnage went on till the final Peace Accord was signed between the two warring groups in 1998. This ethnic feud was often called as the "Kuki-Zomi" conflict because of the fact that under the organizational name of Zomi, not only Paite but the Vaiphei also got involved in it, while on the other side, the Thadou and Gangte tribes were together in one camp. The Zou, Simte and Hmar and Lushai-Mizo remained neutral to the conflict though quite sizable number of them got murdered, kidnapped and displaced.

Table 26.1: Zomi victims in Zomi-Kuki Conflict (1997-98) in Churachandpur

Nature of Incidents	*No. of Persons*
Deceased persons	342
Kidnapped and Killed	16
Injured persons	92
Displaced persons who returned homeless from Mizoram	7000
Displaced persons who returned homeless from Myanmar	1000
Displaced persons who returned homeless within Manipur	25,000

Source: Memorandum to the Prime Minister of India by the Zomi Council Manipur, 1998.

The conflict has far reaching consequences to the people living in Churachandpur. There were hundreds and thousands of displaced persons during the incidents. Thousands of people were rendered homeless. More than 1000 houses were burnt down and hundreds of people from both sides were dead. There was almost no Kuki or Zomi village that was left without being attacked by either group in and around Churachandpur district. In general, the conflict has gravely affected the economic, social and political environment as well as the emotional well-being of individuals in Churachandpur. It took more than five years to reconstruct the havoc caused by the conflict. In a real sense, this issue has been much conceived as an internal dissension among the kindred Zo tribes rather than a conflict between two different enemies.

Peace Accord and its Aftermath

The incessant rampage continued for almost one year when, after suffering grievously, all felt the need to stop it in order to live a normal life once again. Under the initiative of the State Government, leaders representing both the communities were brought to a negotiating table. A Memorandum of Understanding (MoU) was signed on March 26, 1998 followed by a ceasefire agreement which was extended thrice till the last and final agreement was arrived on 1st October, 1998. Then, on the 1st October, 1998, both ZC and KIC signed a written agreement in the presence of W. Nipamacha Singh, the then Chief Minister of Manipur. Both leaders of the parties agreed that every individual or tribe shall be given liberty to be either Kuki or Zomi or have any other identity. These nomenclatures cannot be imposed to anyone by force; that, the Kuki and Zomi militants should not collect fund and "taxes" from anyone other than the person of their own 'affiliated' tribes or groups which includes government employees, the public in general, contractors and businessmen.

Peace prevailed once again in Churachandpur district but not without bringing in a new vigour of ethnic consciousness, dialectal chauvinism, and mutual distrust among the Zo people. In regard to the aftermath of conflict, the situation among the tribes of Kuki-Chin-Mizo (Zo) was best described by Nepram (2002): "With the two terms 'Zomi' and 'Kuki' coming in and propagated mainly by two major tribes (Paite and Thado) of the Chin-Kuki-Mizo group, other minority tribes like the Zous, Vaiphei, Gangtes, Simtes, and Koms are in dilemmas" to accept if Zomi or Kuki identity as nomenclature." The immediate effect was found on the Gangte tribes who had been embracing the Kuki nomenclature for a long time, had shifted their allegiance from Kuki identity to Mizo in 1999. Some of the Thadou speakers also shifted their political affiliation from Thadou to Paite which detrimentally became a setback to the Kuki unification. Nevertheless, the Zomi unification process also was under turbulence when some of its affiliated tribes in the armed groups were disappointed for alleged unfair treatment meted out to them and started to defect from the outfit.

Growth of Ethnic Militant Groups and Alliances

Although no more ethnic clash occurred in the aftermath of the final peace agreement, the people had no real harmony in their mind because of frequent factional fights between the underground groups. Tribal identity consciousness regained importance among the people and more so with the militant groups. Thereby, the need was felt to foster the spirit of brotherhood and safeguard their territorial control from the possible aggression of expanding valley based militant groups, a new alliance known as Indigenous People's Revolutionary Army (IPRA) was formed among the Kuki-Chin militants on May 27, 2000. IPRA comprised the ZRA, KNA, KNF (MC), KNF (P) and HPC (D). The allegation that IPRA was formed basically to "fight unitedly against Naga and Meitei insurgent groups in Manipur", the organisation strongly denied and termed it "baseless version of disinformation". The organisation, then, stated that it was formed with the main objective of the indigenous peoples to live together and not to disturb each other. It however, lasted for a few years.

The KNF was split in two to three more factions followed by internecine feuds among them. In Sadar hill areas of Senapati district, Kuki Revolutionary Army (KRA), a new Kuki militant came into being from the run-away faction of the KNF (MC) with the help of the NSCN (IM) in December 1999. The primary objective of the KRA is to secure a "separate State" for the Kuki tribe within the Indian Union and the unification of all scattered Kukis in the new homeland. In Assam, its declared objective is the creation of the "Kuki National Council", an autonomous administrative council for the Kukis in the Karbi Anglong district. However, in August 2007, the KRA underwent a split with the formation of the KRA-Unification in the Karbi Anglong district of Assam. Again, due to various election rows in Chandel district another outfit, United Kuki Liberation Army (UKLF) was formed in March 2000 allegedly to counter the operations of the KNA. To protect the Komrem identity, the United Komrem Revolutionary Army (UKRA) was formed in 2006.

The Zomi integrity was also shaken when disputes occurred among the cadres of ZRA. In 2005 most of the Vaiphei in ZRA deserted their camp in Singngat subdivision of Churachandpur and took shelter under the Meitei militant groups. Thereafter, they formed a new armed organization known as United Socialist Revolutionary Army (USRA). The formation of Vaiphei underground group has given a complicated situation for the Vaiphei People's Council (VPC), the apex body of the tribe, which has been an active member of the Zomi Council (ZC) for long time. The USRA was against the VPC's merger in the Zomi Council. The outfit says: "As our tribe identity has been challenged (by ZRA), USRA believes the Vaipheis need not submerge themselves in the so called community, 'Zomi'." Then, it joined the KNO armed wings. The ZRA again faced a setback when another group of Paite defected to form a new armed outfit called Zomi Revolutionary Front (ZRF).

On the other state of affairs, around 2002, the United Zou Organisation (UZO), the apex body of the Zou tribe, declared its affiliation under the Zomi Council (ZC) like that of other sister tribal organisations of the Paite, Vaiphei, Simte and Tedim-Chin. The membership under ZC was reacted with disapproval by some section of the Zous who wanted to join neither the Kuki nor the Zomi umbrella organisations. Consequently, the discontented section of the Zou floated an armed outfit known as Zou Defence Volunteer (ZDV) under the support of Meitei militant groups. ZDV was also said to be formed as a consequence of the Kuki-Zomi conflict in 1997. During this ethnic clash, a number of Zou had become victims under the warring groups. Despite being neutral to the conflict, several Zous were killed and hundreds of their villages were burnt down. On account of this situation, the ZDV was formed with the main agenda of protecting the Zou tribe against any possible attack from other armed groups. Soon after in 2005, ZDV snapped ties with the Meitei militants and linked with the Kuki National Organisation.

Therefore, it can be understood that the tribal unification movement in the name of Zomi did not seemingly sail well in view of the mentioned disagreement within each of the Vaiphei and Zou communities. While each politically apex bodies are in association with the Zomi organisation, the extremist groups ostensibly representing the peoples, i.e. the USRA (Vaiphei) and ZDV (Zou) are affiliated to the Kuki armed union. The nationalist movements under the Kuki confederation also suffered severe blows due to 'abnormal' proliferation of so many armed groups and incessant clashes among the groups. There are more than ten militant groups under the name—Kuki. In regard to political ideologies and agendas, one finds no difference among them – the creation of a Kuki homeland, however, the reason as to why so many groups have existed, is hard to explain. Internally, there have been immense problems within the Thadou (Kuki) themselves.

All Chin-Kuki (Zo) extremist groups signed Suspension of Operation (SoO) with the Central Government in August 2005. The ceasefire attained its complete shape in 2008 when the State government also agreed to join it. One interesting development about it is that all the Kuki-Chin or Zo militants after long period of conflict between one another, finally, came under two apex bodies: The Kuki National Organisation (KNO) and United People's Front (UPF). The KNO group presently consisted of eleven militant organisations while the UPF is composed of eight groups, all of which signed SoO under the name of these two apex bodies.

Table 26.2: Various Zo Militant groups under Kuki National Organisation

Sl. No.	*Name of the Militants*
1.	Kuki National Army
2.	Kuki National Front (Military Council)
3.	Kuki National Front (Zogam)
4.	Kuki Liberation Army (Manipur)
5.	Kuki Liberation Army (Assam)
6.	Kuki Revolutionary Army (Unification)
7.	United Old Kuki Liberation Army
8.	United Komrem Revolutionary Army
9.	United Socialist Revolutionary Army
10.	Zomi Revolutionary Front
11.	Zou Defence Volunteer (KNO)

Source: Haokip, P.S. (2008). Zalen-gam: The Kuki Nation, p. 378.

Table 26.3: Various Zo Militant groups under United People's Front

Sl. No.	*Name of the Militants*
1.	Hmar People Convention (Democratic)
2.	Kuki Revolutionary Army
3.	Kuki National Front (President)
4.	Kuki National Front (Samuel)
5.	Kuki Liberation Army (UPF)
6.	United Kuki Liberation Front
7.	Zomi Revolutionary Army
8.	Zou Defence Volunteer (UPF)

Source: *The Telegraph-North East*, December 20, 2008.

Conclusion

The process of ethnification of the Kuki-Chin-Mizo or the Zo people had already started since a long period of time even before India's independence. Importantly, the wave of ethnic revival resurfaced in the post-independence era which ultimately led to adoption of separate identities by all the tribes of Manipur in general and the Zo people in particular. Based on the concept of common history, culture and tradition, a lot of efforts have been made by the leaders of the tribes to unify them in a common nomenclature, but sooner than later, they failed to achieve the anticipated dream. The first and foremost attempt to unify under the Kuki National Assembly failed and gave birth to the formation of Khulmi Union which, however, did not succeed. The failure of Kuki National Assembly and the Khulmi Union led to the formation of various political organizations by each tribe. This was followed by recognition of all tribal groups in Manipur by the Indian Government under the Constitution of India where all the Kuki-Chin-Mizo tribes were given the status of Scheduled Tribes. The Mizo Union with its main aim of unifying all the Zo people under the Mizo nomenclature and creating greater Mizoram by integrating all the Zo inhabited areas of Manipur, Mizoram and Assam failed to fructify. The Zomi National Congress, with a much higher ambition of unification for all the Zo people in India, Bangladesh and Burma, came into the picture but existed momentarily.

Nonetheless, the Kuki-Chin-Mizo people are one and the same people historically and anthropologically where past historians have also proved so in their writings and records. But the main predicament lies in identity and unification. The main stumbling block of unifying force has been the question of a common nomenclature. The terms like Kuki, Chin, Mizo, Zomi or Zo have been the bone of contention and issue among them. Based on the writings of imminent scholars and records of the British writers, ZO seems to be, perhaps, much genuine and appropriate term for these groups to come to a common platform.

In congruence with the moderate political spectrum, the wave of ethnic revival has already been high in the extremist advance. In fact, the wave of extremism became strong when some of the non-violent movements failed. HPC was formed in Mizoram in 1986 seeking for integration the Hmar inhabited areas and set up a separate administrative body. KNA and ZRA have also existed in the 1980s and 1990s respectively in a move to unite all Zo ethnic groups under either Kuki or Zomi nomenclature and create a separate homeland. These objectives have not been realised till date. Unifying the "scattered" people in a radical and extremist approach does not seem to make it in practice. More often than not, the innocent people are subject to terror, harassment, displacement and death caused by the extremist militants on the one hand and the state on the other hand.

Ethnic fanaticism and its resultant ethnic conflicts caused the proliferation of various armed groups among the tribes for desperate self-defence. To assert their identity and protect themselves from harassment by other groups, minor tribes like the Zou, Vaiphei, Komrem, etc. have formed armed organisations too. There are presently around 20 armed organisations belonging to the Kuki-Chin-Mizo tribes alone. Moreover, formation of armed groups for the much-hyped 'assertion of ethno-nationalist identity' on one hand and purported 'political goal' on the other hand has placed Manipur in the mist of turbulence where the wheel of socio-economic as well as human developments have been impeded.

The present unification of the extremist groups belonging to the Kuki-Chin-Mizo (Zo) people under two umbrella organisations: Kuki National Organisation and United People's Front, and the observation of ceasefire or SoO by them with both the State and Central authorities have been a welcome and positive move. It is being anticipated by all citizens to see a positive sign of development in all spheres of life in the State-Manipur provided the extremist groups shun violence and work for the cause of human welfare and development. Nonetheless, every citizen should be on guard from being swayed away by ethno-nationalist and extremist obsession which could unconsciously develop as a woe to society as a whole.

REFERENCES

Gopalakrisnan (1996): *Socio-Political Framework in North East India,* Delhi: Vikas Publishing House, pp. 148, 150, 153, 154.

Goswami 1979: *The Mizo Unrest – A Study of Politicisation of Culture,* Jaipur: Aalekh Pub., p. 58.

Grierson, G.A. (1904 reprint). *Specimens of the Kuki Chin and Burma Groups,* 'Linguistic Survey of India', Vol III, Part III, Calcutta, pp. 1, 5.

Grierson, G.A. (1995 reprint). *Languages of North Eastern India,* 'A Survey' — Vol II, Part Delhi: Gyan Publishing House, p. 1.

Haokip, P.S. (2008). *Zalen-Gam the Kuki Nation* (revised ed.), Kuki National Organisation Pub., pp. 1, 376, 378, 379, 381.

Khai, Singkhaw (1995). *Zo People and Their Culture – A Historical, Cultural Study and Critical Analysis of the Zo and Ethnic Tribes,* Churachandpur, p. 1.

Lehman (1963). *The Structure of Chin Society,* Urbana: The University of Illinois Press, p. 30.

Nepram, B. (2002): *South Asia's Fractured Frontier – Armed Conflict, Narcotics and Small Arms Proliferation in India's North East,* New Delhi: Mittal Pub., p. 81.

Ray, Asok Kumar, *et al.* (2007). *Terrorism and Peace Initiatives in North East India,* NEICSSR, New Delhi: Om Pub.m p. 22.

Sangermano, Vintentius (1833). *A Description of the Burmese Empire,* John Jardine (ed.), Rangoon: 1884, p. 43.

Vaiphei S., Prim (1995): *The Kukis in Manipur* in 'Manipur: Past and Present', Vol. III, Sanajaoba, N. (ed.), New Delhi: Mittal Pub., p. 128.

Vumson (1983). *Zo History – With an Introduction to Zo Culture, Economy, Religion and Their Status as an Ethnic Minority in India, Burma, and Bangladesh.*

Zomi Council Manipur (1998): *Memorandum to the Prime Minister of India,* Zomi Council Headquarter, Lamka, Manipur.

Zou, David Vumlalallian (2005). *Raiding the dreaded past: Representations of headhunting and human sacrifice in North East India.* Contributions to Indian Sociology (n.s.) 39, 1, New Delhi, Thousand Oaks/London: Sage Pub., 89.

27

Extremism, Poverty and Socio-economic Backwardness

Prakash Sarma

One of the major extremist groups of Assam is United Liberation Front of Assam (ULFA) formed towards the end of the 1980s. This outfit does not believe the Constitution of India and wants to liberate Assam from the so-called colonial rule of India. To achieve their goal, they have picked up gun in their hands against the Indian Government. As they are now banned by the Indian Government for their anti-Indian activities, they are now operating their activities from the foreign soil and hideouts. They usually enter Assam dividing into small groups and select poor remote and backward villages for sheltering. These extremist groups spend lavishly in name of fooding and lodging during their stay. The host is also benefited as he enjoys a share of the lavish expenditure. Because of the financial supports received from the extremist groups the poor villagers are seemed to provide heroic welcome to the anti-Indian elements. The young children of the poor and backward villagers especially the school drop-outs are attracted towards the luxurious style of living adopted by the cadres of the banned outfit and some of them even joined in the organization as revealed in the police records. Consequently, these villages are now identified as red areas in the Assam police diary. The Assam police along with Indian army and para-military forces often initiate combing operation against the extremist groups in these villages turning the area into virtual battlefields. As a result, the common and innocent people have to suffer a lot. Sometimes, they have to succumb death in the cross firing between the Government forces and extremist groups. It is viewed that these unwanted incidents could be avoided, if the backwardness of the villages is addressed properly. Keeping this point in mind, poverty as a cause of extremism in some parts of Assam is discussed in this chapter.

Introduction

So far the United Liberation Front of Assam is concerned, it is basically a rural based organization. This fact is also applicable in case of so many other extremist groups of North East India. No doubt, most of the remote and inaccessible backward villages of Assam are the breeding ground of extremist groups including ULFA. The extremist groups basically use these villages as their hideout, communication and enrolment of cadres into their organization. Now the question arises, why these areas are easily falling pray to the extremist groups. Since, the words like 'colonialism', 'deprivation', 'exploitation' used by so called extremist groups against Indian Government has no meaning to the common illiterate and poor people living in rural areas under backward condition. Is geo-poverty and there any socio-economic factor responsible for the ever growing tendency of extremism in the socio-economically backward areas? Here, we shall try to find out the answers of these questions taking a remote, socio-economically backward village as an example.

Methodology

To achieve the objectives of this chapter, one remote and inaccessible and economically backward village is considered for conducting house to house survey, for which appropriate questionnaire have been prepared in order to collect data. To understand about the extremist related problem, the senior citizens of the village including the grown-up boys and girls are elaborately interviewed. The collected data are processed using SPSS soft ware to draw meaningful inferences.

Study Area

The village Eratari under the Paka Betbari Developmental Block of Barpeta District of Assam is taken for case study. The village is located approximately ten kilometres west of Sarthebari famed for bell metal industries. The place is also not far from the River Brahmaputra used as corridor to Bangladesh by the extremist groups. The village characteristically flood prone separated from its surrounding immigrant villages by some *beels* (swampy low lying area). It is mainly inhabited by low caste Hindus who belong to Scheduled Caste. However, a few numbers of families belong to Scheduled Tribes. The village has witnessed several incident of killing ULFA members in the anti-insurgency operation conducted by Indian army. Even some members of the same group are being killed because of differences of opinion and internal conflicts. It is also recorded that the village was once used to keep conceal the prisoners hijacked by ULFA. Keeping all these points in view mentioned above, this terrorist affected village is taken for case study.

Analysis

The index selected to gauge the standard of living of the villagers' are—

1. Demographic characteristics, and
2. Availability of sustenance amenities and health awareness.

Demographic Characteristics

The village Eratari is lagging behind much in terms of a number of important aspects of well-being and social progress. The village is characterized, *inter alia,* by high level of mortality, fertility, under-nutrition, illiteracy, and a slow pace of poverty decline. Ethnic verities are few; there is absence of general class people. The village is Scheduled Caste dominated. The percentage of Scheduled Caste in the village is 88.94 and the rest is Scheduled Tribes.

Age-Sex Distribution

Male outnumbers female in the village in terms of sex ratio. Much like other poor villages of Assam, the age group of 0 to 15 claims highest. This age group is not an earning group. They are the dependants. Economic burden is too much among most of the families. They have to spend the major part of their hard earnings for basic needs, i.e. for food. Under such a precarious situation, if some organization comes forward to help them, they readily accept it. This way, the villagers have fallen pray to the extremist groups. Table 27.1 indicates life expectancy in the village is short in comparison to other areas.

Table 27.1: Age-Sex Group

Age Group	*Male*	*Female*
0-15	238	220
15-60	390	350
>60	31	27
Total	**659**	**597**

Total Households: 190.
Source: Surveyed by Researcher, 2008.

Family Size

As per the survey report, family size of sixty per cent families of the village is within 5 to 10. The widespread extreme poverty have considerable influence on the high birth rate in the village. Moreover, social factors like relatively low marriage age result in prolonged period of fertility, lack of education, absence of birth control measures are the cause of large size family. Women have very little control upon their reproductive life.

Table 27.2: Family Size

No. of Persons Per Family	*No. of Families*
2 - 4	45
5 - 10	123
11 - 15	14
17 - 21	8
Total	**190**

Source: Surveyed by Researcher, 2008.

Literacy Level

Table 27.3 presents comparative figures of male and female literacy rates in the Eratari village. As far as the specific issue of literacy is concerned, the most sobering feature of the educational situation in the village is pathetic. There persists high level of illiteracy even in the younger age group (30%). Educational facilities in the village are very poor except a primary school. For post-primary education, the village boys and girls have to cover at least five kilometres from their home. Such situation is never encouraging for academic upliftment. The pity is that only one teacher has been assigned to teach the students right from class-I to Class-IV. Hence, the expectation of high quality human resource from such a school is beyond imagination.

Table 27.3: Level of Literacy in the Village

Level of Literacy	*Male*	*Female*	*Total*
Illiterate	138	235	373
Primary level	176	141	317
Middle School	95	88	183
Secondary level	184	113	297
Higher Secondary	46	17	63
Graduate	18	6	24
PG	1	1	2
ITI	1	0	1

Source: Surveyed by Researcher, 2008.

The Occupational Structure

The occupational structure of Eratari's population reflects clearly the backwardness of the village. It is recorded that 66.67 per cent population of the village is non-worker. They have to depend for their subsistence on the 32.33 per cent of working population of the village. Out of the total population, 8.51 per cent are cultivators. The fact is that, agriculture is not the main stay of life; neither remains the sole source of income. As the village is located in the flood prone area, the agro-yield from the cultivable lands is uncertain. It is astonishing that 7.48 per cent population of the village manages the two meals a day from their daily wages. The fishing and pisciculture, therefore remains one of the important occupations of the villagers. In a nutshell, the present occupation pattern of the village is not enough to manage two square meals a day.

Table 27.4: The Occupational Pattern

Occupation	*No. of Persons*	*Percentage*
Non-Workers	830	66.67
Cultivators	106	8.51
Agri. Labourer	29	2.33
Casual Labourer	93	7.48
Non-Farm Labourer	20	1.61
Government-Services	21	1.69
Private-services	31	2.49
Self-employed	67	5.38
Contractor	3	0.24
Fishing	45	3.61
Total	**1245**	**100.00**

Source: Surveyed by Researcher, 2008.

Availability of Village Amenities and Health-Care Facilities

An attempt has been made to understand how far people are aware to take advantage of the existing resources and amenities available in the village and around.

Electricity Connection

One of the major policies of Assam Government is to make available electricity connection to all the family under its jurisdiction. But so far the electricity connection is concerned; such a novel endeavour of Government has been measurably failed in the village. In spite of having electricity network in the village, only 15 per cent families of the village have access to the facility. The rest is yet to be connected with this facility because of their poor financial condition.

Table 27.5: Electricity Connection

Electricity Connection	*No. of Family*	*Percentage*
No	162	85.26
Yes	28	14.73
Total	**190**	**100.00**

Source: Surveyed by Researcher, 2008.

Sources of Drinking Water

The major source of drinking water in the village is tube well. The

Table 27.6 presents that 94.64 per cent family of the village receive water from tube well. No effort is made so far to provide drinking water facility from the government side. The interesting feature is that the villagers have no habit of taking boiled water. Even family having water from the open pond for drinking purpose don't boil before taking it. It might be a major cause of various epidemics and diseases in the village.

Table 27.6: Sources of Drinking Water

Sources of Drinking Water	*No. of Family*	*Percentage*
Pond	8	4.21
Well	2	1.11
Tube Well	180	94.68
Government Supply	0	0.00
Boiled Water	0	0.00
Total	**190**	**100.00**

Source: Surveyed by Researcher, 2008.

Sanitary System

A major rural problem in India is poor sanitary system. Erąțari village is even worst. In the modern age too, 58 per cent family of the village use open space around the village. As per concerned record, the villagers have to suffer often from the gastrointestinal and jaundice problem. The major cause may be open space latrine system. The number of family having sanitary latrine system is 6.32 per cent only.

Table 27.7: Sanitary System

Sanitary system	*No. of family*	*Percentage*
Pakka Latrine	12	6.32
Kachcha latrine	68	35.79
Open ground	110	57.89
Total	**190**	**100.00**

Source: Surveyed by Researcher, 2008.

Infant Mortality and Vaccination

The survey report shows that social problem like infant mortality is still very high in the village. Table 27.8 presents that 14.74 per cent families of the village have the high rate of infant mortality. Because of the remoteness and poor affordability of the people may be some of the reasons of high infant mortality. The villagers have yet to respond whole-heartedly to the vaccination programme launched by the health department of Government of Assam.

Table 27.8: Health Awareness

Health Awareness	*No. of Family*	*Percentage*
Infant mortality records	28	14.74
Response to Child's Vaccination	159	83.68

Source: Surveyed by Researcher, 2008.

Conclusion

The poverty and backwardness of the people in all the socio-economic fronts have rendered the village a play ground of extremism. In order to let the village free from all extremisms, the only way out is to elevate the village socially, economically and educationally at least promote peace in the locality and well-being of the people. It is important to note that if proper education could be provided to the new young generation, that will definitely work positively in the long run to eliminate extremism from the backward village.

Index